Towards a New Community
Culture and Politics in Post-Totalitarian Europe

Edited by
Peter J.S. Duncan and Martyn Rady

School of Slavonic and East European Studies
University of London
LIT Verlag, Hamburg and Münster
1993

Towards a New Community

Culture and Politics in
Post-Totalitarian Europe

Cip-Kurztitelaufnahme der Deutschen Bibliothek

Towards a New Community:
Culture and Politics in Post-Totalitarian Europe
Peter J.S.Duncan and Martyn Rady (Ed.)
– Münster ; Hamburg : Lit 1993
    School of Slavonic and East European Studies
    ISBN 3-89473-362-4

NE: GT

© LIT VERLAG   Dieckstraße 56   48145 Münster   Tel. 0251-235091
                Hallerplatz 5   20146 Hamburg   Tel. 040-446446

CONTENTS

Preface vii

Introduction ix
Martyn Rady

Part One: Passages from Totalitarianism

1 Our Understanding of Totalitarianism 3
  Andrei Sakharov

2 Stalinism and Pluralism: Two Pathways from the
  Enlightenment 13
  Gale Stokes

3 Democracy and the Nation State in Contemporary
  East-Central Europe 27
  Paul G. Lewis

4 The Russian Myth: Empire and People 37
  Geoffrey Hosking

5 Metamorphosis in the Czechoslovak Economy 45
  Václav Klaus

Part Two: The Recollection of Identity

6 Nationhood and Self-Recollection: Ways to Democracy
  after Communism 53
  Ghia Nodia

7 The Reconstruction of Community in Late
  Twentieth-Century Europe 65
  Anthony D. Smith

8 Culture and the Intelligentsia: Forms of Cultural Revival 75
  Elena Nemirovskaia

9 What Price an Orthodox Revival? The Dilemmas of
  the Russian Church 81
  Simon Dixon

10	The Post-Revolution Conflict Between the Orthodox and Eastern-Rite Catholics in Romania *Fiona Tupper-Carey*	93
11	Convergence versus Divergence in Romania: the Role of the Vatra Românească Movement in Transylvania *Dennis Deletant*	101
12	Reconstruction as Deconstruction: the Case of Yugoslavia *Mark Wheeler*	121

Part Three: Language: Death and Resurrection

13	Language and Politics in Bulgaria *Blaga Dimitrova*	133
14	Soviet Language Laws: 1989-1990 *Michael Kirkwood*	147
15	Language and Nationalism in Georgia and the West's Response *B.G. Hewitt*	161

Conclusion 　　　　　　　　　　　　　　　　　　　　177
Peter J. S. Duncan

Notes on Contributors 　　　　　　　　　　　　　　　192

PREFACE

In December 1990, the School of Slavonic and East European Studies (SSEES), of the University of London, celebrated the 75th anniversary of its foundation with a major international conference, 'Towards a New Community: Culture and Politics in Post-Totalitarian Society'. Although arranged around such themes as 'The Myth of Nation', 'The Cult of Culture', 'Language: Death and Resurrection', 'The Past and its Uses' and 'The Search for a Belief', the conference was overwhelmingly concerned with exploring the patterns of disintegration in Communist systems and with analysing the dynamics of political and cultural change in post-totalitarian societies. During the course of the week-long conference, which was generously funded by the British Academy, the British Council and the Ford Foundation, some ninety scholars from the United States and Europe, including the USSR, presented and discussed papers or chaired sessions.

The present volume brings together a small selection of papers delivered at the conference. The editors are grateful for the advice of Lindsey Hughes and Robert Service who helped with the initial identification of papers suitable for publication, and for the willingness of contributors both to agree to publication and to revise their papers accordingly. The editors would also like to thank Sarah Safraz, who helped with the typing of the chapters; Sonia Kanikova and Robert Pynsent, for their help in translating one chapter; and Diane Nicholls, for translating the two Russian contributions. Particular thanks are due to Radojka Miljević, SSEES's Publications and Conferences Officer, who not only organized the conference in the first place, but also undertook the subsequent labour of seeing the present volume to press.

Peter J.S. Duncan
Martyn Rady

August 1993

INTRODUCTION

Martyn Rady

The School of Slavonic and East European Studies celebrated its Seventy-Fifth Anniversary in 1990. To mark the event, an international conference was held at the School under the title 'Towards a New Community: Culture and Politics in Post-Totalitarian Society'. The conference was one of the first in Europe to analyse and debate the process of transformation in contemporary Eastern Europe within the broad context of the region's history, politics, society, literature and languages. It drew together over 200 scholars from Europe and the United States, and was supported by a variety of cultural events and exhibitions.

The present volume includes a small selection of papers taken from more than seventy delivered at the conference. Some of the papers published here have been revised by their authors to take into account further developments in Central and Eastern Europe. Others have been left in the form in which they were first delivered on account of the high level of insight which they demonstrated at the time.[1] The editors have also added an entirely new piece on the disintegration of Yugoslavia, and a paper from Václav Klaus on the Czechoslovak economy which was originally delivered in November 1991 at the University of London's Senate House. A concluding essay by Peter J. S. Duncan analyses some of the main changes in the region since the conference and discusses their relevance to co-operation and security in Europe.

Notwithstanding their differences in background and discipline, almost all the participants at the conference were united in their belief that a decisive shift towards democracy and the market economy had occurred in Eastern Europe. Despite one attempt to rally support for co-operative socialism, little

---

1 The contributions of the following are thus published in an unrevised form: Blaga Dimitrova, Elena Nemirovskaia, Fiona Tupper-Carey, A.N. Sakharov, Anthony D. Smith.

sympathy was expressed for 'third way-ism'.[2] In the opinion of most contributors and discussants the countries of the former Soviet bloc were 'returning' to Europe; their economies and constitutions would, henceforward, seek to replicate those of the West. As Gale Stokes put it, the 'hyper-rationalist genre' of state socialism had failed as much as its National Socialist 'anti-rationalist' counterpart. Henceforward, the pluralist model would prevail, *faute de mieux*.

Yet, at the same time, the fact of nationalism had to be accepted as the principal 'legitimating power ... upholding state authority' in the region (Anthony Smith). This had obvious implications for the movement towards European union. As Smith explained, 'It is one thing to speak of the possibility of European institutions playing a role in conciliating parties to ethno-national disputes ... It is quite another thing to predict a large-scale shift in allegiances away from *ethnie* and ethnic identities to Pan-Europeanism and a truly European community.' Moreover, Smith presciently warned that the emancipatory aspects of nationalism might all too readily give way to more virulent and intolerant forms which threatened the pluralist model of community.

Even at the time of the conference there were indications that the nationalism of which Smith spoke was likely to impede a satisfactory transition from totalitarianism. In Transylvania violence between ethnic Romanians and Hungarians had flared in March 1990 and a sharp contest was already evident between Orthodox and Uniate believers in Romania. Both Dennis Deletant and Fiona Tupper-Carey warned of the 'divisive and confrontational' atmosphere in Romanian society and stressed that mutual trust was a precondition of democratic transformation. In Serbia, Slobodan Milošević had recently consolidated his own power and had pushed through a new constitution removing even the shadow of autonomy from Kosovo and Vojvodina. In the Transcaucasian republics of the Soviet Union fighting had also broken out between Armenians and Azeris, and George Hewitt (correctly, as it turned out) anticipated an escalation of national tensions in Georgia. Elsewhere in the Soviet Union, Russia had declared its own sovereignty and announced the primacy of republican legislation over enactments issued in the name of the Union. Within the whole edifice of the Soviet state, furthermore, a contest was already evident between what A.N. Sakharov referred to as 'revolutionary totalitarianism' and 'the private ownership alternative' which sought the 'entirely peaceful assimilation of revolutionary totalitarianism'.

In the months following the conference, the pace of disintegration doubled. Following the abortive coup of August 1991 and the 'catastrophic collision' of which Sakharov warned, the Soviet Union collapsed. It left behind a myriad of disaffected national communities in its ruin. Georgia, Yugoslavia and Moldova

---

2 Robin Blackburn, 'The Revolutions of 1989: A Socialist Response'. This paper was subsequently published in a revised form as 'Fin de Siècle: Socialism After the Crash', *New Left Review*, 185, 1991, pp. 5-66.

dissolved into civil war, and Czechoslovakia broke in half. As Mark Wheeler indicates in this volume, the instability once confined to Europe's 'southern tier', the Balkans, has now spread northwards. 'An arc of discord' presently reaches from the lands of the former Yugoslav state through Moldavia to the Crimea and onwards to Central Asia. And the newly-sovereign Slovakia may provide an entry-point for instability in Europe's northern tier, particularly if the Mečiar government starts behaving in a discriminatory fashion towards its large Hungarian minority.

The participants at the conference could not of course have predicted these more recent developments. The conference was among the first to investigate the transition from Communism, and the contributors were keenly aware that their field of enquiry was an entirely new one. Whereas there had been passages from Empire, there had never before been passages from Communism. As Ghia Nodia explained, 'The peculiarity ... is that the point of departure in this transition is not the traditional but the Communist society. What is going on in the former Communist countries has never occurred in history.' Nevertheless, individual contributors were able to indicate the wider problems which existed in the new Eastern Europe and which were likely to impede the transition to stable, liberal democracies. For convenience, these problems may be placed under three main headings: the historical nature of the East European state which influences the contemporary passage from totalitarianism; nationhood and identity in Eastern Europe as it is being recollected today, and the legacy of totalitarianism particularly in respect of culture and language.

It was increasingly apparent during the course of the conference that the type of state structure in Eastern Europe may historically have borne less resemblance to West European norms than the easy slogan of a 'return to Europe' allows. This point was strikingly made by Paul Lewis who argued that in contrast to those in the West, the states of Eastern Europe were weak ones analogous to the countries of Latin America. As he explained, 'One of the major legacies of totalitarianism in East-Central Europe has been the persistence of relatively weak states with limited powers of autonomous development and few sources of internal strength.' Lewis does not elucidate what he understands by 'weak state' other than that the concept 'relates to the unity, effectiveness and reach of [the state's] apparatus overall'. Nevertheless, the characteristics of the 'weak state' may be thought to include the following: overly rigid structures which are incapable of adaptation; institutions lacking the capacity to implement their goals and to aggregate group interests; a high concentration of political power at the centre; and an absence of mechanisms for the orderly transfer of this power between generations and between élite groups.[3]

---

3   This last point is stressed in particular by Merle King, 'Towards a Theory of Power and Political Instability in Latin America', *Western Political Quarterly*, 9, 1956, pp. 21-35.

Lewis confines his account to the experience of this century. Examination of their history relative to the West suggests, however, that the East European states have been weak for a rather longer period.

One of the distinguishing features of West European development is that by the early nineteenth century its representative institutions had triumphed decisively over the government of the prince. Even in Britain, where the *ancien régime* showed a greater tenacity and longevity than its French counterpart, no election has been 'made' by the crown since 1830. In Eastern Europe, however, the very reverse trend seems to have occurred. As László Péter has pointed out, even in Hungary the crown continued to wield an extensive authority right up until 1918. Thus while the government of Hungary may have been constitutional and responsible, 'it was not parliamentary in the sense in which parliamentary government was understood in Western Europe'.[4]

A yet more extreme case occurred in Russia where the entire apparatus of rule had necessarily to be organized 'top-down'. Even the most primitive village institutions were, as Geoffrey Hosking shows, transformed into agencies of the tsarist government, and society became a testing-ground for theories of cameral science. The Stalinist administrative-command system and the notion of 'revolutionary totalitarianism', the origins of which A.N. Sakharov describes, may be thought to mark the culmination of this process.

In complete contrast, therefore, to developments further West, in Eastern Europe the prince prevailed over parliaments, and representative bodies were squeezed by the executive. Furthermore, since both authority and sovereignty were deemed to reside in the ruler, concepts of citizenship and of the *Rechtsstaat* were slower to emerge in Eastern Europe. The consequences for the region were severe, for it meant that Eastern Europe either lacked or lost institutions which were capable of mediating between government and people, which enjoyed popular confidence and which were vested with an authority deriving from notions of contract and consent. Instead, the principle of consultation frequently gave way to the practice of coercion, and the discretionary application of the law rode roughshod over the concept of individual rights. The result was the development in the nineteenth century of states which were 'top-heavy' and therefore inherently unstable.

If the historical experience of Eastern Europe has tended towards the creation of states which were structurally weak, almost certainly this trend received new impetus under state socialism. As Leonard Schapiro has argued, totalitarianism devours the institutions of government as remorselessly as it corrupts civil society.[5] Moreover, by failing to permit civil society to develop,

---

4 László Péter's contribution to the conference, 'Montesquieu's Paradox on Freedom and Hungary's Constitutions 1790-1990' has been published separately in *The New Hungarian Quarterly*, 123, 1991, pp. 3-14; the quotation given here is from p. 8.
5 Leonard Schapiro, *Totalitarianism*, London, 1972, pp. 69-71; more recent studies have concentrated on the erosion of bureaucracy by 'partocracy': thus, Jan Pakulski,

the Communist rulers added to the structural weakness of their regimes, not appreciating the paradox that the 'existence of society outside of the state's control makes the state stronger'.6

Eastern Europe may have rediscovered civil society, but as Lewis explains the process of transition has created new infirmities in the structure of the state. The continued condition of state weakness carries with it a certain danger. As Lewis warns, 'Democracy ... does not seem to thrive in weak states where the challenges of state formation and consolidation remain strong and the state apparatus is not fully unified'. If democracy is to prosper in Eastern Europe and not to degenerate into populism and the tyranny of the majority, it must be firmly grounded in 'a liberal and primarily constitutional order'.

A related supposition informs Anthony Smith's discussion of nationhood and community in Eastern Europe. As the concept of nationality becomes infused in Eastern Europe with ideas of democratic and popular participation, so Smith foresees the emergence of a series of unstable combinations in the region. He thus envisages a type of demotic nationalism which is 'both participatory and decentralizing, pluralist yet mass-mobilizing'. These contrary impulses require hemming in: on the larger scale by the development of a specifically Pan-European identity; on the smaller, by notions of civic and political identity. In other words, the ethnic nationalisms of Eastern Europe need to be constrained and channelled by the same ideas of citizenship and rights as inform the West European concept of national identity. Whether this is best achieved by the formulation of new national myths or by the elaboration of constitutional codes which freeze democratic nationalisms at their emancipatory stage must, for the time being, remain uncertain.

Like much of his work, Anthony Smith's discussion of the reconstruction of community in Eastern Europe assumes the existence of two varieties of nationalism.7 The Western variant tends to emphasize a common territory, laws and institutions, legal equality as citizens and a common, high cultural inheritance. The Eastern, by contrast, stresses a community of descent as manifested in language, customs, religion and rituals. Smith hopes that East Europeans are currently striving for a new type of nationalism which unites these two different strands. As he explains, 'They are groping today towards a new synthesis of history and popular participation, and the type of community they wish to inaugurate is one which combines the vernacular past of each *ethnie* with the active citizenship characteristic of modern social movements and modern nations.'

'Bureacracy and the Soviet System', *Studies in Comparative Communism*, 19, 1986, pp. 3-24.
6 Dan Van Atta, 'The USSR as a "weak state". Agrarian Origins of Resistance to Perestroika', *World Politics*, 42, 1989, p. 149.
7 Anthony D. Smith, *The Ethnic Origins of Nations*, Oxford, 1986, pp. 134-44; *National Identity*, London, 1991, pp. 11-13; 'National Identity and the Idea of European Unity', *International Affairs*, 68, 1992, p. 61.

INTRODUCTION

The distinction between Western and Eastern variants of nationalism is a commonplace, which has been put in its historical context by Hans Kohn.[8] In Western Europe notions of nationhood were grafted on to older concepts of citizenship, natural rights and popular sovereignty. In Eastern Europe, by contrast, these concepts were less well developed and they often lacked an institutional framework for their articulation. Under these circumstances the nation itself became the collective repository of rights to be set against the claims of absolutist or autocratic rulers. The nation thus replaced and subsumed the individual, and civic rights took second place to the doctrine of national rights.

It is largely because writers like Elie Kedourie and Lord Acton failed to distinguish between types of nationalism that they have been so critical of its manifestations.[9] By contrast, those students of nationalism who have grasped its variety, notably John Plamenatz, have appreciated its contribution to the spread of democracy and personal freedom.[10] In this respect, Ghia Nodia's contribution to the present volume is no exception.

Nodia stresses the distinctions between Western and Eastern modes of nationalism. With respect to the Eastern variant, Nodia explains, '[In Eastern Europe] the national legitimation of state power could not just "crown" civil society, since a political community had yet to be created ... Personal and social emancipation did not precede national self-determination'. Yet at the same time, Nodia emphasizes the connection between nationalism and individual liberty and he seeks to turn Kedourie's critique of Kantianism on its head.[11] First, Nodia shows that concepts of nationhood are fundamental to the creation of a 'basic we', which is itself essential to the doctrine of popular sovereignty. Secondly, he argues that the transition from the traditional community involves the simultaneous self-determination of the individual and of the national community. In short, the same processes as create nations also create individuals.

Once, however, the nation had been born (or invented) out of the dissolution of the traditional community, conflict invariably arose between the claims of the individual and those of the *Volk*. In Western Europe, a civil society and political community was sufficiently well established as to prevent the erosion of individual rights. In Eastern Europe, however, where the peoples that sought full nationhood were less 'ripe', the outcome was different.

---

8 Hans Kohn, *The Idea of Nationalism*, New York, 1967 (first published 1944), esp. pp. 329-31.
9 Elie Kedourie, *Nationalism*, London, 1960; J.E.E.D. Acton, 'Nationality', in *The History of Freedom and Other Essays*, eds J.N. Figgis and R.V. Laurence, London, 1909, pp. 270-300 (first published in 1862).
10 John Plamenatz, 'Two Types of Nationalism', in *Nationalism: The Nature and Evolution of an Idea*, ed. Eugene Kamenka, New York, 1976, pp. 22-35.
11 Kedourie, pp. 20-50; see also Ernest Gellner, *Nations and Nationalism*, Oxford, 1983, pp. 130-34.

There, the liberty of the individual was frequently sacrificed to the superior right of the *Volk* with the consequence that nationalism is now frequently perceived as a force hostile to freedom and democracy.

Because in Eastern Europe, the *Volk* has defined itself largely by reference to linguistic affiliation, the issue of language rights has become a measure of the extent to which the master-nation is prepared to give way to those who do not share its mother-tongue. There is no obvious reason, for instance, why the Hungarians of Romania, the Mingrelians of Georgia and the Russians of Estonia should not be accorded the same linguistic rights as are enjoyed by the Welsh of Great Britain or the Swedes of Finland. The concept, however, of the state as the embodiment of the unified *Volk* and as the expression of an indivisible nationhood precludes even symbolic gestures to those of a different linguistic affiliation.

The practical consequences of *völkisch* nationalism for speakers of minority languages are addressed in this volume by George Hewitt and Michael Kirkwood. Both articles make it clear that the formation of new national communities in the area of the former Soviet Union has been accompanied by a heavy drive towards linguistic uniformity. As Kirkwood shows, the implementation of a state language policy in Moldova and Estonia has been pursued regardless of the huge economic costs involved. In Georgia the imposition of Georgian as the exclusive language of state has to be viewed in the context of an increasingly strident Georgian nationalism directed in the main against the non-Georgian half of the population.

Communist totalitarianism not only ate away at the fabric of the state, but it increasingly exploited nationalist passions as a means of obtaining popular legitimation and social integration. Having abolished all institutions capable of mediating between government and people, and having destroyed civil society, the Communist rulers had to reinvent nationhood as a way of binding together and mobilizing an otherwise atomized society. To the old association of state with nation was thus added the new configuration of nation and party. In the Soviet Union this identification was made at the expense of traditional Russian patriotism, which Geoffrey Hosking defines in this volume by reference to the epithet *russkoe*. As he argues, the imperial *rossiiskoe* notion of Russian identity prevailed over the *russkoe* as a way of explaining and justifying the hegemony of the party-state. The persecution endured by the Russian Orthodox Church, which is discussed in this volume by Simon Dixon, may be partly explained in terms of the conflict between the National Bolshevik *rossiiskoe* concept of the state and the *russkoe* idea of a Holy Russia.

Party, nation and state were similarly confused by Ceauşescu in Romania as a way of shoring up his increasingly beleaguered regime. The chant 'PCR' (which stood equally for 'Communist Party of Romania' and 'The People, Ceauşescu, Romania') had its counterpart in Ceauşescu's ritual baying at the Hungarian minority and in his sponsoring of antisemitic publicity. The consequence of his nationalist propaganda remains all too plain in contemporary Romania. As Dennis Deletant explains, the notion of the Romanian national unitary state and the old slogan 'Romanians must be masters in their own home' are still employed as devices against the minorities. Moreover, the quotation he gives from a spokesman of the nationalist *Vatra* organization ('We should all unite. Let there not be a Transylvanian Romanian who is not a member of Vatra Românească, so that when we have more than six million members there will be no need to declare ourselves a party, because then we shall be the Romanian nation itself, dignified and free, upright and tolerant') suggests the continued interchangeability of the concepts of state, nation and mass political party. Similar overlaps of meaning can also be found in the pronouncements of prominent members of the Hungarian Democratic Forum and may doubtless be demonstrated for Croatia, Serbia and Slovakia as well.

Communist rule not only distorted notions of state and nation but also influenced the realm of cognition. As Blaga Dimitrova argues here, Communism both altered the meaning of individual words and phrases and affected the syntax by obliterating tenses and moods. It replaced complexity of expression with clichés and superlatives, and concealed reality behind a hedge of verbal codes. Until the language is restored, perceptions of reality will remain incomplete and the possibility of effecting genuine change will be limited. Elena Nemirovskaia warns, however, that the recovery of language may occur unevenly in society and actually widen the cultural gap between the intelligentsia and the majority. As she explains, the language of the 'informal culture' which is now replacing the 'institutionalized culture' of the Soviet period, 'is as inaccessible to the man in the street as is the language of the thinking intellectuals'.

A part of Ghia Nodia's contribution serves to amplify Dimitrova's theme. As he suggests, the years of exposure to ideology have created their own form of ideological fetishism: 'The slogans in the name of which communist régimes are being dismantled ... seem to be to a greater degree borrowed ideological figures rather than verbal expressions of real inner demands of society. Society is deprived of the means even to articulate and to express its demands because language is monopolized by ideology.'

As Nodia suggests, the monopolization of language by ideology means that terms such as 'pluralist democracy', 'free market' and 'rights of the individual' may take on the character of slogans. Moreover, for those schooled in the clichés of Communism these slogans soon acquire an absolute value as certainties whereby the external world may not only be understood but mastered as well. The conviction that a political and economic system may be obtained 'sufficient to satisfy the harmonious physical and intellectual needs of man' is a conceit which is surely not confined to Communists. It may also be found among those new democrats and free-marketeers who fail to appreciate Gale Stokes's advice: 'Pluralism is messy. It does not offer formulaic solutions. It is an open-ended process rather than a system.' Or, in the words of Václav Klaus: 'It would be a great oversimplification to interpret the events in the real world as an exercise in applied science ... We know that the world is run not by human design but by human action.' In short, political pluralism and the market do not offer the same ideological and theoretical certainties as scientific socialism; that, however, is their strength and why they may be thought to work rather better.

In the inaugural lecture which he delivered in 1915 at King's College, London, on the eve of the School's foundation, Tomáš Masaryk outlined the problems facing the 'small nations' of Europe.[12] History, Masaryk explained, 'is a process of integration, but at the same time of disintegration; the double process appears as the strengthening of individualism and the simultaneous growth of collectivism'. By collectivism, Masaryk understood the development of nation-states, these being 'natural organisations of homogeneous individuals'.[13] The reconciliation of state and nation with individual liberty proved more elusive than Masaryk could have imagined in 1915. As the contents of this volume suggest, its complete achievement is still one of the tasks confronting Eastern Europe today.

Martyn Rady

---

12   Thomas G. Masaryk, *The Problem of Small Nations in the European Crisis*, The Council for the Study of International Relations, London, undated.
13   Ibid., pp. 20-21.

PASSAGES FROM

TOTALITARIANISM

CHAPTER ONE

Our Understanding of Totalitarianism

A.N. Sakharov

Totalitarianism is a terrible, all-embracing concept which swallows up the personality, life and fate of generations, with millions of victims, mad hopes and tremendous failures, the hysteria of nations and international deadlock.

This concept arose in Mussolini's circle in the mid-1920s and called for the total subjection of the individual to the state in the interest of accomplishing certain lofty, eternal and national goals. Later, Friedrich von Hayek in *The Road to Serfdom* with reference to German Fascism and Stalinism linked totalitarianism with socialist teachings and with the degeneration of the great world social utopia. Still later, Theodor Adorno in *The Authoritarian Personality* attempted to show that it is the 'atomized individual' which gives rise to the syndrome of totalitarianism, while Hannah Arendt linked totalitarianism with the model of Nazi concentration camps.

Zbigniew Brzezinski in 1956 on the basis of his study of totalitarian regimes around the world identified six basic characteristics of totalitarianism: the existence of a single mass party led by a leader-dictator; an official ideology reigning in society; a monopoly of control of the mass media; a monopoly of the armed forces; a system of terroristic police control; a central system of control and direction of the economy.

George Orwell in *1984* and Evgenii Zamiatin in *We* presented their readers with a frightening image of totalitarian society in the twentieth century in a generalized literary form.

Not so very long ago in the USSR a broad debate took place on the problems of totalitarianism in the course of which (supported by Western and Soviet research) several new approaches were put forward. It was noted that totalitarianism in general, and Soviet totalitarianism in particular, included absolute individual power, indoctrination of the population, a general amorality and a total contempt for the individual. Also, in the light of the writings of Hayek and other Western writers, totalitarianism was also discussed as a synthesis of elements of Asiatic despotism and radical ideological doctrines, and as being defined by its orientation towards the future, its appeal to the masses, its incredible ideologization and its reliance on external expansion.

There was only one subject on which both the eminent Western theorists and their present-day successors in the USSR were silent: that is, the social essence of all forms of totalitarianism, and the role played by the people in the formation of totalitarian regimes.

It is these points I would like to examine both in connection with the problems of Stalinism and with the creation of a totalitarian state in the USSR.

By 1920, according to our historians' data, only 58% of the urban population and 33.5% of the rural population were literate. All inhabitants of the outlying districts of the nation were illiterate. But even if part of the population had been literate, that would not mean that it had culture. This great mass of illiterate and semi-literate, frankly primitive, people, who did not even come close to the heights of culture, entered on to the historical scene after 1917. This was the terribly high price that Russia had to pay for its backwardness, for tsarism and for the persistence of remnants of feudalism.

Demographic data reveal that at this time the young, that is those aged between twenty and twenty-nine years, comprised 30% of the male and 35% of the female population. Taking into account the fact that they were also from the lower social classes, we have the following phenomenon: the masses were practically all uncultured, semi-literate and young, but they were energetic and passionate. This was precisely the material with which the Bolshevik leadership — Stalin — was working.

Furthermore they were semi-rural masses, bound to the soil: they were proletarianized peasants. During the First World War, these masses learnt to wield weapons. They were armed. Millions of soldiers returned from the war owning rifles, machine-guns, grenades and even heavy duty guns. During the civil war and its attendant social upheaval, millions of them went into the towns and there set up the social circumstances with which the revolutionary government of Russia was confronted.

It is also important to remember that, according to Soviet experts, at the end of the 1920s (up to and including the start of collectivization) more than 200,000 of those who were either awaiting dispossession or who had been dispossessed one way or another moved into the towns. These were the strongest, the most vital, the most prepared and strong-willed members of the rural population. They were for the most part peasants in their full bloom of strength; together with their young offspring, they represented a new generation. All these 200,000 or more people dispersed into the towns, and there, on the strength of their purely personal qualities, they took up certain positions in society.

In his post-revolutionary works Lenin repeatedly said that the Party and the country would build a new society, founded on the highest cultural achievements of mankind. His was a theoretical and conceptual approach to the future development of the country.

The fact remains, however, that his concept suffered total failure. In practice it did not happen. This was not because Lenin did not want to bring it into being; events developed instead in such a way that the bearers of the old culture were practically wiped out. They were destroyed by the revolution itself.

The conventional explanations for this are well enough known. It should, however, be considered that in our country, as the revolution evolved, a colossal historic trap was set into which Soviet society fell: the people who were to become the foundation of the future culture and who were to provide cultural support for those semi-literate sections of the populace who hungered for a new happy life, disappeared. They came before firing squads, emigrated, were killed in the civil war or were sent into exile in 1922.

One might raise the objection that, for example, in 1922 approximately 300 people in all were exiled. But what sort of people were they? Each one of them was a tremendous personality; behind each was his own school of thought, his own highly developed scientific, cultural and humanist mentality. The very spiritual élite which gave life and nourishment to all generations living in Russia at that time perished. Lenin could not, of course, have foreseen this 'trap'; hence, his passionate appeals to study, his harsh references to our lack of culture and to our primitiveness, which began to run through his works at the start of the 1920s when the intoxication of 'war Communism' had already begun to pall. He sensed that we were in that blind-alley, in that historic trap which threatens the country with incredible cataclysms, when rising, embittered, vengeance-seeking masses, lacking specific cultural guidelines, lofty spiritual and moral values and constraints, are capable of any social transgressions and may agree to any decisions which indulge their passions.

So it turned out that the most radical revolution in the world, the only victorious radical revolution in the world, began to be tinged with the environment in which it took place. This 'detail' cannot be discounted when talking about totalitarianism, about Stalin, Ordzhonikidze, Kirov, Kaganovich, Khrushchev and about all those who from then on rallied around Stalin and formed the so-called Stalinist guard.

When we speak of the people, we sometimes have a very curious image of how they were drawn into the revolution. As a rule, we think that in 1917 during the October Revolution the masses rose up to a new life and took up certain positions in the fields of economics, politics, culture, etc. In reality, nothing of the kind took place.

In 1917 and 1918 those who entered into these positions were those who had carried out the revolution with weapons in their hands. They were peasants and workers, 'dressed up in soldiers' greatcoats', and detachments of the Red Guard and sailors: they were the Party. But the millions of the masses in my opinion only joined the revolution later. The vast Russian expanses, the provinces, the outlying regions of the nation entered it gradually. For them even the civil war was just a noise overhead.

Russia only began to enter the revolution 'for real' — and this was a consequence of the country's incredible geographic dimensions — somewhere around the mid-1920s. It was in this period that the corners and the periphery rose up. Each village, each factory, where there had hitherto been neither Whites nor Reds, where there had not been civil war or, if there had, where it had been superficial or short-lived, woke up. The ordinary citizen entered the revolution.

The revolution began to trickle through to even the most remote places when the barely cultured, unfortunate, poor and destitute people realized that they could not only rise to the level of the rich and propertied, but could also rise above them in the social hierarchy by owning their houses, property and means of production, either collectively or as individuals. This sense of social revolution was the most genuine result of the October Revolution.

It seems to me that in reality the masses did not so much as get close to social freedom or a taste of the new social world in 1917; instead, the 150 million rose slowly. Decree by decree and year by year, the revolution slowly, but surely, extended in stages to the lower classes. It was the incorporation of these 'secondary' and 'tertiary' masses into the revolution with which the government of the country and Stalin had to deal. These were the very lower classes, which, in theory of course, had no idea what Marxism was or what socialism was, but which instinctively felt that their time was approaching. By their reckoning, the moment had come for social revenge for the decades and maybe even centuries of oppression.

But how could somebody from the depths, from the village, the country, the suburbs, somebody from the lower classes of the people, realize these social opportunities? The slogan of social justice was an abstract slogan for him. Dearer to him were the slogans of universal equality and of social egalitarianism. As these strata were politicized, the slogan of social justice which the socialists followed was reborn in the masses as a slogan close to social equalization.

While the revolutionary theorists were building castles in the air, the people were deciding everything in their own way. This 150 million-strong mass had its own mentality which quite clearly had its own guidelines: the new regime should give them what they did not have before. At whose expense? At the expense of the 'bourgeois counter-revolutionary' on the one hand, which was to be achieved through their participation in the new system of government. They therefore joined the Party, the Soviets, the committees and tribunals, and began to obtain the benefits which the new system in all its poverty could give them. The tremendous social revenge which the people hankered after was realized. This phenomenon should not be underestimated.

To think that the vast masses, which could not read or write, lived by lofty social ideals, is simply not to understand history.

And it was on this vast canvas of Russia that those 'betters' were advanced who were 'best' in that particular milieu — not better in our present-day understanding of the word (more intelligent, prepared, literate, humane, etc.) — but, the most cunning, relentless, go-getting and ardent, and the most resolute.

In this connection it seems to me that the notion that Stalin manipulated the people is rather naïve. Instead the people manipulated the Party in that period and they manipulated their leaders. These same lower classes, these vast layers, this pressure from below in many ways also determined both the image of the leaders and their thinking. It was, one might say, a reciprocal manipulation. Lenin was right when he said, 'In the mass of the people we are all like drops in the ocean and we can only govern when we correctly express that which the people can acknowledge.' Of course, the government did manipulate the masses, who were not only politically ill-prepared but also thirsty for social revenge, social benefits and advancement to the top of society. But the masses too exerted pressure on their leaders and moulded their collective image. As Bukharin put it, in a speech at the 1926 22nd Leningrad Province Conference: 'In Russian conditions the Soviet model of socialism can only be backward socialism.'

Today we are talking about deformations of socialism, about its distortions and other such things. But of what deformation are we speaking when dealing with the 150 million-strong masses which flooded the expanses of Russia? What deformations can we speak of when these people not only could not read Marx, but could not read at all?

In the USSR at the moment there is serious debate on whether Trotskii was a possible alternative for the leadership of the country, whether Trotskii could have led the Party and whether he could have led the people. This, in fact, was impossible. The masses would never have followed the intelligent, reflective Trotskii. Certainly, they followed him when he came to them with an armoured train and with inflammatory speeches, when he called them to arms and to death. But his books, his style, his imagery and intellectualism were totally alien to them in other, more peaceful circumstances.

In speaking about the people who created the cultural medium for those manipulations which Stalin brought with him, it is necessary to bear in mind the behaviour of the leaders themselves. Consider how Lenin and Trotskii retreated into the shadows, how the moderate Stalinists left the proscenium and allowed people of a different nature to come into the foreground: people whom we figuratively call 'men in boots'. They were leaders who were close to the people, who came from among them. They understood what the people wanted and the people in turn understood them. They were poorly educated, desperate, shrewd politicians who had been through the school of penal servitude and exile. They did not play chess with Lenin in Capri and did not study at the school of Longiumo.

The further the selection of 'leaders' went along this path, the further the intellectuals and the so-called representatives of the Lenin guard slipped away. The Stalin guard was created and a new type of leader evolved: leaders who were closer in image to those millions who rose to public life towards the mid-1920s.

In connection with this, the term 'administrative-command system' is a profoundly anti-historical and totally ideologized term. It does, of course, take into account the character and form of government in our country from Stalin's rise to power, when the administrative-command system began to blossom, up to the present day, when it still exists and is only slightly camouflaged behind the cardboard façade of democracy. The concept of 'administrative-command system' fails, however, to take account of the most important factor. The nucleus is omitted which was the *raison d'être* of Russia; that nucleus comprising the revolutionary origin of the people, their revolutionary mentality, their revolutionary passion, their cultural narrow-mindedness and their illiteracy, which together account for the popular revolutionary phenomenon which arose in the USSR in the 1920s. What was in place, then, should not be defined as an 'administrative-command' system, but as true revolutionary totalitarianism. It was the totalitarianism of the people. It was not an abstract dictatorship of the proletariat but an absolute system which was based on the hatred of the oppressed people for their enemy. It was based upon the hatred felt by a person from the lower classes who had tasted the nectar of power. It was a totalitarian system basing itself on the cult of force and on the cult of power which was realized not by Stalin nor by Ordzhonikidze, nor by Kaganovich, nor by anybody else, but by each specific individual in his own particular place. It was the cult of the victorious 'I'. The cult of strength and of power seeped upwards into every cell of society: hence, the terror and excesses which became a part of the system from 1917 onwards.

These days there is a lot of discussion about morality. We condemn much of what we term immoral. But name for me one single revolution which was moral and which was guided by moral norms! Maybe elements of moral norms were seen in the Paris Commune, but did they not render it 'soft as wax' and doom it to failure? Now in a peaceful, renewed, intellectual environment, we may begin to look for what was moral and what was immoral in 1917 and during the civil war. But to understand that era requires a great deal; it is necessary just for a moment to put oneself in the position of those 150 million who overthrew the old order.

The question is whether we condemn all the excesses associated with the social avalanche? Do we condemn this revolutionary totalitarianism? I think that the historian should not condemn, but should understand and feel acutely this process and reveal how in this environment people were formed and how the leaders of this environment evolved.

In this connection the old guard of revolutionary theoreticians, practical workers and semi-intelligentsia was doomed to pass away. Primitive, simple, and in many ways utopian slogans on the one hand, and on the other, the real values of social revenge were destined to triumph. And they did triumph and with them rose a people befitting these slogans and values. These people were intoxicated with victory and with their own strength. They were struck dumb by their own theory of building socialism in one country and were proud of being the first. Stalin came to power on the wave of rejection of the NEP, when it revealed all the dangers it posed for the ordinary people and threatened a return to social inequality. And while Lenin, Trotskii and later Bukharin were trying to find a way out of the left-hand blind-alley of the revolution, Stalin turned it into a broad corridor to the future.

What did the Party, which Stalin used as his instrument in the struggle for power, represent? By 1921 90% had joined the Party during the civil war. The Party at that time was the product of a militaristic culture. This fact should not be overlooked. Kaganovich in his address to the 16th Party Congress (1930) put forward the following data: 88.4% of the leading cadres of the Party represented at the Congress joined the Party after 1917. They were simple workers and peasants and sailors to whom Lenin had appealed in his time and to whom Stalin could also appeal in every way. It was these same simple, coarse, boot-clad masses that made up the basic backbone of the Party from the 1920s to the start of the 1930s.

I want to ask a question which has never arisen so far in our historiography — about the combination of the old and the new guard, and about the combination of the Russian and the *émigré* revolutionary guard. I want to offer a very curious illustration. In 1925, at the 14th Party Congress, K.E. Voroshilov attacked Zinov´ev (who was favoured by the workers) and accused him of 'leaderism' and of anti-NEP deviation. He added the following highly significant sentence: 'This concept is, you know, based on old, long-forgotten foundations and on *émigré* notions of organization. Comrade Zinov´ev sits abroad somewhere and, on Comrade Lenin's orders, scribbles down a memo: do this, do that, send someone there.' The ardent Stalinist Emilian Iaroslavskii, referring to Zinov´ev and Kamenev, said: '... many of us could not be abroad at that time and close to Lenin because we were building the Party here and working here'. Voroshilov's anger at Zinov´ev could only have been exhibited once power had passed to those such as himself, when the Stalin guard was already formed.

What kind of people were the Stalin guard? They were for the most part Bolsheviks — ex-convicts and revolutionaries who had spent a fair amount of time in prisons and living in exile. That is not to say that the *émigré* section of the Party did not spend time imprisoned or in exile, but the differences between the *émigré* sector and the Russian sector had become fairly clear by

1917. The emigration supported Lenin, Zinov'ev, Trotskii and others, while the Russian group, I think, recognized Stalin and those who followed after him as their true leaders. These were Russian revolutionaries who had not experienced Western emigration and who had an entirely different revolutionary approach to phenomena and processes. At some time both these and others were united by the authority and will of Lenin, but when that uniting force crumbled, a rift between them became inevitable. This dynamic was understood perfectly by Stalin, who leaned in his personal struggle for power on that section of the Party which unequivocally supported him.

The evolving totalitarian regime and its leader were a product of the revolution, of penal servitude, of the underground and of the civil war.

Lenin valued Stalin for his firmness, brutality, resolution and relentlessness; for the same things for which he valued Trotskii, Sverdlov and other leaders of the revolution. We need only recall the action of Stalin in Tsaritsyn during the defence of Petrograd and we immediately sense that iron fist which Lenin actively encouraged.

These were all people from the same revolutionary clan, with the same revolutionary style, and their revolutionary brutality and 'exaggeration' were an integral part of a general revolutionary process rooted in the rage of the people. When they stopped along the way, expressed doubts, reflected and tried to find an alternative to the left-hand blind-alley which was inapplicable in peaceful circumstances, they lost the support of the masses.

The greatness of Lenin consisted in the fact that, when the country began to settle into peaceful times, he was the first to sense the danger of these genies which came out of the lamp during the revolution. And he was the first to attempt to put the chief, most relentless, most resolute genie, Stalin, back into the lamp. But it was already too late both for Stalin and for other 'leaders'. And this was where the tragedy of Lenin began, which ended with his defeat; not only his physical death, but also his political downfall. He was the first to understand the danger. He understood that of all the others, Stalin was the most resolute, the most dangerous, the most unprincipled and brutal. Lenin sensed that Stalin could actually become his successor and carry further that revolutionary and military line which was now no longer appropriate for the leadership of the country.

And this is where the knots were tied in that tragedy which in many ways contributed to the rise to power of Stalin.

The first signs of it came to light when Lenin was wavering politically during his illness and was later dropped from the revolutionary centre stage.

His fall was definitely cataclysmic. By 1921 Lenin, who for a long time at the beginning of the twentieth century was on the left wing of the revolution, no longer represented that left wing. There were forces which attempted, in the struggle with the NEP, to galvanize the militarist system of the civil war period and wanted to go even further to the left. They wanted to realize a naïvely utopian concept of socialism, dictated by their wretched images of the course of the historical process. For these people, Lenin was already right wing.

Trotskii introduced the term 'thermidor' for what happened in 1929. Today these words are repeated in many articles and books. But what 'thermidor' are we referring to? For do not all the roots of the Stalinist regime extend back to 1917? 'The Iron Tread of Millions' guaranteed the success of Stalinism. The people-torturers became people-martyrs under the heat of Stalin without even realizing it and whilst praying to their idol.

Terror formed the foundation of the triumphant, relentless revolution of the lower classes. The notion of 'enemy of the people' and the model of the gulag were also founded in the same revolution. The bitter war was fought on all fronts, including the spiritual front. There was also the elementary struggle for a place in the sun which was fought by the lower classes, leaning on their own government.

Of course, that was 1929. After that some years went by. Was it many or not? If it was many, then the people who made use of all these models created before their time were utter criminals. If it took little time for them to change their revolutionary thinking, then they were simply continuing the logic of revolutionary totalitarianism, flavoured with the struggle for personal interests, personal prestige and the struggle with personal enemies. It is impossible to answer this question unambiguously. I believe that seven to ten years is too short a time for people to essentially alter, especially if they are of limited intellect.

Moreover we also cannot, of course, abstract ourselves from the fact that Stalin introduced into this genuine revolutionary totalitarianism so much malevolence, so much dark intrigue and so much cruelty that it even went beyond the 'normal' bounds of the most brutal revolution. Although he was also limited, he proved to be the most resolute, brutal, cunning of revolutionary leaders, who exploited the situation and mood of the people and the party masses in his struggle for personal power. He was not gifted with Lenin's understanding. In his struggle with his opponents and his struggle for personal power he followed previously formulated systems and structures. Consequently, the revolutionary totalitarianism inherent in all great revolutions grew into a personal dictatorship.

But in this matter too it would be naïve to simplify historical phenomena. The Stalinist regime, which today we call an administrative-command system, did not, however, entirely do away with the notion of revolutionary totalitarianism. On the contrary, Stalin skilfully utilized the revolutionary upsurge in the people and it can scarcely be thought that he himself, despite all the monstrousness of his crimes of the 1930s and the following years, renounced it entirely. In the Stalinist regime, despite all its outrages, repressions and firing squads, and despite the presence in power of primitive, pitiful, coarse, envious people, elements of revolutionary totalitarianism continued to exist. It is hard for us to understand this nowadays. It seems strange to us that during a period of repression the people cheered and called for the execution of 'enemies of the people'. The image of the dictatorship of the proletariat, revolutionary totalitarianism, continued to be enormously significant. It all lived on in the consciousness of the people. While twenty million were in prison and labour camps and several million drank from the bitter cup of dispossession and subsequent famine, cursing Stalin and his collectivization, one hundred million believed themselves victorious. They received crumbs and believed themselves rich. That is the tragedy and triumph of our society.

The most curious thing is that even today we have a continuation of all that has gone before, but this time in a new edition. Our society, as at some time at the end of the 1920s, has split. Some preach the line of revolutionary totalitarianism. This line never lost popularity with the people. It is a powerful, terrible, brutal line which may engender new catastrophic collisions. And the stronger the 'NEP-style' private ownership alternative grows, the more it will gain strength, gathering under its banner all those from the lower classes who have not benefited from policies so far.

On the other hand the revolution has ended, has come to nought and now the people are beginning to chew over and swallow this fact. And, of course, the end of the revolution is incompatible with revolutionary totalitarianism. This is the situation which will slowly and painfully be overcome and express itself through many present-day leaders of society. And in that situation the historical figure of Mikhail Gorbachev is the most tragic figure today. He is tragic because he combines within him the incompatible: both elements of revolutionary totalitarianism of the old society and elements of a new and entirely peaceful assimilation of revolutionary achievements. In his time Lenin perished as a political figure precisely due to the incompatibility of these elements. But in those days revolutionary totalitarianism was totally invincible. Today the correlation of forces has changed.

CHAPTER TWO

Stalinism and Pluralism: Two Pathways from the Enlightenment[1]

Gale Stokes

The most fundamental event of the past few hundred years is the great environmental revolution brought about by humanity's discovery of how to extract energy systematically from non-living things.[2] The mastery of gunpowder and steam, and the fundamental changes put in train by related developments, placed such an enormous amount of controlled power into human hands that agricultural society became obsolete, just as the discovery of how to extract energy from living things systematically, agriculture, made hunting and gathering obsolete. We are still in the first generations of coping with the literally incomprehensible changes in all aspects of our lives that this great transformation made necessary, and in fact are still using the ideas and forms invented, or at least brought to widespread consciousness, only within the past ten or so generations during which the transformation has been under way.

I would like to suggest that three basic sorts of solutions to the fundamental challenges of this transformation, all first broached in the eighteenth century, have characterized the twentieth century. I would call them the anti-rationalist genre, the hyper-rationalist genre and the pluralist genre. Only one of these, pluralism, has proven minimally adequate to the social and technological demands of the past two hundred years. This does not mean that pluralism has

---

1 This article was written in part while I was a fellow at the Woodrow Wilson International Centre for Scholars in Washington, D.C., which I would like to thank for its hospitality.
2 Some readers of a draft of this article have suggested that it is reductionist to single out energy in this way, since communications technology and other phenomena are also of fundamental significance in creating the modern world. I agree that the concept is reductionist, but I invite those who think it is too much so to perform what Rousseau might call a thought experiment: attempt to conceive what might happen in Europe and America if it were possible for sixty days to shut down completely all internal combustion engines and turn off all electricity.

adequately solved the modern problematic. When we observe the misery of not just most people in the Third World, but a large number of persons in the First World, we understand that many issues remain on the agenda of pluralist societies, not the least of which is the problem of finding a plausible framework for opposition to injustice in political systems that are suffused with self-satisfaction. The great message of the twentieth century is not the positive accomplishments of pluralism, although there are many, but the negative message of the other two genres: we have not learnt what works as surely as we have learnt what does not work. Pluralism has its problems, but the other two genres are dead ends.

I do not intend to spend much time on the first of these dead ends, the anti-rational solution. By this term I mean, of course, those movements of rage and rejection in the first half of the twentieth century that craved the technological power put into their hands by the industrial revolution but believed, as Schelling did, that the universe held 'a primal, non-rational force that can be grasped only by the intuitive power of men of imaginative genius'.[3] Nazism and Fascism rejected reason for power, individuality for *sacro egoismo*, virtue for vainglory, transparency for obscurantism, constitutions for the *Führerprinzip*, humanitarianism for racial fanaticism, objectivity for prejudice, and, in the end, the guillotine for the gas chambers.

If 1945 demonstrated the futility of this genre, 1989 demonstrated the futility of the hyper-rationalist genre. Stalinism may be understood, in my opinion, as the *reductio ad absurdum* of Descartes' assertion that we humans can 'render ourselves the masters and possessors of nature'.[4] It is not difficult to construct a historical pathway from Descartes to the ecstatic Hungarian author of 1961 who said socialism was on the verge of 'the final manoeuvres ... for the ultimate conquest of the material world'.[5] The pathway would lead through Engels, who spoke of humanity becoming the 'conscious lord of Nature',[6] and through Stalin himself. Robert C. Tucker calls Stalin a 'transformist', denying all spontaneity and autonomy that would 'impose limits upon the extent to which [something] could be transformed from without'.[7] In

---

3   Isaiah Berlin, 'The Counter-Enlightenment', in his *Against the Current*, Henry Hardy (ed.), New York, 1982, p. 19.
4   René Descartes, 'Discourse on the Method of Rightly Conducting the Reason', in Elizabeth S. Haldane and G. R. T. Ross (trans. and eds), *The Philosophical Works of Descartes*, n.p., 1955, vol. 1, p. 119.
5   Mihály Váci, quoted by Ivan Berend, *The Hungarian Economic Reforms, 1953-1988*, Cambridge, 1990 (hereafter *Hungarian Economic Reforms*), p. 148.
6   Friedrich Engels, 'Socialism: Utopian and Scientific', in Robert C. Tucker, *The Marx-Engels Reader*, New York, 1972, p. 637.
7   Robert C. Tucker, 'Stalin and the Uses of Psychology', in his *The Soviet Political Mind: Studies in Stalinism and Post-Stalin Change*, New York, 1963, p. 93. Cf. Rousseau: 'Whoever ventures on the enterprise of setting up a people must be ready ... to change human nature, to transform each individual ... into part of a much greater whole, from which that same individual will receive, in a sense, his life and his being' (*Social Contract,* translated and introduced by Maurice Cranston, Harmondsworth, 1968, p. 84).

his most extreme and mature phase, Stalin believed implicitly in the ability of the human actor (namely himself) to create a rational economy, produce new ideas in linguistics and even transmute nature itself, denying that there was anything arbitrary, subjective, risky or unpredictable about the schemes for transformation that [his] regime put forward'.[8]

In delineating the pathway from Descartes to Stalin, of course, we must remain clear that it is not an unobstructed freeway leading to a known destination for which the concept emerged in the seventeenth century, but engineering plans were drawn in the nineteenth century. Instead we confront an utterly undriveable road of convoluted twists and turns built without blueprints by squabbling construction crews who had no idea of their destination and most of whom quit in any event to start their own roads. The way to Stalinism is not preordained or inevitable, but neither is it just another one of the infinite number of narrative paths that could be constructed. Alternatives were possible at every juncture, and many took them, but the set of branchways that produced Stalinism constituted a massive test of one particularly narrow understanding of how humans construct their world.

This view is connected with the new answer that the eighteenth century proposed to St Augustine's classic question, 'Where then is evil, and what is its source?' Augustine, and most Christians who followed, answered his question by means of the parable of the Garden of Eden. Man and Woman, punished for seeking to obtain God's absolute knowledge, had been cast out into the mortal world carrying their ineradicable burden of original sin. Evil is an inherent human characteristic that cannot be eliminated but must be regulated or suppressed by authority when it inevitably bursts out into socially disruptive behaviour. The gloomy implications of this position are best represented by the savage pronouncements of the conservative Catholic Joseph de Maistre, who proposed that 'the whole earth, perpetually steeped in blood, is nothing but a vast altar upon which all that is living must be sacrificed without measure, without pause, until the consummation of things, until evil is extinct, until the death of death'.[9]

Rousseau completely rejected this view. For Rousseau, the corruption of human morals was not an insoluble problem of the soul, but a paradoxically direct consequence of humanity's most vigorous and conscious efforts to civilize itself. Only when compassionate natural man had created private property and thereby entered into civil society, with all of its 'crimes, wars, murders, ... misery and horror', had evil proliferated.[10] Rousseau's vision was vastly more optimistic than the Christian one. By placing the sources of evil outside of us, in the institutions that humans themselves had built for their own

---

8 Tucker, 'Stalin and the Uses of Pyschology', p. 94.
9 Quoted by Isaiah Berlin, 'Joseph de Maistre and the Origins of Fascism', *New York Review of Books*, 27 September 1990, p. 62.
10 Jean-Jacques Rousseau, *A Discourse on Inequality*, translated with an introduction and notes by Maurice Cranston, Harmondsworth, 1984, p. 109.

purposes, by bringing the sources of evil to the surface, so to speak, Rousseau made modern politics possible.[11] To the extent that we believe that social problems can be ameliorated through the political process, whether by reform or by revolution, we are all today Rousseau-ians.

But how was one to fix ancient and culturally embedded institutions? From the time of Voltaire's *Philosophical Letters*, there was little doubt among most eighteenth-century thinkers — one must seek out the natural laws of human interaction through the application of reason and turn the knowledge thus gained to good use. The assumption of rationality did not mean that each individual acts rationally all the time, but that there must lie deep inside of each person a true sense of what is good. When all the people together use this sense to make a decision concerning their governance, they express a general will of society that will be 'always rightful and always tends to the public good'.[12] The general will is not only an expression of human rationality, therefore, but of humanity's fundamental virtue as well. This true understanding, this general will, can be achieved, however, only in conditions of real freedom, that is, only when we are living under laws to which we have given our full consent. 'Obedience to a law one prescribes to oneself', said Rousseau, 'is freedom.'[13]

Essential to Rousseau's view is his assumption that the people, at least when asserting their general will, are a homogeneous and virtuous whole, not a plurality of factions and individuals pursuing partial interests. This is in fact what differentiates the general will from partial wills — it is the single view on any given issue that truly reflects the virtuous will of the generality. This notion that the people had one view that could be both virtuous and rational was very common in the eighteenth century, in part because of the general acceptance of the idea of mixed government, in which the people were considered a single element that contrasted with the other two elements, the aristocracy and the king. Thinkers as diverse as Edmund Burke, John Adams and the Abbé Sièyes subscribed to the notion.[14] It is, however, the Trojan

---

11 Of course he was not the only one to do so. For example, by substituting defence of property for defence of privilege as the proper function of government, Turgot and others entered into what François Furet calls 'a very modern discourse', basing their justification of the state on defending the interests of society rather than on the abstract general will, as Rousseau did (François Furet, *La Révolution française de Turgot à Jules Ferry 1770-1880*, Paris, 1989 [hereafter *La Révolution française*], pp. 34-35).
12 Rousseau, *The Social Contract*, p. 72.
13 Ibid., p. 65. Cf. Immanuel Kant: '[The rational being] is free as regards the laws of nature, and he obeys only those laws which he gives to himself' (*Grounding for the Metaphysics of Morals*, translated by James W. Ellington, Indianapolis, 1981, p. 41).
14 Edmund Burke said 'parliament is a deliberative assembly of one nation with one interest, that of the ... general good, resulting from the general reason of the whole'. Gordon S. Wood, *The Creation of the American Republic, 1776-1787*, Chapel Hill, North Carolina, 1969 (hereafter *The Creation of the American Republic*), p. 175. Sièyes held that legislators 'are not the representatives of portions of society, their electors for example, but of the entire nation', (*La Révolution française*, p. 64). John Adams maintained his

horse that permitted revolutionaries to turn Rousseau's undoubted passion for freedom into structures of unfreedom.

Rousseau's idea of a virtuous people expressing its general will contained what might be called an origination flaw. If freedom was obedience to the laws written on the basis of the general will and at the same time the condition for expressing the general will, how could the first law be written? Since it could not be written under the conditions of freedom that only it could establish, it could not be a true expression of the general will — there is no way to start the process. In 1789 the French found a way out of that dilemma — revolution. The French Revolution itself, the revolutionaries concluded, created 'the natural public virtue necessary for the exercise of national sovereignty'.[15] The reign of egotism was over, Saint Just claimed in his maiden speech, now that the people were sovereign.[16] This is why the revolutionaries made an early decision to dispense with traditional political forms, such as a senate, in favour of a unitary state unmediated by corporate structures of any kind.[17] Only such a state could reflect the virtuous people's will without hindrance, transparently as it were.[18]

But if the people were virtuous and if the general will was rational, what was one to make of the opposition? Rousseau's answer was that since a law passed in accordance with the general will was a rational expression of human freedom, disobedience to such a law could only arise from obstinacy or ignorance. In either case the duty of the magistrates was the same: to compel the deviants to obey, either by force or through education.[19] When an 'opinion contrary to my own prevails [as the general will]', Rousseau said, 'this proves only that I have made a mistake'.[20] During the French Revolution Robespierre, Saint Just and the others turned the 'mistake' of differing with

---

idea that the people were the virtuous single order of a mixed government until his death (Wood, *The Creation of the American Republic*, pp. 589-90).

15   Keith Michael Baker, 'Fixing the French Constitution', in his *Inventing the French Revolution: Essays on French Political Culture in the Eighteenth Century*, Cambridge, 1990, p. 286.
16   Carole Blum, *Rousseau and the Republic of Virtue: The Language of Politics in the French Revolution*, Ithaca, 1986 (hereafter *Rousseau and the Republic of Virtue*), p. 174. This is Blum's paraphrase of St Just's remarks.
17   The view expressed here is based on the school of François Furet. For a critique of that school, see Isser Woloch, 'On the Latent Illiberalism of the French Revolution', *American Historical Review*, 95, 1990, pp. 1452-70.
18   Jean Starobinski introduced the term transparency to describe the fundamental thread that runs through Rousseau's work, which was to recapture the immediacy of childhood experiences in the highly mediated world of adult life. Jean Starobinski, *Jean-Jacques Rousseau: Transparency and Obstruction*, Chicago, 1988, orig. pub. 1957; François Furet, *Interpreting the French Revolution*; Lynn Hunt, *Politics, Culture and Class in the French Revolution*, Berkeley, 1984.
19   Rousseau said the deviants 'shall be forced to be free' (*Social Contract*, p. 64). Cf. Lenin: 'We must crush [the oppressors, the exploiters, the capitalists] in order to free humanity', *State and Revolution*, New York, 1932, p. 73.
20   Rousseau, *Social Contract*, p. 153.

them into treason punishable by death. As Albert Camus put it, whereas in the ancient world 'there were more mistakes than crimes', in the modern world 'there are no longer any mistakes, but only crimes'.[21]

The contributions of Rousseau and the French Revolution, therefore, are profoundly paradoxical. If the source of human evil lies in the structures of society then it should be possible, assuming as the Rousseau-ians do that human beings can be rational, to improve society by changing these structures. For this to be possible political action must create the conditions whereby understanding can be expressed without being distorted by mediating institutions. Once those institutions have been eliminated, as by a revolution for example, the state can count on the rationality and virtue of the general will. And since it would be logically absurd to believe that a truly rational decision could injure the interests of those who make it, decisions made by recourse to the general will by definition support the public good. Anyone who dissents from such a law is either uninformed or damaging to the public good and must be re-educated or disciplined. Revolution breaks the old system of partial interests, of egoism. The virtuous people seize the reins of power and choose leaders who are emanations of their unquestioned virtue.[22] True rationality in politics — real freedom — consists of the efforts of these leaders to bring the recalcitrant members of society, those who choose not to count themselves among the people, to virtue.

If this thumbnail sketch of an eighteenth-century phenomenon sounds eerily familiar in the twentieth century it is because, among other reasons, Marx and Lenin passed it on to us dressed in a new form. A creature of class analysis breathed to life by dialectical materialism, the proletariat is none other than Rousseau's virtuous people. Marx did not use the vocabulary of virtue and he considered the Christian view of evil a prime example of false consciousness. The contradictions of capitalism do not grow from the greed of the capitalists, although they are greedy, but rather from their self-interested efforts to produce structures in which to live, just as Rousseau suggested. But Marx did consider the proletariat the 'special and essential product' of capitalism, the 'self-conscious, independent movement of the immense majority'.[23] It was the class that would, by seizing the means of production, eliminate the category of class itself and create a humanity that was fully free, no longer alienated by the anarchic constructs of market exchange. Such a world would be historically without evil as we have known it. History, to paraphrase Fukuyama, would be at an end.

---

21   *The Rebel*, New York, 1956, p. 173. To break with Marxism, David Horowitz says, 'was not a simple matter, like abandoning a misconception or admitting a mistake. It was more like accusing one's comrades. Like condemning a life' ('Socialism: Guilty as Charged', *Commentary*, December 1990, p. 17).
22   The phrase is from Blum, *Rousseau and the Republic of Virtue*, p. 223.
23   'The Communist Manifesto', in Tucker, *The Marx-Engels Reader*, p. 342.

Marx's entire project is a deeply eighteenth-century one — to comprehend the laws of human society and to show how this understanding can create a truly human society. Marx called the method by which he arrived at his insights scientific, which is just the word Condorcet used to describe what the eighteenth century meant by rational.[24] Neither Marx nor the philosophers meant by this term 'thinking clearly', although they did think clearly about many things. Instead they meant 'thinking as I, the one who understands these things, do'. Reason is for them metaphysical, not pragmatic, which is to say that Marx did not think of his views as one theory among many. Because he based his ideas on what he considered 'real' foundations, that is, relationships that grew inevitably out of humans' unique attribute as producers, and because he elaborated his views in terms of the dialectical method, which he believed scientifically verifiable, he and Engels considered their views simply correct. 'Marxism is not a philosophy of history', the French philosopher Maurice Merleau-Ponty said, 'it is *the* philosophy of history, and to renounce it is to dig the grave of Reason in history'.[25]

In the eighteenth century Rousseau believed that whereas the people were fundamentally good they were also weak, and so they needed a lawgiver, education, and even, on occasion, coercion. In the twentieth century Lenin believed that whereas the proletariat was the only class able to create the unalienated society of the future, it was prone to error and therefore needed a mentor. 'The people is never corrupted', said Rousseau, 'but it is often misled.' 'The history of all countries', Lenin wrote, 'shows that the working class, exclusively by its own efforts, is able to develop only trade-union consciousness.'[26] In the republic of virtue the people's representatives were fully rational because they represented the virtuous nations. In the republic of socialism the vanguard party was the repository of reason because only it truly understood the interests of the historically progressive class. As Evgenii Zamiatin put it with heavy irony in the last sentence of his novel *We*, 'I am certain we shall win. For Reason must prevail.'[27]

When Reason with a capital R did prevail in 1917 there was little doubt in the minds of the Bolshevik revolutionaries that they would be able to produce a 'new Soviet man'. If under capitalism the worker was unable to see his own interest with perfect clarity, under Communism the structures that had prevented proletarian virtue from shining forth would be eliminated and the Rousseau-ian vision would be complete. And what if the new Soviet man seemed just as prone to quibbling and disputatiousness as his old capitalist

---

24 Furet, *La Révolution française*, p. 35.
25 Quoted by Tony Judt, 'The Dilemmas of Dissidence: The Politics of Opposition in East-Central Europe' (hereafter 'The Dilemmas of Dissidence'), *Eastern European Politics and Societies*, 2, 1988, p. 231.
26 Rousseau, *Social Contract,* p. 72; V. I. Lenin, *What is to be Done? Burning Questions of our Movement*, New York, 1943, pp. 32-33.
27 Eugene Zamiatin, *We*, translated by Gregory Zilboorg, New York, 1959, p. 218.

counterpart? Education and coercion would come to the rescue, just as Rousseau proposed.

The French revolutionaries faced the paradoxical problem of leading to virtue a people that were by definition already virtuous; the Russian revolutionaries faced the problem of creating a new and unalienated Soviet man out of a proletariat that was only potentially unalienated. But the Russian revolutionaries thought they had an advantage over their French predecessors because they possessed an elaborate plan of centralized economic planning supported by a highly organized and disciplined party. But despite that advantage, 1989 has shown us unequivocally that they failed.

The view that this depressing culmination of the Marxist experience is an outgrowth of a sterile kind of rationalism characteristic of an Enlightenment overestimation of human capacities has led to harsh judgments. Václav Havel considers the approach in 'which people are first organized in one way or another (by someone who always knows best "what the people need") so they may then allegedly be liberated' is depraved.[28] 'The Marxist myth', Tony Judt has suggested, 'is not simply the error of our time, it is the inevitable consequence of a belief in the possibility of a cognitive grasp of the external world. Rationalism has not given rise to our problems — it is our problem.'[29] This judgement is not dissimilar to the one made during World War II by two critics of the anti-rationalist genre of modernizing solutions. 'The Enlightenment', said Theodor Adorno and Max Horkheimer in the opening sentences of their 1944 work, 'has always aimed at liberating men from fear and establishing their sovereignty. Yet the fully enlightened earth radiates disaster triumphant.'[30] These judgements, and others like them, have naturally focused on the débâcles characteristic of the failed genres. The cost of their failures to assimilate the industrial revolution has been so immense as to defy description, so that students of the year 2000 will look back on the twentieth century with the same sort of incomprehension earlier generations looked back on the religious wars of the sixteenth and seventeenth centuries. But these same students will not look back on every outgrowth of the eighteenth century with the same incomprehension, because there they also will find the third genre of coping with the energy revolution, pluralism.

If Rousseau is the father of the rationalizing genre of solving the political and social issues of the energy revolution, Adam Smith is the father of the pluralist genre. Smith started from the obverse of Augustine's question that motivated Rousseau. He did not ask 'Where then is evil and what is its source',

---

28 Václav Havel, 'The Power of the Powerless', in his *Living in Truth*, Boston, 1989, written 1978, p. 90.
29 Judt, 'Dilemmas of Dissidence', p. 237.
30 Theodor W. Adorno and Max Horkheimer, *Dialectic of Enlightenment*, New York, 1989, p. 1.

but the potentially more constructive question 'wherein does virtue consist'.[31] Given the enormous passions that drive human beings toward self-aggrandizement, how is it that people can and do form moral judgements? His answer was that although pursuit of their own interests pits human beings against each other, their capacity for sympathy, imagination, reason and reflection 'provides them with the rational and moral faculties to create institutions by which the internecine struggle can be mitigated and even turned to the common good'.[32] These institutions do not emerge directly as a result of leaders putting into effect a systematic and rational plan based on a general will. Smith had no faith in men of system, as he called them.[33] Whatever virtues society had were rather the unintended consequences of the internal struggle between self-interest and morality that work themselves out under the guidance of the natural laws of individual human interactions. The arena in which this play of invisible forces went on, of course, was the market.

Adam Smith had much less influence on the American Revolution than Rousseau had on the French Revolution, but it is in the American Revolution, specifically in the Constitution of 1789, that we find the innovation that gave political expression to the pluralism latent in Smith's notion of the market. The revolution of 1776 played the same function initially for Americans as the revolution of 1789 did for the French: in the minds of the revolutionaries it transformed a divided people into a republic of virtue in which the chronic divisiveness of the colonial era would disappear. Gordon Wood puts the American confidence as follows:

> Enlightened men could believe ... the new habitual principles ... could be created and nurtured by republican laws, and that these principles, together with the power of the mind, could give 'man's ideas and motives a new direction'. By the repeated

---

31 'In treating of the principles of morals there are two questions to be considered. First, wherein does virtue consist? ... And, secondly, by what power or faculty in the mind is it, that this character, whatever it be, is recommended to us?', Adam Smith, *The Theory of Moral Sentiments*, edited by D. D. Raphael and A. L. Macfie, Indianapolis, 1982, p. 265. Note the similar view of that great opponent of the hyper-rational genre, Václav Havel: 'I am not interested in why man commits evil; I want to know why he does good', *Letters to Olga*, translated by Paul Wilson, New York, 1989, p. 232.
32 Robert L. Heilbroner, 'Adam Smith', *Encyclopedia Britannica*, fifteenth edition, vol. 16, 1976, p. 905.
33 'The man of system seems to imagine that he can arrange the different members of a great society with as much ease as the hand arranges the different pieces upon a chess-board. He does not consider that the pieces upon the chess-board have no other principle of motion besides that which the hand impresses upon them; but that, in the great chess-board of human society, every single piece has a principle of motion of its own, altogether different from that which the legislature might chuse [sic] to impress upon it' (Smith, *Theory of Moral Sentiments*, p. 234).

exertion of reason ... it seemed possible for man to recover his
lost innocence and form a society of 'habitual virtue'.[34]

When the revolution came, therefore, one of the first acts in every colony
was to write a new constitution that severely limited the power of the king's
surrogate, the governor. The revolutionaries firmly believed that the state
legislators, once they were freely elected by a virtuous people to protect its
interests against the tyrannical governor, would be incapable of passing laws
damaging to the public interest.

But just as Robespierre found a bit later and Lenin much later, the people
turned out to be far from homogeneous, legislatures did not always do the
right thing and disinterested natural leaders were few and far between.
Tyranny on the part of the state legislatures, the first decade after 1776
showed, was just as real a possibility as tyranny on the part of colonial
governors. When the people are 'loosened from their attachment to the ancient
establishments', Alexander Hamilton remarked, '[they were apt] to grow giddy
[and] more or less run into anarchy'.[35] 'We have, probably, had too good an
opinion of human nature in forming our confederation', George Washington
observed.[36]

Here is the crucial point at which the Americans found a new solution to
the problem of popular sovereignty. Private interests have always disrupted
stable government and threatened political leaders. The almost universal
reaction has been to suppress unruly demands and pretensions. The rich
mythology of human sinfulness standing at the centre of Christianity justified
social restraint in the name of order. Repression in the name of a virtuous
people or in the name of the proletariat, therefore, was in a sense nothing
more than a new wrinkle in a very old pair of trousers, a secularization of
repression that can be seen as simply another chapter in the demystification of
the world.

In the decade after 1776 Americans unexpectedly re-wrote this chapter in
their own way. The articles of Confederation were not working because the
theoretically virtuous people were refusing to pay federal exactions,
repudiating debts, printing cheap money and generally running amok, at least
in the eyes of the men who considered themselves the natural leaders of the
revolution. James Madison knew that the traditional method of dealing with
such disruptions was repression, but his originality, and the originality of the
federalists in general, was to look the obvious fact that no society had ever
been homogeneous straight in the eye.

'As long as the reason of man continues fallible, and he is at liberty to
exercise it', Madison said, 'different opinions will be formed ... The latent

---

34   Wood, *The Creation of the American Republic*, p. 120.
35   Quoted in ibid., p. 67.
36   Ibid., p. 472.

causes of faction are thus sown in the nature of man.'[37] Agreeing with the Christian view that original sin was an inherent human characteristic, Madison rejected the Christian solution. Government must not suppress divergent opinions, he argued, because doing so would destroy the very freedom that is the ground for producing them. 'Liberty is to faction what air is to fire. But it could not be less folly to abolish liberty, which is essential to political life, because it nourishes faction, than it would be to wish the annihilation of air, which is essential to animal life, because it imparts to fire its destructive agency.'[38] Instead of ignoring the fact of human contentiousness in a search for unity and harmony, Madison and his federalist colleagues proposed to contain the effects of faction by creating a republic in which the powers accorded to the state were 'so divided and balanced among several bodies of magistracy as that no one could transcend their legal limits without being effectually checked and restrained by the others'.[39]

This solution, in which it is important to note that powers were not only separated horizontally among the three branches of government, but vertically among several layers of local, state and federal governments, broke with the idea of a homogeneous people possessing a single interest. The people remained sovereign in the Constitution of 1789, as they did in the French and Russian revolutions, but their sovereignty did not inhere in any single institution, such as a legislature or a party, not in fact in any institution at all. The people retained their entire sovereignty, only dispensing 'such portions of power as were conceived as necessary for the public welfare ... to such bodies, on such terms, and under such limitations, as they think proper'.[40] This was the essential innovation of American political pluralism. All organs of government in the American system were, in their separate spheres, equally possessed of the people's sovereignty, a situation expressly forbidden during the French Revolution.

The contrast with the principles of homogeneity characteristic of the hyper-rationalist genre is stark. The Le Chapelier Law of 1791, for example, stated in its preface the following: 'Sovereignty being one and indivisible, and belonging to the entire nation, no administration of a department [i.e. local government], no district, no municipality, commune or section of a commune, nor any section of the people ... has the right to execute any act of sovereignty.'[41] Instead of fearing a division of sovereignty, as did the eighteenth-century authors of the Le Chapelier Law, the designers of the

---

37 Alexander Hamilton, John Jay and James Madison, *The Federalist Papers*, edited and with an introduction by Clinton Rossiter, New York, 1961, pp. 78-79.
38 Ibid., p. 78.
39 Ibid., p. 311.
40 Thomas Paine, 'Dissertations on Government, the Affairs of the Bank, and Paper Money', in Michael Foot and Isaac Kramnick (eds), *Thomas Paine Reader*, New York, 1987, p. 168.
41 *Le Moniteur universel*, 28 February 1791, p. 503.

American constitution positively revelled in it. We will sow the 'seeds of political warfare ... in the constitution' itself, said Thomas Jefferson.[42] In this way the Americans found a way to cast aside the ancient fear of conflict and recast it into a strength, to rechannel diversity into a strategy of cohesion.[43]

American revolutionaries hoped to seize hold of their world and remake it according to human reason just as much as other revolutionaries. Alexander Hamilton asked 'whether societies of men are really capable or not of establishing good government from reflection and choice, or whether they are forever destined to depend for their political constitutions on accident and force', whereas Leon Trotskii held that 'the Soviet system wishes to bring aim and plan into the very basis of society, where up to now only accumulated consequences have reigned'.[44] But 'reason' for the Americans did not mean 'consistent with the world as we would like to see it', but rather 'consistent with the facts as we think we see them'. They were pragmatic rationalists rather than metaphysical ones. The experience of the decade that followed 1776 convinced them, contrary to expectation, that revolution did not suddenly make human beings virtuous. Therefore, they found it only sensible to construct a political system that enlisted 'the interest of vice on the side of virtue'.[45]

By permitting a plurality of interests to compete within complex and overlapping layers of government, by not assuming that the general will was one, and by not excluding a plurality of viewpoints on the grounds that they destroyed order and harmony, the Americans proved to be profoundly modern. The classical idea is that beneath the flux and chaos of ordinary experience there must exist simplicity and harmony. The task of human reason is to reduce complexity to simplicity. The modern view since Heisenberg, and surely since Einstein, Bohr and von Neumann, is that under the flux and chaos of ordinary existence exist flux and chaos, or at least indeterminacy, complexity and uncertainty.[46] The task of human reason under this dispensation is exactly the opposite as its classical duty — to avoid falling into the reductionist error of making complex things simple, and instead to find ways to understand complexity in all its contradictory confusion.

The Anglo-American pathway out of the Enlightenment is not as clear or as easily traced as the one that led to Stalinism, in part because no European states actually adopted the American system of federalism, but mainly because pluralism itself is by definition so multi-faceted. None the less, pluralist political systems characterized by representative democracy, a politics of

---

42 Wood, *The Creation of the American Republic*, p. 449.
43 These are the phrases of Sacvan Bercovitch in the introduction to his forthcoming book on Hawthorne's *Scarlet Letter*.
44 *Federalist Papers*, p. 33; *The Russian Revolution*, abridged edition, New York, 1989, p. 483.
45 John Taylor, quoted by Wood, *The Creation of the American Republic*, p. 591.
46 See James Gleick, *Chaos: Making a New Science*, New York, 1987.

accommodation in which interests contend openly in the public sphere, parties that compete in contested elections, government that is responsible in some way to the people, an electorate that eventually takes in all adults and legal protection of civil rights, did establish themselves in the European continent by the second half of the twentieth century. To the extent that they base themselves on the insight that political structures must be constructed to contain human error one may speak of them constituting a genre of solutions to the problems posed by the energy revolution.

Why has this genre, which in the past decade has had a significant resurgence not only in Eastern Europe but around the world, proven relatively successful in coping with the forces of the industrial revolution? The fundamental strength of pluralist logic, which is also its prime fault in the minds of systems builders, is its fertile vagueness. Pluralism is messy. It does not offer formulaic solutions. It is an open-ended process rather than a system. Change can occur in pluralist systems. When new situations arise, as they inevitably must, they are not automatically rejected as lying outside the current definition of rationality, although there will be those in the system who attempt to do so. Pluralism temporizes; it equivocates; but it finds a place for new phenomena — not immediately, not easily, and often with a great deal of pain and political struggle, not to mention cant and humbug. But it finds a place.

The most dynamic sphere in which pluralist political structures have permitted progress to occur is of course the economic. Hyper-rationalist solutions to economic problems have sought out an optimal plan for achieving certain social aims. Pluralist political systems, while not abandoning rationality in the sense of utilizing quantitive data and developing sophisticated economic theories, have permitted an enormous variety of solutions to the economic and social challenges posed by the Industrial Revolution to achieve a hearing. Underlying all of them is a Smithian confidence that in the end market mechanisms are the best regulators of production and distribution, but within that general rubric the variety and mix of solutions is enormous: French indicative planning and ownership of large enterprises; Swedish socialism; German co-determination; American mixed economy; Japanese co-operative structures. The flexibility of these systems has been demonstrated with particular clarity in the past decade when the explosive growth of information systems has revolutionized business without threatening the political stability of any pluralist system, while at the same time neo-Stalinist economies were collapsing.

If flexibility is a basic characteristic of pluralism, one of the great failings of the hyper-rationalist genre, and it is a typically eighteenth-century failing, is that its solutions were reified and static. Modernity was a thing, a specific set of material objects that some people knew how to achieve. For young enthusiasts who cut their teeth on Engels' description of working-class Manchester and who experienced serious privation in their youth, modernity was steel mills, coal mines and hydroelectric dams.[47] Build those gigantic factories and fill them with workers in blue smocks and caps and you are modern. But of course life is not static. Least of all are the dynamic economies unleashed by the energy revolution static. Pluralism provided a shiplap hull into which the enormously complex new structures created by capitalism could pour themselves. The ship creaks, grinds, shifts and complains, but it accommodates. A politics in which adjustment to changing circumstances and pressures is not only allowed, but honoured as the fundamental organizing principle, can weather many storms. The politics of accommodation is the great strength of pluralism, and this is what we know better now than we did thirty years ago, when a Hungarian Communist could in good conscience write that his party's envisioned plan would, within twenty years, 'not merely exempt our people wholly from problems of livelihood but allow the attainment of consumption targets ... sufficient to satisfy the harmonious physical and intellectual needs of man', a view the central committee seconded by suggesting that Hungary would shortly arrive 'at a standard of saturation on a society-wide scale'.[48] It is difficult to imagine a world-historical ideology with such extravagant claims as seeming both plausible and modernizing in the near future.

---

47 Every leader of Eastern Europe in the 1970s, including Leonid Brezhnev and excepting Gustav Husák, came from a working-class family at best, and some, such as Kádár, Ceaușescu, and Zhivkov, came from backgrounds of real privation.
48 Berend, *Hungarian Economic Reforms*, p. 147.

CHAPTER THREE

Democracy, Civil Society and the State in Contemporary East-Central Europe

Paul G. Lewis

The establishment and prospective consolidation of democracy is rightfully seen as a major political aspect of the current changes in East-Central Europe. Democracy and the enhancement of social autonomy have been understood as having pushed back and superseded the state-centred dictatorship of the Communist system. Political democracy has been closely linked with the encouragement of market economics and the retreat of the state from the administration of economic processes; liberalism and the principles of free association have taken over from the state organization and the bureaucratization of social life. But this is far from being the whole story. It is not advisable to underestimate the role of the state in the current and future development of East-Central Europe, while in conceptual terms the relationship between democracy and the state should not be reduced to a simple antithesis between liberal democracy and the Communist state.

Even a cursory review of the situation shows that the record of the state in East-Central Europe has not been a wholly negative one. The survival and growing role of the state in the region has been seen as one of the few virtues of the post-Yalta system and a pre-condition for the reassertion of national autonomy in the face of Soviet dictatorship. The existence of states and nations in Eastern Europe after the brief period of unremitting Stalinism again became a 'primary reality in that portion of the Old World' and the historic 'prevalence of the factor of states over political ideologies' was again affirmed.[1] The re-emergence and persistence of 'traditional diversities, historical particularities and sovereign orientations' was an important characteristic of the region throughout much of the post-war period.[2] Neither are

---

1 J. Lukas, 'U.S. policy towards Eastern Europe', in N. N. Kittrie and I. Volgyes (eds), *The Uncertain Future: Gorbachev's Eastern Bloc*, New York, 1988, p. 204.
2 J. Rothschild, *Return to Diversity*, New York, 1989, p. 21.

questions surrounding the role and contribution of the state irrelevant to issues of economic change.

The development of capitalist market economies have, with increasing insistence, been endorsed as a precondition for and concomitant of the development of political democracy. Directions of economic change have been closely linked with the pattern of political transformation. The Conference on Security and Cooperation in Europe which ended in April 1990 formally recognized in its concluding document the relationship between political pluralism and market economics; it emphasized that while political pluralism was essential for the sustenance of economic development, economic wellbeing itself was best achieved through the operation of market forces. Capitalism and democracy were joint partners in the creation of the post-Communist future. The linkage was again affirmed at the CSCE meeting held in Paris during November 1990. Earlier visions of a 'third way' between capitalism and socialism did not long survive once the question of system change was placed on the agenda and structures like the Iron Curtain and Berlin Wall were torn away.

The economic principles of a free market swiftly became associated with those of unrestricted political transaction and exchange in the field of government and political relationships.

Open economies have been identified not just with the development of free policies, but also with the restructuring of state-society relations and the diminution of state powers. But the identity that was rapidly established between these concepts and processes within the context of the East-Central European changes begged many of the questions concerning state-society relations that have been raised in academic discourse.[3] More practical considerations of economic organization and accompanying political arrangements also arise. The relationship between the different processes of change and the various aspects of post-Communist development — between political democracy, economic liberalism and social pluralism, for example, — also require further study. There has been, for example, some danger here of misconstruing the relation of the state both to democratic autonomy and to the development of market economies.

The role of the state and its capacity to intervene in economic processes should not be ignored as a factor contributing to economic growth and it has been understood to be an integral component of successful capitalist development. Its functions are performed in different ways. Conditions facilitating the development of processes of market exchange must be imposed and pre-capitalist élites overthrown or their influence restricted; some institutionalized mechanism will be needed to impose a rationality which is not unduly atomized if rates of accumulation are to be sustained, collective goods

---

[3] A recent example is J. Hoffman, 'Capitalist Democracies and Democratic States; Oxymorons or Coherent Concepts?', *Political Studies*, 39, 1991, pp. 342-49.

provided and negative externalities controlled.[4] The requirements are not necessarily complex and the demands of the situation are often simple to comprehend. Outcomes may also be obvious and some relevant points may be made, for example, simply by asking why Warsaw, unlike Budapest and Moscow, was not able with reasonable speed to acquire a McDonald's outlet once the possibility of international expansion presented itself.

It was not for want of trying by the multinational corporation but could be traced to local organizational conditions and, amongst other things, the fate of the holding company (aptly called Holding Wars, although the name was not intended as a reference to current conflicts) formed by the city administration and Warsaw borough councils to develop links with prospective investors in the Polish capital. Its achievements, however, were minimal — not least because Holding Wars became organizationally isolated as the administration was reformed and then much of it dismantled. The capital's People's Council ceased to exist and the city administration no longer formed part of the central state structure. In the absence of an alternative infrastructure Holding Wars could encourage foreign investors but found it impossible to offer them a physical location.[5] The consequences were clearly negative for the development of retail outlets and economic processes.

Although a minor example, this case does suggest that the state and its agencies should not be neglected as a factor in recent changes. The state and associated administrative agencies may also facilitate capitalist development and assist the establishment and operation of the market economies that have been perceived to underpin the process of democratization. If capitalism is now understood to be a necessary condition of political democracy, the development of market systems should not be thought of in terms of the state being denied all part in the operation of the economy. Neither should the reduced powers of the state be identified too readily with the positive processes of political life. It is too simple a representation to portray recent changes just as the decline of totalitarian state power in the face of a civil society which embodies all the forces of democracy.

Totalitarianism, firstly, only in a loose sense involved the repression of society and civil institutions by state agencies. State institutions and government bodies were caught up and used in the totalitarian drive against society but, it may be argued, the offices and organizations of state were used by totalitarianism rather than embodied its essence, and state as much as society in East-Central Europe was its victim. The idea of the state, in one formation, brings into play a number of factors: patterns of power and rights

---

4 D. Rueschemeyer and P. B. Evans, 'The State and Economic Transformation: Towards an Analysis of the Conditions Underlying Effective Intervention', in P. B. Evans, D. Rueschemeyer and T. Skopcol (eds), *Bringing the State Back In*, Cambridge, 1985, p.45.
5 *Polityka-Eksport-Import*, Warsaw, 9 September 1990.

exercised by responsible officials, a complex of offices rather than sets of personal relations and accompanying networks of legal authority, rule-governed processes and the accountability of power. To describe totalitarianism in terms of the increasing encroachment by the state on society, in this view, is to miss the point of what happened in Nazi Germany or Stalin's Russia with reference to the state and its institutions. Leonard Schapiro argued that totalitarianism, embodied in the person of the leader and his apparatus of control, ate its way into the fabric 'of *both* state *and* society. It was here that the real nature of the "totalitarian" regime was revealed.'[6]

Civil society, as these remarks suggest, is not necessarily antithetical to the idea of the state and exercise of its authority — although civil society is usually now defined in opposition to the state. A more considered definition, however, suggests rather that civil society is 'located outside, though not disconnected from, the institutional framework of the state'.[7] Other views and evidence from different parts of the world suggest, indeed, that the scope of civil society may extend in concert with growth in the power of the state, although there is certainly no direct one-to-one relationship and the complexity of state-civil society relations needs fully to be taken into account. One analysis concerned regimes 'beset both by problems of political legitimacy and by an apparent inability to deal with the international economic context of the 1980s', difficulties which 'stimulated new interest in the interaction between civil society and the state in authoritarian contexts'.[8]

The particular cleavages that divide civil society and the growth of horizontal ties that bring its different sectors together are clearly important, as is the definition adopted by the state of its role and policy and the contradictions and conflicts that develop within the state apparatus itself. These points have been developed with particular reference to the political and historical record of some Latin American countries, although their general implications may well have relevance to other contexts. This line of argument is certainly reflected in the views of some other writers. Decisive political action has been identified as a necessary condition for the survival and expansion of civil society, while, in similar fashion, sovereign state power may be seen as an 'indispensible condition of the democratization of civil society'.[9] The precise relationship of the state with civil society nevertheless remains a matter of some debate both empirically and in normative terms.

The exaggeration of the distinctiveness of civil society and the state to the extent that their development and the kind of values they embody might be regarded as mutually contradictory was a tendency that gained strength during

---

6   L. Schapiro, *Totalitarianism*, London, 1972, pp. 65, 69.
7   J. Frentzel-Zagorska, 'Civil Society in Poland and Hungary', *Soviet Studies*, 42, 1990, 4, p. 759.
8   A. Stepan, 'State Power and the Strength of Civil Society in the Southern Cone of Latin America', in *Bringing the State Back In*, pp. 318, 340.
9   J. Keane, *Democracy and Civil Society*, London, 1988, p. 22.

the 1980s — but one conditioned more by the resurgence of liberal principles in the West and the reorientation of its economic principles than by insight into the conditions developing in Eastern Europe or consideration of the changing parameters of social life there. Neither are the interests of democracy necessarily best served by discounting the role of the state or minimizing the conditions for its development. Ironically, the links so rapidly forged between civic freedom, democracy and the capitalist market following the collapse of Communism throughout East-Central Europe and the limited value placed on autonomous state action recall the highly specific and restricted conceptions both of civil society and the state found in the Marxian account.

While the state, for Marx, was often regarded as little more than the instrument of bourgeois dominance, so civil society was the realm of commodity production and exchange and contained little of the social autonomy and civic freedom currently foreseen and whose development is so strongly desired in the wake of Communist dictatorship and the social deformations it brought about. The idea of civil society has, indeed, been subject to considerable variation and applied in a wide range of social contexts. Few social and political concepts, noted Z. Pelczynski, 'have travelled so far in their life and changed their meaning so much'.[10] Comparative experience suggests further linkages between the establishment and consolidation of political democracy and the development of state structures. They relate, in particular, to the existence of social conditions that favour the development of stable democracy. While these refer to the circumstances of modern society, the origins of democracy as idea and form of political practice lie, of course, in ancient times.

The rise of modern, liberal, mass democracy came much later and has until recently been a fairly rare phenomenon, one broadly restricted to the post-World War I period and very narrow in its scope until after 1945. It implies a fairly restrictive definition of the democratic order, one denoting states with representative governments chosen by an electorate made up in principle of the whole adult population — each of whose votes carries equal weight and the members of which are permitted to vote in line with their political preference without fear of state intimidation. By these criteria the United Kingdom did not become a democracy until 1928 with the passage of adult female suffrage and Switzerland not until 1971 by the same token. In the United States literacy and poll tax requirements kept many out of the voting booth; it was only around 1970 that the Fifteenth Amendment was enforced in the South and black adults were routinely given the vote.[11]

---

10 Z. Pelczynski, 'Solidarity and the Rebirth of Civil Society', in J. Keane (ed.), *Civil Society and the State*, London, 1988, p. 363.
11 G. Therborn, 'The Rule of Capital and the Rise of Democracy' (hereafter 'Rule of Capital'), *New Left Review*, 1977, 103, pp. 4, 16-17.

This view of democracy, it might be argued, rests on an excessively stringent definition and might be accused of confusing political practice with constitutional order in a world which is never capable of perfection. Nevertheless, experience of Soviet practice must warn against taking constitutions at their face value (the Stalin Constitution of 1936, for example, was on paper undoubtedly the most democratic in the world). It must also be considered whether — in the 1990s — we would regard as democratic, say, states in Eastern Europe which removed the political rights of Gypsies, Jews or women (the significance of this question being by no means wholly rhetorical). The main point here is that democratic practices have only been greatly extended during the twentieth century, particularly since 1945, and that the criteria by which we judge the political practices of democracies have become more strict. All this, of course, represents a major form of progress.

The advance of democracy has had a quantitive as well as qualitative character. Just between 1975 and 1985 the number of democracies rose on one count from forty-three to fifty-three worldwide.[12] That figure could well be placed higher now. Leading US political scientists have pointed to a major surge of democratization in the 1980s, a process dated by some back to 1974 with the end of the Portuguese and Greek dictatorships. By the middle to late 1980s Dahl and Huntington were able to identify around fifty democracies.[13] But the issue of democratic stability is also a significant one. The question of the survival of democracy is an important one itself, but regime stability obviously has greater salience when a major characteristic of the political order is its capacity to secure the peaceful transfer of power from one group or generation to another whilst at the same time taking effective account of citizens' preferences. The conditions for stable democracy, it was argued in an influential work published over three decades ago, were most likely to be found in the countries of north-west Europe and their 'English-speaking offspring in America and Australasia'.[14]

There, too, were to be found some of the earliest drives towards political democracy in the early modern period. After the Glorious Revolution of 1688 English development did not deviate from the form of a constitutional monarchy and it was the American Revolution that first created the modern forms of representative government. Some of the earliest of the modern democracies were established in Australasia. The contribution of the French Revolution should not, of course, be ignored — but Lipset's judgment on the origins of modern democracy and the conditions of its stable development has not been near the mark. Despite the critical view he has taken of Lipset's work

---

12 *The Economist*, London, 8 June 1985.
13 R.A. Dahl, *Democracy and Its Critics*, New Haven, 1989, p. 234; S. P. Huntington, 'Democratization and Security in Eastern Europe', in P. Volten (ed.), *Uncertain Futures: Eastern Europe and Democracy*, New York, 1990, pp. 36-37.
14 S.M. Lipset, 'Economic Development and Democracy', in *Political Man*, London, 1963, p.71.

and the Marxist underpinnings of his own discourse, Therborn also clearly recognizes the close relationship between capitalism and democracy and tends to imply in practice the empirical primacy of its 'bourgeois' form along the broad lines established in that outline.[15]

But the general thrust of democratic forces was by no means restricted to the Anglo-Saxon areas and their neighbours in Scandinavia and the Benelux countries. The anti-colonial movements that liberated Latin America from Spanish and Portuguese rule in the early nineteenth century were frequently responsible for the formulation of democratic constitutions at the same time or even earlier than analogous developments in Western Europe. Universal male suffrage was introduced for Mexico in 1857, Panama in 1904 and Argentina in 1912. Economic development accompanied the emergence of aspects of a modern social structure and countries like Chile and Uruguay developed strong party systems. Latin American democracy, however, has proved to be highly unstable, its political life unpredictable and violent, while the paths of economic development laid down there have generally been drastically derailed.

Many factors, of course, influence a specific path of historical development, but one critical aspect of Latin American development was the fact that the process of nation and state formation was broadly contemporaneous with the movement to democracy — from the Latin American perspective a dominant characteristic of advanced capitalist democracies is that the 'most basic problems of establishing a *state order* had been solved before the struggle for democracy began'.[16] It is certainly not necessarily the case that established or strong states develop into democracies — though some tendency in this direction has been evident over the past decade and modern capitalism does seem to have developed a closer affinity with political democracy. Democracy, however, does not seem to thrive in weak states, where the challenges of state formation and consolidation remain strong and the state apparatus is not fully unified. It may seem strange to put it in these terms (and it certainly goes against the grain of some popular conceptions of recent developments), but one of the major legacies of totalitarianism in East-Central Europe has been the persistence of relatively weak states with limited powers of autonomous development and few sources of internal strength.[17]

The issue of state sovereignty is clearly an important one and, while formal sovereignty is now established and national autonomy goes unchallenged, it is evident that the weak economic base of the post-Communist states now greatly restricts freedom of manoeuvre and limits their capacity in practical terms for independent development. It was, paradoxically, the very isolation of the

---

15 Therborn, 'Rule of Capital'.
16 G. Therborn, 'The Travail of Latin American Democracy' (hereafter 'Travail'), *New Left Review*, 1979, 113-14, p. 96.
17 Compare with D. Van Atta, 'The USSR as a "weak state": Agrarian Origins of Resistance to Perestroika', *World Politics*, 42, 1989, 1.

Eastern countries from the world economy and their pursuit of economic autarchy that has placed them in a position of relative weakness and puts a question mark over their capacity to exercise national autonomy in any real sense.[18] In this, their situation may be compared with the problems that have faced Latin American democracy and the consolidation of state structures under economic conditions of dominated incorporation: dominated because the Latin American countries were enmeshed in situations of capitalist dependence and occupied a subordinate position within its international system; incorporation because they were linked with and dependent on the international system without being effectively integrated within it or possessing the capacity to use its energies for the purposes of national society.[19]

This condition imposed powerful obstacles to the unification of the Latin American states and the consolidation of their structures of rule, the position of key officials for example resting to a large extent on external sources of power and leaving them with highly selective relations with respect to national or local groups. The comparison between East-Central Europe and the Latin American countries should not be laboured or over-emphasized. Nevertheless, the links drawn between Latin America's unsatisfactory experience of political democracy, the problematic position it has occupied within the international capitalist order and its record of 'weak' statehood may well have some relevance for current developments and the future of East-Central Europe. State weakness in this sense relates to the unity, effectiveness and reach of its apparatus overall rather than to any insufficiency of power on the part of particular agencies, and it is precisely such questions of unity and structural consolidation that have emerged as an important factor in the transition from Communist statehood to democratic forms in East-Central Europe.

A major legacy of the Communist period has been the inheritance of a large cadre of government, party and state officials whose credentials and effectiveness have been open to much doubt, particularly under the new conditions characteristic of liberal democracy. Developments here have not just concerned the process of replacing existing officials and employees and strengthening the state apparatus, but also involved controversies and conflict over the issue itself which made their own contribution to the problems facing the new leaders of post-Communist East-Central Europe. The pace of change in this area and the replacement of the Communist *nomenklatura* was a major bone of contention in most post-Communist countries and contributed in Poland, for example, to the weakening position of Prime Minister Mazowiecki and his failure in the presidential elections of 1990.

The State's ability to maintain its monopoly of the means of repression and defend its position against external and internal challenges to its authority is

---

18 P.G. Lewis, 'Democratization in Eastern Europe', *Coexistence*, 27, 1990, 2, pp. 254-57.
19 Therborn, 'Travail'; pp. 99-101.

also one of the most basic components of its institutional power. Complex procedures were adopted in some countries to ensure that former officials did not consolidate their position within the new structures of the democratic state: of the 22,000 members of the former Polish security service, for example, 14,000 reapplied for employment and had to be vetted.[20] Commissions of enquiry, however, performed very differently, with 75% of candidates being rejected in Poznań province but only 8% in Gdansk. The task of constructing a new state apparatus, providing conditions for its coherent operation and securing its institutional unity was clearly not a simple one. The development of new state forms and even the strengthening of state powers and governmental capacity may well be necessary, however, if the new democracy is to be consolidated and conditions for the successful development of market economies put in place.

State intervention has by no means been irrelevant or antithetical to the successful development of capitalist economies, and the dislocation of existing state structures surviving from the Communist period is by no means an unqualified benefit if there are no alternative institutions in place to perform the necessary functions. Neither should the existence of strong institutions of state be regarded as a replication of the totalitarian experience or, necessarily, as an obstacle to the further development of civil society. Democracy, too, has put down strong roots where the modern state became established at a fairly early stage and the pressures of democratization did not have to be faced at the same time as those associated with state-formation. Mass political democracy and the establishment of full democratic rights is, indeed, a very recent phenomenon while, as Latin American experience suggests, movement in the direction of democracy has often taken place without leading to a successful outcome or stable conclusion.

The criteria for modern democratic statehood are several and they are by no means solidly established in the regions of post-Communist Europe. Questions of territoriality are not settled and, as developments in the Baltic states and Yugoslavia were the first to show, the issue of who exercises control over the means of violence remains a current one. The task of building a unified state apparatus capable of dealing with the demands of the post-Communist situation remains essentially incomplete. The nature of state power itself also remains on the agenda as the problems of creating a new constitutional order are faced and the process of constitution-making continues in East-Central Europe. The role and problematic status of civil society in East-Central Europe makes its own contribution to this situation and directs attention to the importance of constitutional statehood, taking account of fears that Communist power may be replaced rather by populism than liberal democracy and that civil society unconstrained by the Communist state is capable of exerting its own form of dictatorship.

---

20 *Rzeczpospolita*, Warsaw, 18 August 1990.

The liberal-democratic state currently seen in Western Europe and elsewhere represented initially, it should be recalled, a liberal and primarily constitutional political order; its democratic character was a later development.[21] The recent victory of civil society in East-Central Europe identified and welcomed by many led, however, to a greater concern for the expression of popular sovereignty and social interests than for the less seductive task of defining and qualifying the nature of contemporary democratic statehood. This has increasingly been seen as a source of current and future political problems. Populism is a response that is all too natural under the conditions of post-Communism. It has not only been seen as a natural response to misery, 'the years of humiliation and a low standard of living, but also the fruit of a servile mentality, of faith in the omnipotence of the state'.[22] The desires and aspirations of a greater fraction of society might be better satisfied by the political arrangements arrived at within the post-Communist order — but this is not necessarily the same thing as the establishment of political democracy. There were clear echoes of John Stuart Mill's fears of the tyranny of the majority in complaints aired in the Polish press that 'a state in which morality forms the law is a totalitarian state'.[23]

During the early phase of post-Communism some parts of East-Central Europe were experiencing similar dilemmas and sharing problems related to those faced by the nations of Western Europe during analogous phases of their political development. The political articulation of a civil society offered little guidance in itself to decisions on a constitutional settlement and promised little for the institutional mediation of power relations or the protection of minority rights. The establishment of a modern democratic state is linked with the creation of an impersonal and sovereign political order — and this means not only the abolition of the privileges of the *nomenklatura* and the elimination of party political loyalty as a basis for the holding of public office, but also the divorce of political rights and obligation from traditional privilege, property and religion. The latter factor was by no means significant in a country like Poland and already gave cause for the dismissal of a Deputy Minister of Health in May 1991. The establishment of liberal democracy therefore requires the foundation of an agreed constitutional order and involves the necessity of sovereign state power as a condition also for the democratization of civil society.

---

21 G. Poggi, *The State: Its Nature, Development and Prospects*, Cambridge, 1990, pp. 53-58.
22 A. Michnik, 'The Presence of Liberal Values', *East European Reporter*, 4, 1991, 4.
23 *Polityka*, 29 September 1990.

CHAPTER FOUR

The Russian Myth: Empire and People

Geoffrey Hosking

At the first Congress of People's Deputies in 1989, the writer Valentin Rasputin suggested that, in view of the rising tide of anti-Russian national feeling sweeping the republics, maybe Russia would do well to secede from the Soviet Union.[1] Few people took him seriously at the time: indeed many probably did not understand what he was saying. For nine-tenths of the world's journalists Russia and the USSR were in any case quite simply synonymous.

Yet, almost exactly a year later, what Rasputin proposed had begun to take effect. The Russian Republic had declared its sovereignty, which, while stopping short of actual secession, meant asserting its right to ownership of its own resources and insisting on the precedence of its legal enactments over those issued by the Union (I nearly said 'by Moscow', which would have been confusing, but would have highlighted the paradoxical nature of the situation). This, though little remarked in the West at the time, was a profoundly important moment in the history of Russia. It was the foundation of a Russian nation-state, the first time such a formation has ever existed.

For Russia, as a political entity, has always been an empire, never a nation. Kievan Rus´ was a loose association of duchies, not a nation-state, and long before its successor, Muscovy, had reassembled the peoples of Rus´, it had started to overstep ethnic boundaries and embarked on the road of imperial expansion, absorbing non-Russian territories and tribes. From that time on, perhaps the most important fact about Russia's history is that the empire has always oppressed the nation. State-building has impeded nation-building. Why is this so?

Basically, for geographical reasons. The vast open frontiers of northern Eurasia have been Russia's curse and her blessing, a deadly threat and a limitless opportunity. They enabled the Mongols to invade and devastate her in

---

1 *Izvestiia*, 8 June 1989, p. 6.

the thirteenth century; but they also enabled her four centuries later to reverse that invasion and establish dominion over the largest expanse of territory ever ruled over by any state, an expanse which, moreover, went on growing till the mid-twentieth century. Every time Russia expanded, it did so in order to absorb and control the source of some danger, real or imagined — but very often real. Geopolitical realities compelled Russia to be either a huge dominion herself or a petty principality in someone else's: the equivalent of the Grand Duchy of Riazan, perhaps, or the vassal khanate of Kasimov. The fear of division and impotence, of helpless subjection to ruthless aliens, lies deep in the Russian consciousness, and avoiding that fate became an overwhelming priority. In fact, Russia became in terms of what you might call 'square kilometre-centuries' the greatest of all historical empires, outdoing by a considerable margin her closest rivals, the British and Chinese.[2]

This fact is intimately linked to the overbearing and sometimes grotesque forms of authoritarianism by which Russia has been ruled. Viewed soberly, the empire exceeded by far the capacity of Russia's population to defend and administer it. To do so at all required both extreme concentration of resources and also the co-operation of outsiders. This was the purpose of the formation of that peculiarly Russian type of nobility, the *dvorianstvo*, created by the absolutist state (in part from the aristocracy of conquered peoples) and tied to it by the duty of service. It was also the reason for the relentless fixation of the Russian peasantry: they too were bound to the service of the state, through taxation, military recruitment and through labour duties on a noble's estate. Serfdom, which in most of Central Europe was commercial in motive, was generated in Russia by the needs of the state.

Even the church was subjected to the same imperatives. In the mid-seventeenth century, when Muscovite diplomacy and arms were beginning to achieve success in Europe, the Orthodox Church started to prepare itself for an ecumenical role in keeping with a great empire by correcting its service books and liturgical practices in accordance with what were held to be the best international examples. The state, in the person of Tsar Alexei, overthrew the Patriarch who had decreed these reforms, but all the same enforced them with a ruthless violence which split the church from within, and drove many of its staunchest believers into a schismatic movement which has endured to the present day. At the beginning of the eighteenth century Peter the Great went a stage further by abolishing the Patriarchate, which had been the symbol of the church's independent standing, and reduced the church to a department of state charged with securing the welfare of the common people, providing basic education for some of them and keeping all of them in quiescent obedience towards the powers that be. Catherine II completed the process by

---

2 R. Taagepera, 'An overview of the growth of the Russian Empire', in Michael Rywkin (ed.), *Russian Colonial Expansion to 1917*, London,1988, pp. 1-7.

expropriating the Church's landholdings and submitting it to financial dependence on the treasury.

Nobles, peasants, church ... : these are normally the pillars of a nation, especially in the seventeenth and eighteenth centuries, before the industrial and democratic revolutions. In Russia they were subjugated to a state which exploited them for the needs of empire. One of the most remarkable testimonies to the predominance of the imperial ethos is the way in which the tsars recruited Germans to staff the military and civil service. The Germans, especially the landowners from the Baltic, responded with enthusiasm, rose in quite large numbers to the highest ranks, and became some of the Tsar's most dedicated servitors. Germany in the seventeenth and eighteenth centuries was the home of Kameral-Wissenschaft, the science of public administration, but no German principality, not even the Kingdom of Prussia, remotely offered the scope for the exercise of such skills as the diverse territories and people of the Russian Empire, 'ripe for development', to use the jargon of a later age. By the reign of Nicholas I something like a third of the highest official posts were occupied by Germans, most notably perhaps the long-standing Count Nesselrode, who could not even speak proper Russian, and of whom Freiherr von Stein (certainly no Slavophile!) remarked: 'He has neither homeland nor mother tongue'.[3] Bakunin caustically dismissed the whole set-up as 'Knuto-germaniya'.[4]

Of course, many empires in history have co-opted foreigners to help with trade, administration or military affairs. One has only to think of the Ottoman empire, which did this to a greater extent even than the Russian. But, unlike the Ottoman, the Russian Empire was not as a matter of principle a supernational or even purely dynastic entity: it bore the Russian name, professed the Russian faith and bore on its banners the symbols of Russia. When in the early nineteenth century Count Kankrin (himself Greek by nationality) proposed to end this anomaly, to remove the ethnic designation and rename the empire Romanovia, the proposal was rejected.[5] Konstantin Aksakov may have felt that, since the time of Peter the Great, Russia had been a nation occupied by an alien bureaucratic regime,[6] but we cannot take so simple-minded a view. There was an imperial consciousness which was genuinely Russian. Some nineteenth-century writers were its exponents, the greatest of them Pushkin.

---

3 John Armstrong, 'A mobilized diaspora in Tsarist Russia', in J. Azrael (ed.), *Soviet Nationality Policies and Practices*, New York, 1978, pp. 75-76; A.E. Presniakov, *Emperor Nicholas I of Russia: the Apogee of Autocracy, 1825-55*, Gulf Breeze, Florida, 1974, p.45
4 M. Bakounine, 'L'empire knouto-germanique et la révolution sociale, 1870-1', *Archives Bakounine*, Vol. 7, Leiden, 1981.
5 N.V. Riasanovsky, *Nicholas I and Official Nationality in Russia, 1825-55*, Berkeley and Los Angeles, 1986, pp. 225-27.
6 Andrzej Walicki, *The Slavophile Controversy*, Oxford,1975, p. 251.

The truth is that we should recognize that there have always been two forms of Russian national consciousness, an *imperial* one, which focuses on the state, and an *ethno-cultural* one, with a tendency to alienation from the state. This dichotomy is confirmed by the Russian language, which has two epithets for them, respectively *rossiiskoe* and *russkoe*. There is, furthermore, plenty of evidence for the existence of a persistent patriotic awareness in Russia focused on the people and hostile to, or at best suspicious of, the state. The historian Michael Cherniavsky has shown that the notion of Holy Russia was oppositional in its implications and grew out of the sense that the Muscovite state was losing its moral bond with the people over which it claimed to rule by divine right.[7] This legend was taken up and given added emphasis by the archpriest Avvakum and the Old Believers, who regarded the doings of the state and its puppet Nikonian church establishment as the work of the Antichrist.

In the eighteenth century the anti-governmental current in Russian national consciousness led a precarious and scarcely perceptible existence among the Cossacks and Old Believers, rearing its head briefly but sensationally in the person of Emelian Pugachev. Perhaps too it endured discreetly in the monastic cells of the Orthodox Church. In general, though, it was not till the nineteenth century that it became again a prominent factor in Russian politics and culture. The first stimulus was the Napoleonic War, for this was not just by the imperial army which had gained so many condign victories in the previous hundred years, but also by the efforts of partisans and armed militia bands drawn straight from the peasantry. The feeling took hold that an imperial patriotism was incongruous which imposed the privations of serfdom on ordinary Russians: that was the chief motivating force among the young army officers who attempted to overthrow the tsar in December 1825. In the following generation a similar indignation pervaded the oppositional ideas of both the Westerners and the Slavophiles.

The Slavophiles were the first to try to formulate the ideas of anti-governmental Russian patriots in a language adequate to the European political and philosophical discourse of the time. Ironically, such was the condition of Russian culture at the time, that they had to borrow heavily from German idealism in order to do so. Significantly, they focused their speculations on the two social orders which had probably suffered most heavily from the demands of empire: the peasant community and the church, seeing in them both manifestations of a *sobornost'*, a spirit of community, which they believed distinguished Russia advantageously from the apparently more successful social and political systems of the West.

---

7   Michael Cherniavsky, 'Tsar and People and Russia', in Orest Ranum (ed.), *National Consciousness, History and Political Change in Early Modern Europe*, Baltimore, 1975, pp. 118-43.

The Slavophiles misread history: the evils they attacked began not, as they asserted, with Peter the Great, who merely radicalized existing tendencies, but with Ivan the Terrible, in fact with Muscovy's first excursion beyond the ethnic borders of Rus´ into rule over non-Russians, that is, into empire. Nevertheless, their focus on the peasantry was deeply appropriate, for the peasantry had indeed kept alive certain principles of community which the Russian state had elsewhere undermined and destroyed.

The peasant community (*mir*) took shape between the sixteenth and eighteenth centuries to suit both the demands of empire and the needs of the peasants themselves. For the state, and the landowners who acted as its agents, it formed a convenient means of organizing the peasants and counting them so that they could be taxed, recruited and compelled to perform labour dues. For the peasants themselves it offered a mode of risk minimization and social security, a means by which the burdens could be distributed in such a way that they fell on those best able to bear them. The landowner usually knew little about agriculture and was content to leave the peasants to cultivate the field and run their own affairs, provided they fulfilled their obligations to him. Accordingly the peasants developed their own form of participatory democracy, whose forum was the *skhod,* or village assembly, in which every head of household had the right to participate. The *skhod* took all important decisions about village life, including the crop rotation to be followed in the fields and the distribution of land between households. It was not democratic in the sense in which we understand the term today: its procedures emphasized consensus, authority and custom rather than human rights and the rule of law. Nevertheless, it testified to a lively participatory spirit at the grass roots: precisely what had been lost in politics at a higher level. The Slavophiles were right to see it as something distinctive and valuable in the Russian way of life.

The first Russian socialists also singled out the *mir* as an institution worth preserving, along with its working-class counterpart the *artel´*, and converting into the corner-stone of a future society. This current was so strong that even Lenin, who despised the *mir* as a relic of the feudal past, had in practice to bring it in as a key element in his revolutionary alliance: in effect, he handed it complete power in the countryside.

If one looks at the Soviet Union, then, it is far from self-evident that it is essentially a Russian empire. The name of the state is not Russian: indeed, it bears no ethnic or geographic designation. Its emblems are explicitly internationalist and its ideology theoretically no less so. More than that, the Soviet regime has wrought such destruction upon the Russian church, Russian culture, the peasantry and the natural environment, that it seems monstrous to think of it as being in any way Russian, as Solzhenitsyn has repeatedly pointed out.

Yet all the same, even here I think that we can discern a definite Russian subtext underlying the symbolism and the power structure of the Soviet state. Certainly, if you ask any non-Russian he will tell you in no uncertain terms that he has been oppressed by Russians for decades and will unhesitatingly identify the Soviet regime as being Russian in its very essence. The core of the party-state apparatus is mainly Russian (or Ukrainian, which in this case means Little Russian); so too are the senior cadres of the armed forces and the security police. Russian has been the language of military command and of most official transactions, as well as of ideology and of much of the education system. Russian history and culture, albeit in bowdlerized form, have dominated pedagogy, at least since the mid-1930s.

I would suggest, in fact, that in the Soviet period the split between imperial and ethnic Russian patriotism has become even more radical. The Soviet state, or rather the Communist Party, has oppressed and exploited Russian culture for the needs of empire even more ruthlessly and destructively than did the tsarist regime. Russian national consciousness has accordingly also been sharply divided into two categories, which the American scholar John Dunlop has clearly identified, and which he labels (i) National Bolshevism and (ii) 'revivalism' (*vozrozhdenchestvo*).[8] The first represents the *rossiiskoe*, the second the *russkoe*.

The touchstone of their differences has been their attitude to Stalin. The National Bolsheviks revere him as the leader who expanded the Russian state to its most grandiose dimensions; the revivalists' viewpoint has a certain internal consistency, though they underrate the extent to which Marxism took on specifically Russian features when it was imported, and to which the Soviet state has inherited Russian traditions. The National Bolsheviks' outlook, on the other hand, suffers from an irreconcilable contradiction. They respect the tsarist state, and they approve both its imperialism and its espousal of Russian nationalism; yet they also revere Communism, which began by destroying the tsarist state, combatting Russian nationalism and encouraging the separatism of the non-Russian peoples. They also have great difficulty in explaining how, in the 'unbroken stream' (*edinyi potok*) which the Soviet leadership has inherited from the tsarist, the Russians are oppressed and exploited. Unlike the other nations the Russians have no 'elder brother' to blame for their sufferings. Some National Bolsheviks do their best to explain away these inconsistencies by invoking the myth of an international conspiracy of Zionists and Freemasons, which corrupted the Communist Party from inside and seduced it into anti-Russian crimes, such as the murder of Nicholas II and the destruction of the Cathedral of Christ the Saviour.

From the mid-1960s to the mid-1980s National Bolsheviks and revivalists moved further and further apart. Since 1985, however, under pressure of political crisis and the greater assertiveness of the non-Russians, the revivalists

---

8 John Dunlop, *The Faces of Contemporary Russian Nationalism*, Princeton, New Jersey, 1983, pp. 242-43.

have split. Some of them, like Rasputin, Belov and Astafyev, have moved closer to National Bolshevism, fearing that no kind of Russian national identity can be preserved without a Russian empire. Others, like Mozhaev, Zalygin and Academician Likhachev, have distanced themselves even further from the traditional forms of the Russian/Soviet state and have joined the democratic camp.

The latter represent, I believe, the true interests of Russia today. Russian national values can best be preserved and extended in a Russian nation-state, such as most European nations succeeded in establishing by the nineteenth or early twentieth century. There will be enormous difficulties in creating such a political entity. The Russian Republic is itself an ethnic patchwork, and some means must be found of ensuring that the national minorities living within it are able to satisfy their aspirations no less than the Russians themselves. Then there is the intractable problem of the twenty-five million Russians who live outside the Russian Republic, in territories whose populations are often now quite hostile to everything that reminds them of their former masters.

But precisely for their sake it is crucial that relations between the Soviet nations remain as peaceful and mutually tolerant as possible. In practice, too, many Russians living outside Russia seem able to detach themselves from the legacy of empire and to embrace the cause of the sovereignty of their present homelands, as can be seen in the various referendum results of March 1991. Certainly, in my view there is no doubt that the appropriate political outlook for Russian patriots today is anti-imperial: they should not be in opposition to Rukh and Sajudis, but in alliance with them.

CHAPTER FIVE

Metamorphosis in the Czechoslovak Economy[1]

Václav Klaus

All of my life I have been a very diligent student of economics. I am a true believer in its basic paradigm (both methodologically and philosophically) and I would strongly argue that there is nothing more practical than a good theory. I would repeatedly stress that without my theoretical background in general economics, in disequilibrium macro-economics, in econometrics and other areas, I would not have been able to do my job for even one day. But the radical transformation of Czechoslovak society and economy is not an exercise of applying economics to a practical problem.

This is a very sensitive issue for me because I have been often criticized at home for implementing an 'extreme and obsolete doctrine of laissez-faire' at the end of the twentieth century. Nothing can be further from the truth because preaching 'market with no adjectives' does not mean implementing it in real life. It would be a great oversimplification to interpret the events in the real world as an exercise in applied science. Moreover, it would be a disaster to impose the dreams, prejudices, constructions and blueprints of ambitious and irresponsible intellectuals upon the real world. That is exactly what I am not interested in doing. We in our part of the world know probably better than anybody else that attempts to implement the ambitions of intellectuals quickly and directly lead to the Brave New World of totalitarian regimes which Aldous Huxley warned us against some sixty years ago.

We know that the world, to the great benefit of all of us, is run not by 'human design' but by 'human action' (to use the Hayekian terminology). We are not so ambitious as to try to dictate the reform process, to plan its detailed sequencing, to fine-tune it, to implement some old or new theoretical doctrines, to realize simple or sophisticated social utopias, etc. We do have our dreams and preferences but these are much less ambitious. We accept and take it as a constant that we live in a complicated world of checks and balances, of unpleasant but existing constraints, and of significantly limited decision-making abilities. We know that in the real world there are millions of our fellow citizens who follow neither our suggestion nor our ideological dogmas, but instead follow their own self-interest.

We know that it is our task to prepare the necessary preconditions for a successful transformation of a centrally-planned, administrative and state-owned economy to a standard market economy based on private initiative and on private ownership.

In my understanding, there are four basic preconditions which must be fulfilled in any country which aims to undergo a systematic change. I would dare to argue that we in Czechoslovakia have already reached that stage in all respects.

First, one must have a vision of where one wants to go and what one holds most crucial. Negativism and rejection are not enough. One must be able to create and sell a country a positive vision of where one wants to go and of what one wants to accomplish.

Secondly, one must have a pragmatic, feasible reform strategy. It is impossible to have a five-hundred-day plan one day, and three stages or any other kind of reform blueprint another day. The pragmatic reform strategy is not a railway timetable. It is more or less a chessgame. One should know the theoretical beginnings and should know how to play chess. However, one cannot forecast a move of the White King after the twenty-seventh move. So the pragmatic reform theory and the possibility of controlling it and of reacting to it is the second necessary precondition.

Thirdly, one has to be able to create a political and social consensus supporting the reform changes. This support is absolutely necessary and I would strongly argue that Czechoslovakia is the only country which has succeeded in this respect.

Finally, the fourth precondition for successful reform is to begin. One has to be able to put together a critical mass of necessary reform measures and begin implementing them, not begin by debating them. We have already put in place the critical mass of reform measures that pushed us over the Rubicon. We simply moved from one economic and social system to another.

What belongs to the critical mass of reforms? I do not speak from a theoretical and *a priori* opinion but from experience. First, lifting off all kinds of controls and the opening up of markets is essential. The crucial moment is price liberalization. In Czechoslovakia, 95% of all prices are now free. This is more than in most European countries ten years ago.

The second part of the critical mass of reform is opening up the economy to the rest of the world. This means foreign trade liberalization and the introduction of at least internal currency convertibility. Both events took place in Czechoslovakia on 1 January 1991. The third cornerstone of the reform process is massive, rapid and 'wholesale' privatization.

What are the lessons which can be learned from the Czechoslovak experience? First, liberalization on all fronts must be completed overnight and residual regulation should be minimized. The faster it is done, the better.

From experience we have discovered that liberalization is much easier to implement than we originally expected it to be. I remember the Sovietologists in the West who ten years ago speculated about the date when *perestroika* would liberalize prices and make the currency convertible. They put this date at the year 2006. I remember ideas about fifteen years of gradual liberalization. They are all nonsense. Liberalization must be done overnight and not doing it fully means introducing new and additional distortions which complicate an already difficult decision and make it more difficult than it was before liberalization.

In this respect, I disagree with the famous and false dilemma between gradualism and shock therapy. No dilemma like this exists. There are reform measures that must be done overnight because their time dimension is zero and there are those reform measures which take time. Privatization takes time and therefore it is impossible to speak about shock therapy, similarly with liberalization. All the fancy theoretical articles discussing the optimal sequencing, or gradualism versus shock therapy, are missing the point.

The second lesson which can be learned from the Czechoslovak experience is that the economic fundamentals expressed through the macro-economic policy must be very conservative. There must be a balanced budget and very cautious and slow monetary growth. After having surplus budgets, probably the only country in Central and Eastern Europe to do so, for 1990 and 1991, we are having trouble balancing the budget for 1992. However, we are convinced that it is very important to have a balanced budget for many old-fashioned textbook reasons.

The third lesson relates to the exchange rate. The Czechoslovak crown is fixed against a basket of five major currencies. The exchange rate must be viable and defendable even at the expense of having the rate far from purchasing power parity. One must be prepared to explain a hundred times a day that there is a difference between these two variables. A question which is repeated more often than any other is exactly this one. One must be willing to undertake and justify a dramatic devaluation. This is the only way to stop hard currency regulation, the black market and all similar distorting phenomena.

The final lesson relates to privatization. Privatization must combine standard and non-standard methods. Using only the standard methods described in textbooks would take not years, not decades, but centuries. If we moved as fast as your country under Margaret Thatcher in the 1980s, we would privatize the Czechoslovak economy in about six hundred years. We cannot afford to privatize two, three or four firms a year. We have to privatize two, three or four thousand firms a year. Therefore, we have to combine the standard methods with the so-called non-standard methods; one example is the famous voucher privatization scheme created under my auspices as a method of artificially augmenting the savings of the population and accelerating the privatization process.

The voucher booklet was first put on sale to the Czechoslovak public for the symbolic price of about an average weekly salary. After registration, we expect millions of Czechs and Slovaks to participate in this simple process. Vouchers will be exchanged for shares of the privatized state-owned firms in a highly sophisticated, nationwide and computerized 'silent' auction. This is a unique and a very specific approach. We are convinced that there is no way of privatizing a formerly centrally planned and fully state-owned economy without such a device.

Now a few words about the results of the process outlined above: what does one see, witness and feel in a country undergoing such a dramatic therapy? First of all, one sees a visible, spectacular change in mentality and in the whole social climate. We really live now in a different world. One feels it permanently, just walking on the street.

Scholars of disequilibrium macro-economics know that switching from an excess demand regime to an excess supply regime is of the utmost importance. Ten years ago when we were modelling on our computers, the idea of switching was just of theoretical interest to us. I must confess that I could not imagine the actual switching. Price-liberalization can be done immediately and overnight. One escapes from the world of shortages, of repressed inflation, of permanent excess demand to the world of excess supply. It was done even faster than in theory and it was a complete surprise for me. One discovers that all the economic agents change their behaviour and activity overnight. Instead of searching for goods, which is a standard task for consumers in a shortage economy, the economic agents are searching for markets or for jobs. It is a very deep change.

I must confess that I was afraid of what the prices would do after lifting all controls after forty years of rigid, administratively controlled prices and of repressed inflation. Our macro-economic studies indicated that the rate of disequilibrium in Czechoslovakia was lower than in other Central European countries. After liberalizing the prices, the rate of inflation on a monthly basis was 26% in January. Inflation was 7% in February, 4.7% in March, 1.95% in April, 1.85% in May, and after that in July, August, September and October inflation was zero. It becomes evident with a restrictive macro-economic policy that one can let prices go. The prices are until now more than favourable and this disinflation record has not yet been repeated by any other country. There are some small price increases in November as a result of the new harvest but in spite of these, the price story is very favourable.

Less successful is the output development in which we face the unavoidable J-curve. We are still on the decline. With all the inaccuracy of the statistics, we expect GDP to decline 12-14% this year. The decline is unavoidable and to my great regret will continue. We expect that we will reach the 'transformation bottom' after the completion of the first privatization wave at the end of 1992. We hope to have the first positive quantitative macro-economic results in 1993. This decline is very hard for some parts of the population to accept. However, there is no other way.

Finland, a neighbour of the Soviet Union, is not undergoing a major systemic change, privatization, liberalization, introduction of currency convertibility, legislative changes, or anything else. But this country had an important share of market in the Soviet Union. If I am not wrong, the GNP of Finland will decline 5-7% this year. The Czechoslovak decline of 12% with a much higher share of trade with the Soviet Union and undergoing all the above mentioned reforms does not seem so major. The decline is simply unavoidable.

There are public auctions in the so-called 'small' privatization process permanently taking place every weekend all over Czechoslovakia. Every weekend tens of public auctions all over the country take place where hundreds of small businesses are privatized. I should point out that these small businesses are not so small. A week ago, I was asked to cut the ribbon in a newly opened department store in the suburbs of Prague. I asked the owner how many employees he had and he said 126. Last Saturday, I was in Hodonin in Moravia. A man who had just become the owner of a brick kiln told me that he employs 155 people. Small privatization is not just privatization of cafes or small shops. It is a very important process which complements the 'large' privatization which mostly deals with standard industrial firms.

I am sure that you know about the very unpleasant coincidence of events of which we are victims. We are introducing our own reform at a time when the full disintegration of COMECON and especially the Soviet Union is occurring. This year we lost about 60% of our Soviet market. In this respect macroeconomic performance is extremely good. Imagine, the East Asian dynamic, aggressive, eastern tigers (Japan, S. Korea, Taiwan, and Singapore) overnight losing 60% of their American export markets. They would economically collapse. They are not undergoing privatization, liberalization and all of that at the same time. Therefore, finding Western markets is of the utmost importance for all of us.

I always stress that we need business more than we need aid. We are not interested in financial assistance because we should not be using loans to buy our own products. What we really need is business and trade. Recently, I was in the United States with President Havel. We visited the White House, the Capitol and the State Department and three times we discussed the US import quota on Czechoslovak cheese. We were informed that we were exporting to the United States one seven thousandth of one per cent of American cheese consumption. Nevertheless, there is an import quota against Czechoslovak cheese. Regardless of all the rhetoric in the West about co-operation, aid, help, assistance, etc., my cheese story paints a different picture. Our metamorphosis is, however, under way. We still have a long way to go but I would argue that we have already crossed the Rubicon.

1   This paper was delivered as the Stamp Memorial Lecture at the University of London on 26 November 1991 when the author was Deputy Prime Minister and Finance Minister of Czechoslovakia. The author introduced his paper as follows: 'I was honoured to have been invited to present the prestigious 1991 Stamp Memorial Lecture here tonight. I took and take this invitation as a personal honour for someone who until recently would not have even been permitted to deliver a normal lecture at home, let alone a special lecture at a university abroad. The fact that I am here tonight, and that I am able to deliver a lecture similar in content both here and in Czechoslovakia, is the most convincing proof that the basic metamorphosis of Czechoslovak society has already been achieved.

At the same time I take this invitation as a symbolic award to the Czechoslovak people and as a signal that we are moving in the right direction. We appreciate the fact that you are interested in our bold attempt to dismantle the institutions of a non-democratic and an economically extremely inefficient and wasteful system, and to create a pluralist democracy and a market economy. I have to add a qualification which is now widely associated with me. Two years ago I said that we want to build a "market economy without any disqualifying adjectives".

Finally, I take this invitation as a demonstration that our effort has a wider meaning not only for us but also for you. It is significant even for you living in a country with a stable democracy and with a long history of a functioning market economy, because in your country also there have been various periodic attempts to replace such a system with more interventionistic, dirigistic and paternalistic approaches. Even you might have an interest in the historical and unprecedented move of Czechoslovakia back to Europe, back to the European tradition of democratic institutions, and back to a liberal political and economic order.'

THE RECOLLECTION OF IDENTITY

CHAPTER SIX

Nationhood and Self-Recollection: Ways to Democracy after Communism

Ghia Nodia

When a liberal-minded Western intellectual speaks about the 'nation' as something 'imagined', 'created' or 'invented', he claims to stand firmly on the ground which is called 'democracy' or 'the rights of the individual'. The individual and his/her rights are presupposed as something unquestionably 'real' and democracy is considered the best historically-known mechanism created by men to ensure the realization of their rights. Yet democracy is not the only man-made social mechanism: there are also some good, others not so good, or even quite bad. Nation is only one of those inventions. Anyone who wants to determine his/her attitude towards this or any other invention has to assess how good or bad it is. It means that a question has to be answered: does clinging to nationhood or 'nationalism' favour the development of democracy and protection of individual rights, or not? This usually leads to another question: what groups of society benefit from rousing nationalist feelings and what real interests do they follow?

In this respect the liberal individualist outlook is frequently supplemented with the Marxist outlook (I use the word 'Marxist' in a very broad sense, implying different forms of economic determinism and not necessarily a doctrine favouring socialist or Communist values). According to this view, the real interests of men (at least after gaining social and political freedom) are their economic interests. A mode of linkage to these interests determines criteria of 'reality'. Thus, in order to give a rational account of nationhood and nationalism one has to find their roots in economic interests and to derive the former from the latter.

The realm of social life is thus described as a realm of individuals, who want to be free and prosperous, and who create a network of social mechanisms in order to attain these goals. Everything that obscures this clear picture is labelled a social mythology. Social mythology allegedly takes social phenomena which are really created and ascribes to them the same degree of 'reality' and 'naturalness' as to the individual and his/her inalienable rights. Nation is rendered 'mythological' not by its creation (democracy and state institutions are also created), but by its claims to be 'real' or 'natural'. The 'Mythos of Nation' consists in an assertion that nation is a self-sufficient entity rooted in a natural or divine order to which the political reality of the state should correspond. The liberal and Marxist critique of nationalism aims at denouncing this mythos and does its best to demonstrate the created artificiality and epiphenomenality of nation.

The liberal Western understanding of nationhood and nationalism, being based on these general theoretical assumptions, may at the same time be more or less tolerant. The intolerant stream has been especially impressed by German Nazism and considers all manifestations of national feeling in its light. According to this viewpoint, nationalism is by its very essence hostile to individual freedom and human reason, and tends to subject it to the interest of some mystically interpreted whole, which is always just a disguised form of the tribal unity (Popper).[1] The tolerant attitude (Gellner,[2] Anderson,[3] et al.) does not consider nationalism as fatally incompatible with a liberal outlook and democratic political practice, but still presents it as inseparable from a mythological way of thinking. A rational analysis of national consciousness, even in more tolerant and sympathetic mode, sees its objective in its unmasking and exposing the 'true' reality hidden below mythological figures of thinking. It is presupposed that the researcher him/herself is out of this mythological realm and has obtained a safe value-free point from which the national consciousness can be analysed.

I am not going to argue that nation is something natural and primordial, that it is created by God, Nature or even History, and that it can serve as an unquestionable ground for solving political problems. My argument is that the individual with his/her inalienable rights is also created (or 'invented', or 'imagined', etc.), that it is created in the same sense in which the nation is created and, moreover, that the individual and the nation are just two parts of the same invention.

In the Western tradition of political thought nationalism has been criticized not only from the liberal individualist position, but also from the opposite conservative point of view, as, for example, in Robert Nisbet's *Community and Power*.[4] Nisbet considers the mode of human life in modern Western civilization using the major categories of existentialist philosophy: the individual and the society find themselves in a deep crisis which consists of total alienation and a lack of security. The reason for the crisis is seen in a loss of community (Karl Popper would brand such a mood as nostalgia towards the

---

1   Karl Popper, *The Open Society and Its Enemies*, Vol. 2, London, 1957, p. 49.
2   Ernest Gellner, *Nations and Nationalism*, Oxford, 1983.
3   Benedict Anderson, *Imagined Communities. Reflections on the Origins and Spread of Nationalism*, London, 1983.
4   New York, 1962.

lost tribal unity), which in its turn is caused by 'the developing concentration of function and power of the sovereign state'.[5] In the New Age the State has by and by ousted old traditional communities, which provided the individual with some personal status and sense of security. Those were communities based on kinship, faith and locality, the ones which Benedict Anderson would call 'real' rather than 'imagined'.[6] The state and individual became allies in their rebellion against traditional communities: the individual would free him/herself from the communal authority leaning on the state power; the state ignored traditional communities and appealed directly to the individual will. 'State and individual become the key terms of modern political discussion just as surely as the group was the key term of medieval political thought.'[7]

The rise of nations and nationalism is seen as directly linked to the rise of the individual and individualism. The traditional ('real') community has been supplanted by the political ('imagined') community as the basic point of reference with respect to freedom and power, and another name for this political community is the nation. Emancipation of the free individual presupposes emancipation from the power of the traditional community over its members; in order to overcome it an individual has to identify him/herself with the 'imagined' community, i.e. nation, of which he/she is an anonymous, impersonal member. The feelings of insecurity and loneliness are not, according to Nisbet, the only bad thing about supplanting the traditional (real) communities with political ones. The authority of traditional communities effectively counterbalanced the state power. Since they are undermined, there exists no real power able to limit the omnipotence of the state; the latter, being earlier an ally of the individual in his/her struggle against the communal authority, can now in its turn infringe with impunity upon the rights of individuals and transform the political community into the totalitarian one. Communist and Fascist totalitarian regimes represent two examples of that strong and dangerous tendency.

This critique of nationalism seems to me much more consistent than the liberal individualist one. Liberalism and nationalism served as allies in the nineteenth century. It is broadly accepted that the rise of nationhood as the modern political principle begins with the epoch of the French Revolution, and that nationalism as an ideology and as a type of popular movement sprang up first as a reaction to the Napoleonic wars. Of course the Napoleonic conquests themselves cannot explain anything because all previous history of mankind has been the history of conquests, annexations and assimilations. This was the conqueror who paradoxically infected the conquered peoples with the principle of national independence, and so did all the Western conquerors of what is now called the Third World. Napoleon turned out to export the

---

5   Nisbet, *Community and Power*, p. xx.
6   Anderson, *Imagined Communities*, p. 15.
7   Nisbet, *Community and Power*, p. 112.

principle of the nation-state as a general pattern of statehood: the principle of political community that renders itself a sole source of legitimation of power.

The French Revolution was lucky to find a ready-made nation moulded for it by monarchic rule. All it needed was to change the political principle: the legitimation of power 'from above' (God-Monarch-subjects) had to be supplanted by the system working from 'beneath' (People, i.e. Nation — representative bodies). The problem of volume, or internal horizontal limits of any established or would-be nation, which gives rise to nationalism, had yet to spring up. But as soon as other parts of the world tried to follow the proposed pattern, it became clear that not any given multitude of human beings may be considered (or, better, consider themselves) as 'People', whose 'General Will' is there to construct democratic institutions. Before people begin to build up democracy, they must decide (or 'imagine', if you will) that they are a nation, a political community, which needs a political organization of its own in order to express its 'General Will' and arrange its life as it thinks proper. If not — if men do not think that they are a nation, that they are members of the same political community, democratic institutions simply will not work. Decisions of the majority will not be binding for the minority, because the latter will express them as decisions of some 'alien' people who want to impose their rule upon 'us'. Any more or less deep political disagreement will be followed thus by a chain of secessions and/or bloody conflicts: something we view in former Communist 'Unions'. Steady functioning of democratic institutions presupposes a basic consensus, or 'basic we', the general pattern of which is explicit in the beginning of the Constitution of the United States of America: 'We, the people of the United States ...'.

How any given group of men acquires this 'basic we' and why they come to think they are a nation are separate questions. Of course, nations cannot be 'invented' arbitrarily, free of will. But neither are they composed 'naturally', i.e. irrespectively of a people's will to be a nation. The main argument of positivistic (or reductionist) anti-nationalists is absolutely correct: no clear and valid 'objective criteria' of nationhood exist according to which a computer disposed in the United Nations would be able to determine which unit of peoples 'deserves' to be called a 'nation' and to obtain a state of its own, and which does not. Linguistic, geographic, confessional, historical, anthropological and other factors are certainly very important but in no way self-sufficient: they are only valid for peoples themselves in deciding whether or not they are nations.

There are times when some would-be parts of a nation need to be persuaded ('you are ours', 'we have to cling together'), and these arguments serve as a means of persuasion. But persuasion — even when enforced by violence — may fail, and then a given unit of people forms a separate nation or joins another one. A decision to be a nation can never be calculated in a completely rational way; but only groups of people who consider themselves to be nations have until now been able to create democratic political institutions based on rationality. Nationhood is a non-rational prerequisite of rational political behaviour.

Thus it seems correct to say that it is not the nation that produces nationalism, rather nationalism creates nations[8] — in a sense, that nation-formation is a part of the human effort to proceed from a traditional sacralized system of rule to the modern principle of self-rule; it is not that 'naturally' pre-given nationhood is a criterion of self-determination, but that an enterprise of political self-determination shapes definitely a unit of people willing to determine itself. In strictly the same sense one cannot say that individuals create individualism, but individualism creates free, self-sufficed, autonomous individuals with their inalienable rights. Traditional societies know nothing about the 'rights of the individual'.

Saying this, one should be aware of a mistake which may arise from misinterpreting the word 'creation': as if the 'creator' and the 'created' exist as two separate entities. This misunderstanding gives rise to an instrumentalist doctrine of nation-formation, according to which nations are consciously (or at least semi-consciously) created (in a sense — forged) by certain social groups (usually élites) pursuing some 'real' economic or political interests. The so-called 'ordinary people', of whom the nation consists, become the object of mass manipulation. The pair of nationalist élites and manipulated masses thus construed is a direct successor to the famous coupling of the sly priest and the naïve peasant, the former deceiving the latter in order to exploit him effectively — an example used by the Enlightenment atheists for explaining religion. This one-sided rationalist approach fails to explain why the strong seven-decades'-long propaganda led by Communist bureaucratic élites in the USSR did not succeed in moulding a single Soviet nation (which several years ago some people in the West considered to be already created), while the first small steps towards democracy gave rise to the strongest nationalist movements.

Another premise of this attitude is the belief that 'primordialism' can be the only alternative to instrumentalism. The notion of the 'createdness' of nation does not necessarily imply that it was created by somebody in order to obtain something; 'being created' stands here just for 'not pre-given'. Nation-formation is an act of self-creation or, to put it differently, of self-determination. The pattern, according to which this act of self-creation proceeds, is self-determination of human personality. Or, one may say, national self-determination is an extension of personal self-determination on to the horizontal level of civic and political life. The meaning of self-determination consists in delimiting a piece of space free from the divine and traditional determination of human action. The struggle for it may be traced

---

8 'It is nationalism that engenders nations, and not the other way round' (Gellner, *Nations and Nationalism*, p. 55).

back to the Renaissance and is both rooted in the Christian understanding of Man, as an image of God, and directed against theocracy in the sense of the submission of human individuality to religious institutions. Self-sufficing human individuality as opposed to the traditional community is by no means something 'natural' or 'self-evident', but 'created' or 'imagined' thanks to a definite interpretation of the Christian religious tradition. Application of the same mode of thinking to the social reality produces a notion of the self-determination of the nation, or nationalism. In the case of human individuals the rational and moral self makes use of its own 'natural' substance in order to build a free and self-sufficing personality according to the pattern of Divine Personality. In the social domain the politically self-conscious part of society makes use of existing ethnic (linguistic, cultural, historical, etc.) ties in order to build a nation as a political, historical and cultural personality. Self-determination of human personality serves as a blueprint for social and political self-determination. National self-determination is a principle of state-building in a world where the autonomous and self-sufficing person plays the principal part.

The existence of a direct line leading from the free individual to the free nation may be illustrated both logically and historically. European liberalism encouraged an idea of national self-determination from the very beginning; a number of modern treatises on nationhood and nationalism cite John Stuart Mill, who said that 'it is in general a necessary condition of free institutions, that the boundaries of governments should coincide in the main with those of nationalities'.[9] But the reverse does not necessarily hold true. Popular movements that claimed freedom for persons and for nations often actually neglected the former and gave birth to regimes that suppressed the human individual in the name of national integrity and power. After the downfall of German Nazism in World War II, European liberals categorically denounced nationalism as something essentially hostile to freedom and democracy, a source of tensions inside states and between them. Earlier co-operation between liberals and nationalists was explained as based on misunderstanding, as a failure of nineteenth-century thought to discern hidden demons present in nationalism from the very beginning.

What is the root of the paradox? As I have said, there exists a difference between the countries which created the blueprint of 'national independence' and those who tried to follow it afterwards. In the latter the relationship between state and civil society differed from that in the former. Peoples that sought full nationhood were frequently not 'ripe' for it socially (which meant that structures of civil society were absent or underdeveloped) and/or politically (which meant no political community had been previously shaped and substantially consolidated like that in monarchial France). The national

---

9 J. S. Mill, *Considerations on Representative Government*, New York, 1958, pp. 232-33.

legitimation of state power could not just 'crown' civil society, since a political community had yet to be created in order to legitimate the national idea — which demanded a strained effort 'from above'. Personal and social emancipation did not precede national self-determination. Thus, although all or almost all national movements have championed sincerely both values of freedom and independence, freedom was often sacrificed to independence embodied in a strong state. The principle of the nation-state is easier to 'import' than personal freedom and civil society. Newly emerged nations were undemocratic not because they exceeded in nationhood, but because they lacked civil society.

Today the word 'democracy' is usually linked in our minds to the word 'freedom'; it is understood as a set of institutions which guarantee protection of individual freedom. It is thus generally implied that totalitarianism is something opposed to democracy as its external enemy. But if we go back to the original understanding of the term we will recall that 'democracy' is primarily connected with 'power', not 'freedom'; namely, it is a system of power legitimated 'from beneath', by the 'General Will' of people. It so turned out that this system of power also gives the best historically known possibilities for the protection of individual rights; but this cannot be derived from the general principle of democracy itself. Democratic procedures adopted by the modern pluralist democracies present just one possible way of asking the 'General Will' what it says in concrete; and a procedure which endows the opinion of fifty-one per cent of those who decided to vote with the status of the 'Will of the People' is not a very good one, but it has proven itself so far to be better than any other. Both Communist and Nazi totalitarianism claimed to speak and rule on behalf of the People, but presented different interpretations of the general democratic principle: they sought the 'General Will' in a different way.

The main problem of emerging democracies is not just to acquire by an act of rational choice institutions and procedures which have proved to be effective elsewhere, but to form political communities, which implies a certain mode of human mentality and is prior to any concrete rational choices. Precisely speaking, the twentieth-century totalitarian regimes do not represent some distinct anti-democratic forces, but children's diseases of democracy-formation. Robert Nisbet was much more pessimistic, in his above-mentioned book,[10] about the inevitable degeneration of political community into the total community than we are today, but it seems doubtless that this tendency of totalitarian degeneration is an intrinsic, though not fatal, danger of democratic evolution. And the danger of nationalist totalitarianism or authoritarianism is a particular expression of this danger, just as the striving for national self-determination is a particular expression of the general democratic movement towards social, political and personal self-determination.

---

10 Nisbet, *Community and Power*, pp. 189-211.

I think this general reasoning is useful for an understanding of what is happening and is going to happen in the former Communist countries, especially the USSR. That Communist totalitarianism finds itself in a state of collapse is only a negative description; but if the events have also some positive meaning, one may speak about a 'Rise to Modernity'. What peoples freeing themselves from Communism are trying to do is to acquire a universal blueprint of modern civilization which consists of both national and liberal-democratic principles in building state and society. The peculiarity that makes this effort unique is that the point of departure in this transition is not the traditional, but the Communist society. What is going on in former Communist countries has never occurred in history.

Communist rule has not only been founded on repression and dictatorship. The history of mankind has known many kinds of repressive regimes, but they were interested only in exercising power, as arbitrarily as possible, in a given social reality. As to Communism, its main objective has been to bring any social reality in conformity to ideas once elaborated by intellectuals. Communism is an effort to change the 'nature' of society and the 'nature' of man. That is why it is hostile to everything 'natural' and 'organic', nature in the proper sense included. In an endeavour to achieve a supreme reign of ideology it cannot annihilate reality completely, but it can 'bracket' it (which is a parody of the Husserlian sense of the term) and build a phantomized reality of ideological fetishism. What is left of reality proceeds in the shadow of these fetishes, as real economic relationships are preserved only in the 'shadow economy'. Having not succeeded in killing reality, it succeeds in creating an ultra-fetishist mentality which is the main product of Communist rule.

Dismantling Communism is primarily an ideological process as much as Communism itself has been an ideological phenomenon. Denouncing ideological fetishism is more essential for the post-Communist mind than solving problems which a modern man is used to calling 'real'. This may be illustrated by the wave of destroying monuments in Eastern Europe and the USSR which may seem strange, and even barbarous, to the civilized and enlightened mind, but is absolutely coherent for those born and bred under Communism. Real anti-Communism cannot help being iconoclastic.

The primacy of ideology inherited from Communism by the post-Communist world also refers to positive values which are being set off against the Communist dogmatics. The phantomized ideological world destroys the foundations of civil society where they had earlier existed and prevents their formation where they had been absent.

Thus, the slogans in the name of which Communist regimes are being dismantled — 'pluralist democracy', 'free market', 'rights of the individual' — seem to be to a greater degree borrowed ideological figures rather than verbal expressions of the real inner demands of society. Society is deprived of the means even to articulate and express its demands because language is monopolized by ideology. This last sentence may sound somewhat Frankfurt-like, but I doubt whether anyone in Frankfurt could ever imagine the degree of 'linguistic alienation' in Communist society.

Where are the inner resources on which society may lean in its effort to gain freedom from Communist fetishism? Since the current social reality is unrecognizably distorted, one thing society can do is to recollect itself and to try to restore the social and national self that was once there. A 'frozen history syndrome' is created which is deeply characteristic of the post-Communist mentality. As the Communist regime tried to 'bracket' social reality as non-existent, so the anti-Communist reaction tends to imagine a period of Communist rule as a historical non-entity, the period when history was 'frozen'. The objective now is to 'defrost' it, that is to pull history directly from its freezing-point. A wave of restorations in the former 'Eastern Bloc' countries and especially in the Soviet Union is complementary to that of monument-destructions. Points of controversy between parties or movements concern not so much current reality, but parts of the historical past that should be recollected and hence restored in the first place. It is frequently mentioned that the opposition movement in Russia began with two groups, one pro-Western and another anti-Western, the first of which called itself 'Memorial' and the other 'Pamiat'', which means 'memory' in English. The main argument of the monarchists in Georgia is not that a monarchy is a better kind of rule, but that Georgia must restore itself not from 1921 when it was re-annexed by Soviet Russia, but from 1801 when it was first annexed by the Russian Empire.

The national-independence movements in the USSR usually follow this recollection-restoration formula. Almost no one speaks about founding a new independent state; every nation seeks restoration of the independence of which it was deprived by force five or seven decades ago. The insistence of the Baltic states on their juridical continuity may be understood from the reality of international politics: many leading countries have recognized the incorporation of the Baltic states in the USSR as unlawful. Yet, even their behaviour cannot be reduced to rational political calculation. The point is more symbolic than political, and it is just more evidence of the 'frozen history' and 'self-recollection' mentality. It consists in the belief that the real choice, the real act of self-determination had already been made and that a period of Communist non-history could in no way diminish its validity. Nations that now seek full independence think that since they once acquired this universal nation-state pattern — whether for two decades, like the Baltic states, or for three years, like Georgia — and have been forcibly deprived of it by external force, have only now to return to the path they never gave up of their own accord. It means that they have already formed themselves as full political personalities in the course of real, not ideological history and need not begin the process anew.

This kind of insistence on restoration, not foundation, has its valid historical arguments. Disintegration of the Russian Empire after World War One came in the first place as a result of an anti-monarchical revolution. It was not caused by national-independence movements, which were not strong enough at the time. But still, the fact that former provinces of the Empire used the power vacuum to form new nation-states has not been a historical fortuity. It expressed the world-wide tendency of spreading the nation-state principle as a universal blueprint of state-building. Once the *ancien régime* was destroyed, it was in complete conformity with the political situation that peoples would 'determine themselves' along national lines and thus join the 'Family of Nations'. Russia just shared the fate of the Austro-Hungarian and Ottoman Empires. Had Russia followed the European way of political evolution after that, the emergence and development of new states would have seemed completely natural. But a supra-natural ideology gained victory in Russia and, in the course of several years, almost all the newly emerged states were forcibly incorporated in the new 'proletarian' empire.

Although this concept of restoration, not foundation, of normal social life in general, and of nation-states in particular, is valid both juridically and historically, the 'self-recollection' and 'frozen history' attitude linked to it preserves its dangerous aspect. Communist rule did not arrest history in reality. Something real and irreversible happened to nations in the Communist period. What the 'frozen history' syndrome does to their mentality, is that it frees men from a sense of historical responsibility for their evolution under a totalitarian regime. Thus, the 'frozen history' syndrome finds its continuation in the victimization and 'external enemy' mentality; anything undesired in the life of a nation is projected to the activity of some external enemy, while 'we' are always just victims and cannot bear responsibility for the process of social, economic, mental or moral corruption that person and society undergo under Communism. 'Bolshevism has nothing to do with Russia; it has come to our country in a sealed coach', one can hear from a Russian intellectual, who hints at Germans paying Lenin for undermining Russia and letting him travel through Germany to Russia during wartime. If a Russian says this, what should Lithuanians or Georgians, who really fell victim to the export of the Bolshevik revolution, think? But the distinctiveness of the Bolshevik regime is, as I have said, that it not only dominates society, but makes every person an accomplice in the whole crime on which the system of power is founded. The 'frozen history syndrome' ousts this universal guilt feeling and directs its energy to the search for scapegoats, producing thus a perfect ground for the development of right-wing authoritarian tendencies.

After all, what is real and what is unreal in the post-Communist world? One thing may be said for sure: if we try to analyse the situation from the viewpoint of problems which are called 'real' by the Western mind, we have little chance of success. The course of events is to a considerable degree defined by something that may be called the 'post-Communist mentality' and that is the reality, even the basic reality of the post-Communist world. It means that the future development of a post-Communist nation to some degree really depends on what kinds of social and political traditions they have to 'recollect' and 'restore'. And in order to cure themselves from an inadequate understanding of social reality and to obtain a sense of historical responsibility, peoples living in the post-Communist world must really restore what is worthy of being restored and make sure they are really independent socially and nationally. It is the only way to disclose a horizon of understanding screened from them by ideological fetishism.

CHAPTER SEVEN

The Reconstruction of Community in Late Twentieth-Century Europe

Anthony D. Smith

With the demise of Communism in Eastern Europe and its current transformations in the Soviet Union, the received patterns of political community have suddenly been undermined, if not fatally damaged. A whole structure of European and global politics and social relations has, it seems, been fragmented and shattered: a structure that Communist ideology and practice, as well as the Cold War, had held together. The Communist decades suddenly appear as merely an interlude between successive acts of the nationalist drama; at the same time, they bequeathed a legacy from which Europeans, especially in the East, are unburdening themselves at different rates and in varied ways.

Here I am concerned with one aspect of this legacy and its possible replacements: the problem of community and solidarity in both Eastern and Western Europe. Three questions inform my argument. First, what kind of effect did Communism have on community-formation in Europe, mainly in the East? Second, what kinds of community are now open to Europeans, East and West, since the demise of the Communist state and its shrinkage in the Soviet Union? Finally, what is the likely impact of the new types of national community, and especially of the ethnic revival, on the Europeans, or non-Europeans and minorities? Through some attempted answers to these questions I shall try to show that the higher levels of active political participation and ethnic self-renewal which characterize current quests for reconstructed community in Europe hold dangers, as well as promise, for Europeans and non-Europeans alike. For the central problem has now, and increasingly will, become how to manage the popular ethnic nationalism unleashed by the demise of Communism and the fluctuations of capitalism.

The Communist legacy

I shall deal briefly with the first question, since it has been the subject of considerable debate.

For my purposes, we may somewhat crudely characterize the Communist legacy as facing two ways: on the one hand, as an aspiration for a new 'utopian' kind of community, which breaks dramatically and radically with the national past immured in 'pre-history', and on the other hand, as underpinning and even legitimating the identities and boundaries inherited from that same national past, with *realpolitik* modifications where appropriate. Put another way, the ruling Communist parties froze many large ethnic identities and national boundaries, while attempting to dilute and alter their contents. This was to be achieved in two ways. The first was through proletarian mass-mobilization. The 'masses' or 'workers' were to be mobilized for national-social goals proposed by the CPSU leaderships, the Party vanguard. Yet, at the same time, this was no 'movement from below'. Mass-mobilization was to be incorporated into the central Party and State institutions and guided by a centralizing programme and unilinear ideology.

Moreover, it was not the total national population that was to be so mobilized and incorporated from above; it was the workers and the peasants, in their national dress, who were to be standardized and co-ordinated, not the nation and people *per se*. In other words, Communism proposed a very specific reading of the nation, its social composition and its goals, one that was in some ways antagonistic to a looser, more traditional nationalism, while at the same time resembling nationalism in its evolutionary belief structure and eschatology.[1]

That eschatology retained the hope that, one day, the socialist content of national aspirations would eventually render national boundaries and identities otiose; but under the impact of events and the continuing evidence of national and ethnic resilience, that hope in a future fusion of nations was, if it was ever seriously entertained, increasingly consigned to an imaginary future and postponed *sine die*. By the 1970s it was clear that the nation and its ethno-national contents and boundaries had remained fairly intact, particularly in Eastern Europe, and that it continued to provide the only real basis for both popular action and state policy.

New types of European community

Given this nationalist base and Communist legacy, what kinds of community appear to be widely acceptable in a post-Communist Europe? What are the

---

1   For the Leninist mode of incorporation, see Samuel Huntington, *Political Order in Changing Societies*, New Haven and London, 1968. For some resemblances between the belief-structures of nationalism and Communism, see Anthony D. Smith, *Nationalism in the Twentieth Century*, Oxford, 1979, ch. 5.

characteristics and forms of a future, reconstructed community in today's Europe?

We can perhaps explore some answers to these questions by distinguishing four types of community, according to whether they are 'traditional' or 'utopian', and whether their mode of integration is 'centralist' or 'pluralist' in character.

1. *Traditional-centralist*: these communities claim a long history and political tradition, as did the dynastic and bureaucratic states of Western and Central Europe. These states are also characterized by varying degrees of centralized authority, unlike say the plural character of integration in the United States, Canada, Belgium or Switzerland. So the first kind of community, the one with which Europe has been long familiar, is both traditional in the sense I have indicated, and also fairly centralist in its mode of integration.

2. *Traditional-pluralist*: a second variety of traditional communities is a looser, more pluralist type. Its modes of integration tend to be of the consociational and/or federal variety, as in Belgium, the former Yugoslavia and Switzerland. Whereas the centralist type of community is held together 'from above', by the central state institutions and their political traditions, the pluralist variety is based far more on constitutional devices emanating from compromises between constituent ethnic communities and/or regions. In that sense, state institutions and élites depend far more for their legitimacy and efficacy on popular and sectional groups and interests, i.e. 'from below'.

In both types of traditional community, however, there is a strong bond emanating from social and political traditions, and a strong sense of community based on a shared past and its collective memories; and an acceptance of these traditions and memories as validating the community and its political institutions.

3. *Utopian-centralist*: in contrast with these traditional communities based on an accepted historical tradition we have two varieties of 'utopian' community. Such communities deny or reject any historical heritage and tradition. Theirs is a revolutionary project for a new type of community, instituted *de novo*, and seeking to remodel human relationships in novel institutional settings.

Of these types, one is centralist in its characteristic mode of integration. The Communist states of both Europe and the Third World exemplified the 'utopian-centralist' type. Here the 'new man' was to be formed 'from above', by Party and State mobilization, in order to create the classless society. To realize this project, there had to be a fundamental break with the national past and all its pre-revolutionary structures, which were tainted with bourgeois and even aristocratic assumptions and practices.

4. *Utopian-pluralist*: the other utopian variety is more pluralist in its mode of integration. It usually lacks a centralized system of control, and its forms are more popular and inchoate. Here I would include the many small-scale experiments in community — communes, sects and so on — that thrive on the active commitments and changing networks of relationships of their members.

The polar extreme is, of course, revolutionary anarchism; but we have also recently witnessed a proliferation of groups, movements and networks devoted to various causes from ecology to feminism and minority rights, in which the break with past traditions is matched by resistance to the modern state and an active desire for new kinds of social relationships.[2]

Which of these types of community can be said to have the most appeal for contemporary Europeans? In the absence of more systematic evidence, continent-wide generalizations must be viewed with even greater scepticism than usual. But I think recent events have demonstrated a widespread disillusion with our third type of community, the 'utopian-centralist' variety sponsored by Communism. In most cases the Communist regimes seem to have failed the test of 'solidarity-creation'. They were unable to win the allegiance, let alone the active collective commitment, of their citizens. And the rites they rehearsed with so much ceremony were increasingly empty.

But neither can it be said that our first type of community, the 'traditional-centralist' variety, commands much enthusiasm from its citizens. The centralized bureaucratic state based on a long political tradition can often appear remote, managerial and élitist, especially to minorities and lower classes. Perhaps that helps to account for the resurgence of ethno-nationalism in the West, in the old, established, industrial and democratic states of Western Europe.[3]

This leaves us with two very different kinds of model community. The one is 'utopian', but generally a small-scale network of active participants shaping their own destinies through popular movements. The other is the looser variety of traditional-historical community, the plural society with its varied historical formations to which people are still attached and which appear to answer to their need for solidarity.

If we regard the recent wave of democratization in Eastern Europe, and the revived ethno-nationalism there and in the Soviet Union, as forming successive phases of a broad popular to demotic ethnic nationalism, then we can begin to glimpse the new forms of community that many Europeans are seeking. They are groping today towards a new synthesis of history and popular participation, and the type of community they wish to inaugurate is one which combines the vernacular past of each *ethnie* with the active social networks and citizenship characteristic of modern social movements and

---

2   For analyses of some of these movements and networks, see the early study by Jo Banks, *The Sociology of Social Movements*, London, 1972, and the more recent one by Alberto Melucci, *Nomads of the Present: Social Movements and Individual Needs in Contemporary Society*, London, 1989.

3   There is a large literature on the ethnic revival in the West. Michael Hechter (*Internal Colonialism: the Celtic Fringe in British National Development, 1536-1966*, London, 1975) emphasizes the bureaucratic remoteness of the modern Western state as a major factor in the resurgence of peripheral Celtic nationalisms; cf. also Milton Esman, *Ethnic Conflict in the Western World*, Ithaca, 1977.

modern nations. From this perspective participation in experimental forms of community based on such networks and movements, such as the Greens, feminism, minority rights and the like, is linked with, even allied to, the renewal of ethnic nationalisms in both Western and Eastern Europe. This in turn requires a diminution of centralized state power, of the kind that both traditional bureaucratic states in the West and utopian bureaucratic states in the East wielded. Only the pluralist version of traditional community can accommodate the decentralization desired by many Europeans today.

Of course, the aspirations and movements of Europeans must operate within several economic and geo-political constraints. The future shape of the continent, and the types of community that are likely to emerge, will be the result of a complex interplay between these ideals and aspirations and the wider structual constraints. But we must not allow our appreciation of these contraints to obscure or underestimate the power and popular basis of democratic and participatory aspirations in contemporary Europe.

A re-ethnicized Europe?
What does the new synthesis of history and participation, vernacular culture and active social movement, mean in practical terms for Europeans, non-Europeans and for Europe itself? Here I can only provide a few sketches of possible scenarios.
1. I start with the Europeans. Broadly speaking, what we may call the emancipatory synthesis I have just outlined will mobilize once again the power of ethnic myths and sentiments in various parts of Europe. We witnessed this in the 1970s in Western Europe — among the Scots and Welsh, the Flemish, Bretons, Basques and Catalans, and others. Now we are watching a similar cycle of popular ethnic nationalism in Slovenia, Croatia and Kosovo, in Transylvania, Bulgaria, the Baltic states, Ukraine and the Caucasus, not to mention in Russia itself. Despite all the differences in starting-point and background, as well as in purely political goals, the ethnic nationalisms in the East share many cultural and social features with their Western counterparts. For they all spring from an earlier wave of popular ethnic nationalism, in which a mobilized, vernacular culture-community, and not just an exclusive aristocracy or merchant class, formed the basis of the future political nation. And these nations and nationalisms hark back, in turn, to a long history of demotic or 'vertical' European *ethnie* in pre-modern times.[4]

This revival of ethnic community implies a certain diminution, but not the demise of state power so often hailed or feared. While particular states may have their powers increasingly circumscribed, and perhaps some of their

---

4 For this ethnic background of East European movements, see Hugh Seton-Watson, *Nations and States*, London, 1977, chs 3-4, and Raymond Pearson, *National Minorities in Eastern Europe, 1848-1945*, London, 1983. For the concept of pre-modern 'vertical' *ethnie*, see Anthony D. Smith, *The Ethnic Origins of Nations*, Oxford, 1986, ch. 4.

territories amputated, the legitimating power of ethnic nationalism will continue to uphold state authority, albeit in a looser manner, in states where there is a single or a dominant *ethnie*. Modern information technology and mass communications may help to sustain dense networks of minority *ethnie*, as Richmond argued, just as they may help to turn into 'high' literary cultures. But these factors, like the processes of vernacular mobilization and cultural politicization on which they are based, can also be appropriated by so-called 'nation-states' and their dominant ethnic majorities. Not only appropriated, but also disseminated in state propaganda to incorporate minority peoples.[5]

But the ethnic revival has been borne on the wave of democratization, both in the West in the 1960s and in the East today. This wave is both inclusive of co-ethnics, and sometimes exclusive of outsiders. It is both participatory and decentralizing, pluralist yet mass-mobilizing. These are unstable combinations of contrary impulses and may yet have serious consequences for European *ethnies* and nations themselves.

2. This is especially true for non-Europeans, but it may also bode ill for European minorities. In the past, indeed, the popular or demotic type of ethnic community was both emancipatory and exclusive, with marked oscillations of mood and purpose. If they could not share in the vernacular culture, outsiders often found themselves relegated, excluded or worse.

Similar situations obtain in many lands today. We can indeed speak of a type of 'ethnic democracy' in which the members of the dominant ethnic community have democratic norms and institutions, but resident outsiders are relegated to second-class citizenship. This has of course been true of various categories of temporary residents, including *Gastarbeiter*, and permanent immigrants from overseas or resident Gypsy communities, which have suffered various kinds of disprivilege and discrimination.[6]

Even where there is a common political citizenship, smouldering antagonism between ethnic communities may lead to outright conflict, flight and expulsions, as has happened in the Caucasus, Bulgaria and the former Yugoslavia. Nor should we forget the recrudescence of an anti-Semitism fuelled by waves of popular ethnic nationalism seeking to 'purify' the community and its territory of foreign elements. These are consequences of the ethnic revival which are not confined to Eastern Europe. The effects of that revival for women remain to be explored; but while they may benefit

---

5 For the argument that a 'post-industrial' age will tend to sustain ethnic nationalisms, see Anthony Richmond, 'Ethnic Nationalism and Post-Industrialism', *Ethnic and Racial Studies*, 7, 1984, 4, pp. 4-18; for the transformation of oral 'low' into literary 'high' cultures, see Ernest Gellner, *Nations and Nationalism*, Oxford, 1983, chs 3-4.

6 For an analysis of the concept of 'ethnic democracy', as it applies to modern Israel, see Sammy Smooha, 'Minority Studies in an Ethnic Democracy: the Status of the Arab Minority in Israel', *Ethnic and Racial Studies*, 13, 1991, 3, pp. 389-413. On the Gypsies, see Thomas Acton, 'Academic Success and Political Failure: a Review of Modern Social Science Writing in English on the Gypsies', *Ethnic and Racial Studies*, 2, 1979, pp. 231-41.

from the emancipatory syntheses of democratic ethnic nationalism in its early stages, a more exclusive, ethnic nationalism, which may turn to armed struggle at the expense of a pluralistic model of community, could well relegate their participation in the nationalist campaign and return them to a traditional supportive, if not subordinated, role.[7]

More generally, as each *ethnie* seeks to re-establish its own cultural heritage and political mythology, the very processes of democratization and popular participation are likely to exacerbate inter-ethnic tensions, even if the apocalyptic scenarios depicted by some critics of ethnic nationalism are unfounded. Nevertheless, the political consequences of reviving the demotic traditions of ethnic nationalism in ethnically mixed areas and states can only serve to increase ethnic tensions, as we have already witnessed in the West as well as the East.

3. Finally there are the consequences for Europe itself. In many ways, the tension between a fissiparous and possibly exclusive ethnic nationalism and the growing movement for greater European unity will become the dominant motif of European politics in the early twenty-first century. In some cases, where different *ethnies* have reached a measure of accommodation between themselves and with the state in which they find themselves, this tension will be constructive and creative. In other cases, where the pre-existing historic antagonisms run deep or where satisfaction of ethnic aspirations has been long delayed, the relationship with a wider Europe will prove problematic, and perhaps conflictual. On the one hand, one can envisage some kind of mediating role for pan-European institutions in cases of inter-ethnic or state-ethnic conflicts, as states begin to cede aspects of their sovereign powers to the European Community. On the other hand, disappointed states and *ethnies* may well turn against a European Community that seems to be unable to accommodate their grievances or understand their problems. In these circumstances, intractable but localized ethnic problems will become European ones, played out upon a continental stage.

Against this scenario, it is sometimes argued that the European Community will in time be able to act as a bulwark against ethnic conflict, and become the vehicle of a 'post-national' era. This argument presupposes a type of 'supranational' community rather different in character from the present state-oriented organization of the European Community, in which a Council of Ministers who represent their respective states ultimately decides the shape and pace of common European policies. Even then, a Europe des Patries has as yet few political teeth. We cannot as yet speak of a European 'super-state', nor

---

7 For the dilemmas of women in modern nations, confronted by the imperatives of nationalism, see Floya Anthias and Nira Yuval-Davie (eds), *Woman — Nation — State*, London, 1989. On the position of Jews in Eastern Europe and the USSR, see Zvi Gitelman, 'Jewish Nationality and Religion in the USSR and Eastern Europe' in Pedro Ramet (ed.), *Religion and Nationalism in Soviet and East European Politics*, Durham, N.C., and London, 1979.

realistically envisage a European 'super-nation' of the kind that is sometimes feared; only a limited pooling of aspects of state sovereignties, coupled with European fora (the European Parliament, the Council of Europe, etc.) and institutions (the Commission) and benign but variable attachments to the European political idea.[8]

This is not to deny the growing impact of regional and global economic institutions and forces like the multi-nationals, the moves towards free movement of goods and labour and perhaps a common currency and banking system, and the interdependence created by telecommunications and mass information technology. Unfortunately, as the history of nationalism shows only too clearly, increased contacts and interdependence may stimulate ethnic antagonism as much as they create the possibility of shared understandings. Local and regional economic disparities, together with unresolved ethnic problems and unrepresentative political institutions, may well fuel endemic national conflicts, particularly in plural states with ancient but insufficiently recognized minority aspirations. The outcome may well be a situation in which three concentric circles of cultural identity compete for primary allegiance: the inner circle of ethno-national identity, the middle circle of national civic and political identity, and finally the outer circle of a pan-European affiliation, which unites institutional allegiances with a gradually forged European political and cultural mythology.[9]

But here lies the rub. On what basis can such a mythology be forged, so that the majority of Europeans will feel a genuine identification with the idea of Europe? Can pan-Europeanism compete successfully with ethno-nationalism and civic-national identities? Given the likelihood of an increasingly exclusive brand of ethno-nationalism, especially in the eastern half of the continent, the chances for such a mass transfer of loyalties and sentiments appear to be slim. It is one thing to speak of the possibility of European institutions playing a role in conciliatory parties to ethno-national disputes, and possibly even mediating in the conflicts of ethnic nationalisms within constituent states. It is quite another thing to predict a large-scale shift in allegiances away from *ethnie* and ethnic identities to a pan-Europeanism and a truly European community.

For the creation of national political communities in Western Europe, let alone in the East, has not succeeded in eradicating the hold of many smaller ethno-national identities and their aspirations for autonomy, despite the passage of many centuries of state-making. The plural 'nation-states', though strengthened in some ways, have nevertheless had to compete for the allegiance of many of their citizens with the ethnic ties which held them

---

8   For the case against the European 'super-nation', see Johann Galtung, *The European Community: a Superpower in the Making*, London, 1973.

9   The links between interdependence and national conflicts were pointed out long ago by Karl Deutsch (*Nationalism and Social Communication*, 2nd edn, Cambridge, Mass., 1966).

together over so many centuries. Even if modern technology and communications telescopes the processes of state-making today, there is little chance of the European Community being able to accomplish over the next century what the European 'nation-states' so signally failed to achieve: to turn the many ethnic minorities of Europe into so many 'ethnographical monuments'.[10]

On the other hand, we should not forget a possible basis for pan-European identity, not in the processes of state-making and institution-building, but in the slower, less planned transformations in the field of culture. In this context, it is not illegitimate to speak of a European 'family of cultures', in which, divisions and 'faultlines' notwithstanding, certain shared legacies of law, religion, artistic and scientific endeavour, and political tradition, combine to form the basis for fashioning a pan-European political mythology and symbolism, without which there can be European co-operation but no 'Europe'.

It would be foolhardy to conclude from such slender hopes and possibilities that 'Europe' will in some sense be realized in the near future, and that it will be able somehow to still the pain of unresolved national grievances or avert the dangers of inter-ethnic or state-ethnic conflict. It is quite clear that, even in the more limited realm of education through the mass media, the ethnic and national context dictates the ways in which international messages are received and perceived. Ethnicity and nationality refract general messages, despite their continental appeal.[11]

Nevertheless, the experimental nature of many 'utopian' social and political movements, and the desire for a more decentralized yet participatory kind of community, suggests that a federal Europe of ethnic communities and nations may provide the longer-term framework for the collective aspirations and varied historical experiences of the peoples of Europe, once the immediate period of national uncertainty and ethnic danger has run its course.

---

10 The phrase is from Engels's *Po und Rhein* (1859); see also Milton Esman (ed.), *Ethnic Conflict in the Western World*, Ithaca, 1977, notably the essay by Walker Connor.
11 These are analysed by Philip Schlesinger, 'On National Identity: Some Conceptions and Misconceptions Criticised', *Social Sciences Information*, 26, 1987, 2, pp. 219-64; see the fuller discussion of the European 'family of cultures' in Anthony D. Smith, 'Towards a Global Culture?', *Theory, Culture and Society*, 7, 1990, pp. 171-91.

CHAPTER EIGHT

Culture and the Intelligentsia:
Forms of Cultural Revival

Elena Nemirovskaia

What happens to culture in a totalitarian country? In a country where the State has entirely swallowed up society? In a country where up to recent times no form of differentiation of social life has existed? How simple it is to detect the near or total death of culture in this country. This is particularly evident at the moment when *perestroika* has been proclaimed from above and *glasnost'* has been authorized from above, when society is no longer dominated by fear of a punitive regime and when a barbarism cultivated for decades has gushed up to the surface. Can there be any hope of cultural revival?

Perestroika has clearly given an impulse to cultural revival, but the process of cultural renewal is long and complex, particularly since the intelligentsia — that sector of society which preserves high cultural norms within its milieu, and by the single fact of its existence opposes cultural entropy — is now becoming disunified. Whereas once it was united by a general hostility to the political regime, now that criticism of the regime has become a commonplace in the mass media and in everyday conversation, it is divided on national, ideological and other grounds. Moreover, people, tiring of pretensions of harmony, are eager to counterpose their individuality and their views to all the rest. This is not always warranted. The language which evolved over many years in this milieu is incomprehensible to the majority. For in this milieu people spoke, reasoned and wrote for only a narrow circle of their peers. There, an almost mystical language evolved.

Nevertheless, the responsibility for reviving the lost culture lies as always with the intelligentsia. It is the intelligentsia that will save or not save that invisible, subtle, spiritual world without which society may not call itself civilized and people may not call themselves people. This revival could follow many basic courses which serve at the same time as lines of self-determination for the intelligentsia and for those who gravitate towards it. These are, at present, as follows:

1. 'Institutionalized culture'. That is academic scholarship, museums, official creative unions, libraries etc. — all these are overseen by the Academy of Sciences or the Ministry of Culture. 'Institutionalized culture' today is no longer being subsidized by the State and must go over to 'self-funding'. But how can it 'pay its way'? Due to a lack of finances and material and technical resources, leading cultural journals are no longer issued, and museums, libraries, concert halls and theatres are closing. In Moscow, the Tret'iakov Gallery and the History Museum are closed, and the Lenin Library is closing. The situation is even worse in provincial towns. There are towns where there are no libraries, theatres or museums at all. The majority of provincial towns do not have their own publishing houses.

The level of State capital investment in culture is a few kopeks per capita per annum. The lack of cultural life in the provinces is provoking a colossal migration of youth which is stripping the country's economy.

The USSR continues to be abandoned by prominent cultural figures, specialists — young people — who embody the creative potential of the country. The reasons for this are instability and the lack of a suitable creative environment. It is clear that the government will not continue to fund culture. The situation could only be redeemed by a well thought-out system of taxation exempting from taxes organizations investing money in culture.

2. 'Informal culture'. This category primarily includes the artistic avantgarde which has been banned for a long time, in addition to the vast layer of artistic, philosophical, theological and political literature. Due to the fact that this culture was banned for a long time, a tremendous 'failure' has occurred; the logical organic perception of cultural values has broken down. People brought up since childhood on Realism, Socialist Realism and Marxist ideologists, suddenly received everything at once: Berdiaev and Solov'ev, Chagal and Kandinskii, Gumilev and Solzhenitsyn. How can one come to terms with all these if one lacks an adequate intellectual and aesthetic foundation? The most likely outcome is that one fails to come to terms with them, to ignore everything, which is what many have done to judge by the number of freely available excellent books on sale which hardly anybody buys, and the vast empty exhibition halls which nobody visits.

'Informal culture' developed for a long time in its own juice, and the fact that it has now come to the surface has nothing to do with the breadth of its dissemination. Its language is as inaccessible to the man in the street as is the language of the thinking intellectuals.

When talking about innovations in this realm, then, the first thing that comes to mind is that previously banned themes such as sex and politics have come to the fore. Here, as well, nothing significant has been done so far. In the process of free dissemination and accumulation of the values of 'informal culture' they must crystallize and build into people's cultural horizons. But for this to take place, at least one generation must grow up in an environment where cultural ideas are freely circulated.

3. Nationalism (*pochvennichestvo*). Seventy years of the Communist regime brought about ethno-cultural genocide among every people of the USSR. And it is natural that with the start of liberalization the most natural (and simple) feelings were most powerfully expressed, i.e. national feelings.

Unlike in Russia, the revival of national consciousness in the Soviet republics (in the Baltic States in particular) always went hand in hand with the freedom movement. The notion of national independence became a synonym for liberation from totalitarian 'central authority'. The struggle for national culture became the struggle against the Communist regime and the manifestos of national fronts are as much political as cultural manifestos.

In Russia, whose language has never been discriminated against and whose culture (though admittedly in mutilated form) was recognized by the authorities as the official culture and was forcibly propagated among other peoples, nationalism and opposition to the regime never coincided as a single notion. Although not long ago nationalists were pursued as fervently as dissidents, today the gap between nationalists and democrats has become even wider. Russian nationalists, as a rule, gravitate towards the right wing of the political spectrum. It is hard to see Russian nationalism, which has aggressive characteristics, as a cultural movement as a whole, although it does have positive trends. It is characterized by a concern with the state of the national consciousness and national culture, with national breadth and with the repudiation of all forms of chauvinism and xenophobia. Will Russian culture manage to find its soil and humanistic potential? If not, the consequences will be 'unforeseeable'.

4. 'Religious culture'. In recent years both traditional and non-traditional religions have become active. The non-traditional ones are for the most part Eastern, i.e. Buddhism, Sufism, Hinduism, etc., which are professed for the most part by young people. It has already been repeatedly noted that Eastern mysticism is dangerous for Russia because its contemplative character inevitably results in the withdrawal from active life of many people, which in a depressed and hopeless situation becomes irreversible. If this is the case, there is nevertheless another side to the coin: on account of the diffusion of literature of non-traditional religions, on meditation techniques, etc., the consciousness is broadened, as are cultural horizons.

As far as traditional religions are concerned, they are today enjoying the growing support of the authorities. This was previously the case during the Second World War when, in a situation of universal demoralization and with the genuine threat of Fascist expansion, Stalin, in order to raise the morale of the people, opened churches and released from detention those priests who were still alive. The current situation in our country is similar in its gravity to the war situation. This is why clergymen freely appear on television calling for love, forgiveness and charity. This is why places of worship, monasteries and Sunday schools which have been boarded up for years are being re-opened, and church literature is being published and sold. Churches and religious organizations can exert a force capable of bringing the vast masses out of a state of spiritual blindness and moral depravity, uniting both people and fragmented political trends. But for this purpose they themselves need to undergo very serious changes. Thus, the Russian Orthodox Church, which dominates on the territory of Russia and which during the years of Soviet power was always in the service of the ruling ideology and politics, should in the opinion of many serious experts repent of a series of grave sins, recognize all new saints (the Tsar's family and other holy people canonized by the Russian Church Abroad), increase the standard of education of clergymen who are often poorly educated, and so forth. But, above all, its positive potential can only be realized when the Church takes up an independent (perhaps even opposing semi-official) position on questions of vital importance, conducting its own cultural and social policies.

Various steps have already been taken in this direction, but very few, and it seems that the Church is as much an inert, sluggish social institution as the Party-bureaucratic apparatus. Furthermore, it seems now that a new form of censorship is emerging — church censorship. Thus, the anthology of spiritual poetry *Voskreshenie,* published in 1990, was sent to the Moscow Patriarch to be reviewed. The approval of the Patriarch was sought for conducting a film festival entitled 'Church and Cinema' (1990) and there was not one film expert on the festival jury.

5. Politicized culture. This culture is represented by the politicized intelligentsia and other politically active strata of the population. Here the situation is the same as at the beginning of the century. The diversity of parties, groups and political trends is duplicated. Russia now has, just as at the start of the century, monarchists, anarchists, Socialist Revolutionaries, Mensheviks, Constitutional Democrats, and so forth. However, political movements are not as a rule culture-oriented at all. Culture does not appear in party manifestos, cultural problems are not touched upon by the 'left wing' of the Supreme Soviet. Probably the traditional stereotype is wearing out: 'first of all we must clean a place, feed and clothe the people, and then we can attend to culture'. But when there is no universal culture, restoration and development of the economy is impossible, any Western aid will run through our fingers like sand, being swallowed up by total unscrupulousness, misunderstanding of the task in hand, dishonesty, greed for money, the sabotage of inertia and obscurantism. People directly involved in culture (writers, artists, musicians, performers, etc.) are all becoming politicians, and even People's Deputies. It is unlikely that either culture or politics can gain from the fact that people of culture are substituting for professional politicians. Political radicalism, the lack of a tradition of liberalism and political culture in general, these are the factors which make 'compromise' impossible as the moral essence of the cultural process. Radicalism closes ranks with reaction and they provoke, sustain and support one another. When a country has outgrown parties (as democratic countries have done in the last

century), when genuine liberalism becomes a reality, only then will *partiinost'* (party-mindedness) in Russia cease to be a factor which destroys culture.

6. Diaspora culture. Only now is it beginning to interact with totalitarian culture. For seventy years the opinion was planted in this country that anything emanating from emigration is evil 'anti-Sovietism' and that *émigrés* are pitiful, spiritually barren people. Russian *émigré* culture, in the meantime, performed an heroic deed. It preserved the cultural values which had been eradicated in this country. It created new cultural phenomena. It transferred a trampled culture from a world of captivity to a world of freedom, and this culture bore fruit. Nabokov, Bunin, Brodskii, Rostropovich, Solzhenitsyn and many other figures, famous throughout the world, are returning to their native land. This and the broadening of contacts with compatriots abroad may have an effect in raising the general cultural standards of the country.

Now there are debates about the diaspora. Some feel that all treasures (icons, pictures, books, etc.), and people too, should be returned to their native country. The existence of the diaspora can be fruitful, however, for culture, partly because the emigration of culture activates preservationist tendencies, and also because there it is particularly open to interaction with other cultures. Evidently the diaspora will increase, both on account of emigration and on account of the separation of the republics, which will come about sooner or later.

The introduction of values preserved and multiplied in the diaspora into the cultural life of the country will help to fill the 'void' which has formed in culture and will create a cultural milieu of great value and diversity.

The ways to resist cultural entropy described here may intersect, duplicate one another and merge, creating new realities. In order for them all to more or less crystallize and define themselves, one or two new generations must grow up, developing in conditions of the freedom of choice of spiritual values. A period of 'primary accumulation of freedom' to live, think and create without the leading role of the Communist Party of the Soviet Union or other parties is necessary.

CHAPTER NINE

What Price an Orthodox Revival? The Dilemmas of the Russian Church

Simon Dixon

'The churches in the Soviet Union have ... survived; they are now also undergoing revival. There may be all kinds of new opportunities for them just around the corner.'[1] So wrote Philip Walters in an essay commemorating the millennium of Russian Orthodoxy in 1988, and his opinion is shared by many. Although Walters's use of the plural is indicative of widespread (and almost certainly over-optimistic) ecumenical hopes, speculation has concentrated on the possible fortunes of one church in particular. Reasons for the focus on the Russian Orthodox Church are not far to seek. In the aftermath of the collapse of the Soviet regime's ideological legitimacy it is difficult to imagine a starker contrast than that between Marxism-Leninism and Russian Orthodoxy. The Russian church can be held up as an icon of everything that was destroyed or submerged by the Bolshevik Revolution. Orthodoxy can serve men and women of radically different persuasions as the ultimate symbol of their rejection of the Soviet regime. As an oasis of Russian national consciousness in the arid desert of Soviet internationalism, it has been courted and symbolically exploited by Boris El'tsin;[2] as a martyr to Soviet persecution, it personifies suffering (and, by extension, can now act as a powerful focus for guilt and repentance).[3] A distinctive current in Soviet literature, derived from the

---

The nature and brevity of this essay have forced me to curtail references, but I have tried to acknowledge my principal secondary debts.

1 P. Walters, 'Religion in the Soviet Union: Survival and Revival' (hereafter 'Religion in the Soviet Union'), in N. Petro (ed.), *Christianity and Russian Culture in Soviet Society*, Boulder, Colorado, 1990, pp. 3-15 (13).
2 For a brief survey, see S. Dixon, 'The Russians: The Dominant Nationality', in G. E. Smith (ed.), *The Nationalities Question in the USSR*, London, 1990, pp. 21-37.
3 The work of Michael Bourdeaux and Keston College has made an unparalleled contribution to our knowledge of the dimensions of suffering. For hints of the potential scope of guilt as a subject, see the striking remarks by R. Beermann, 'The Social

'village-prose' school of the 1970s, has used the image of ruined churches as a metaphor for moral decay, implying that ecclesiastical renovation and the rehabilitation of religion would release into society hitherto repressed creative moral energies.[4] Whether it be as a symbol of nostalgia for a lost past or as a symbol of hope for a better spiritual future, the Russian Orthodox Church, after the unprecedented meeting between Gorbachev and Patriarch Pimen in 1988 which allowed the millennium celebrations to take place in a blaze of publicity which no-one could have anticipated, now has a firmly established public profile in the Soviet Union.

Bearing in mind the tragic recent history of the church, it is understandable to find specialists focusing on two issues: first on the extent of the religious revival among Soviet citizens (and especially amongst the young), which, despite all the State's efforts, eventually made Orthodoxy impossible to ignore; and second on the secular power's corresponding deliberations about the most expedient way to accommodate, disarm and, if possible, exploit this popular sentiment by lifting the repressive legislation which until now has effectively inhibited religious activity of any sort. A consensus is possible on both these matters. Even if precise numbers are hard to calculate, there can be little doubt about the reality of the religious revival[5] (though there may be room for doubt about its chances of prolonged vitality should subscription to religious views lose its cachet as a dissident gesture).[6] Available evidence about the State's intentions suggests that Gorbachev's regime hopes (as the tsarist regime hoped before it) to manipulate Orthodoxy as a much-needed source of moral authority in the cause of social cohesion (and also that it is equally prepared, even anxious, so to exploit Orthodoxy's religious rivals in the Soviet Union).[7] In other words, the rigid supervision of ecclesiastical life formerly exercised by the Council for Religious Affairs is intended to give way to more subtle means of influence. As Jane Ellis has remarked: 'the

---

Psychology of Stalinism: A Literary Approach', *Coexistence*, 27, September 1990, 3, pp. 169-86 (181).

4   G. A. Hosking, *Beyond Socialist Realism*, St Albans, 1980, was a pioneering study. The necessarily allusive treatment of religion by Soviet writers has made interpretation of their work controversial. Compare, for example, the discussion of Aitmatov from a Christian perspective by I. Maryniak, 'The "new god-builders"', in R. Freeborn and J. Grayson (eds), *Ideology in Russian Literature*, London, 1990, pp. 188-204, with A. Olcott's argument that the religious ethic of 'Plakha' is consonant rather with Islam (even though Islam is never directly mentioned in the novel): 'What Faith is the God-Contemporary? Chinghis Aitmatov's Plakha', *Slavic Review*, 49, 1990, 2, pp. 213-26.

5   J. Ellis, 'The Religious Renaissance: Myth or Reality?', in E. B. Shirley Jr. and M. Rowe (eds), *Candle in the Wind: Religion in the Soviet Union*, Washington D.C., 1989, pp. 252-77.

6   P. Coleman's editorial, 'Glasnost for the European Churches', *Theology*, 93, November-December 1990, 756, pp. 435-37, is not at all sanguine.

7   Islam being one of the most important, as J. Critchlow makes clear in 'Islam in Soviet Central Asia: Renaissance or Revolution?', *Religion in Communist Lands*, 18, Autumn 1990, 3, pp. 196-211, esp. pp. 196-99.

consensus among independent church thinkers ... would appear to be that the prominence given to the Russian Orthodox Church amounts to no more than a new form of control over it'.[8] She might well have described it as the revival of an old form of control: there are surely loud contemporary echoes of Synodal Over-Procurator D. A. Tolstoi's verdict on the nineteenth-century Russian clergy as 'no more and no less than a force which should be subject to the government and which a clever government can use expertly for its own aims'.[9]

The danger implicit in this scholarly concentration on popular belief and on the State's legislative straitjacket lies in the temptation to regard the Russian Orthodox Church as a sleeping beauty which need only be released from its enforced dormancy in order that it may legitimately supply the enthusiastic demand for its ministry which so evidently exists. The very vocabulary used by writers on the subject is revealing. Walters, for example, in setting out some of the Church's most obvious opportunities, urges that it should be 'allowed' to involve itself in social welfare work and that it 'ought to be given every opportunity to encourage those enlightened and truly Christian elements in the Russian nationalist movement'. But there is another part of the equation which needs to be considered. As John Anderson has written of Eastern Europe in general, 'the churches' role in the process of change has varied according to the willingness of the State to allow public participation and *the readiness of religious bodies to take advantage of new opportunities*'.[10] It is on the readiness (or lack of it) of the Russian Orthodox Church that I propose to concentrate in this essay, arguing that this is a matter which can properly be judged only from a longer historical perspective than is generally considered.

One way of emphasizing the enormity of the task ahead may be to sketch comparisons with two occasions in history when another Christian church was obliged to come to terms with a markedly unsympathetic secular power: I have in mind the position of the Roman Catholic Church first in France during the Revolution and later in Italy after the Fascist takeover.[11] In the first case, the Church was faced not only with the need for a political accommodation, but also with a virtually complete reconstruction of its pastoral life. Space forbids the detailed discussion that the subject deserves, but three basic points may be made. First, it is worth noting the contrast between the published

---

8 J. Ellis, 'New Soviet Thinking on Religion', *Religion in Communist Lands*, 17, Summer 1989, 2, pp. 100-11 (107).
9 *Vospominaniia E. M. Feoktistova, Za kulisami politiki i literatury, 1848-1896*, Leningrad, 1929, p. 169.
10 Walters, 'Religion in the Soviet Union', pp. 11, 12. Emphasis added. J. Anderson, 'Courtesy towards God: Religion and Change in Eastern Europe', *Religion in Communist Lands*, 18, Summer 1990, 2, pp. 100-23 (119). Emphasis added.
11 Unfortunately, the otherwise outstanding T. Skocpol, *States and Social Revolutions: A Comparative Analysis of France, Russia and China*, Cambridge, 1979, pays little attention to the churches.

Concordat reached by Napoleon and Pius VII and between Mussolini and Pius XI in 1929 and the 'oral concordat' between Stalin and Sergii (Stragorodskii) which produced the metropolitan's notorious declaration of loyalty to the Soviet regime in August 1927.[12] It can scarcely be maintained, in either the French or the Italian case, that the Catholic Church entered negotiations on equal terms with its adversary. Pius VII, whose predecessor had been kidnapped by the Directory, sent Cardinal Consalvi to Paris to negotiate in a situation he described as 'terrible'. Prompted by an unnerving combination of Napoleonic cajolery and courtesy, the Concordat was signed within three weeks of his arrival. Though the Italian negotiations dragged on for more than three years, the Church's power lay only in delay. Yet the very fact of these two negotiations was a public acknowledgement that popular religious protest had made parts of Napoleonic France ungovernable without an accommodation with the Pope, and that Mussolini had to bargain for Catholic votes and for an end to the Roman Question. No such needs troubled Stalin. In Russia there were no negotiations between church and state: Sergii simply succumbed to intolerable pressure, including, reportedly, the threat that more than a hundred bishops would be shot if he did not comply.

Neither the French nor the Italian Concordat was wholly favourable to the Church: a hundred royalist bishops were inadvertently sacrificed in 1801; 1929 saw the Italian state gain an important voice in the appointment to benefices and a considerable measure of control over ecclesiastical property. The twentieth-century political price was the higher of the two: whilst Napoleon healed his breach with the Catholic Church and was crowned by that church, Pius XI healed his breach with the Italian state only at the expense of metaphorically crowning the Risorgimento.[13] Yet, whilst conceding a measure of state intervention in the affairs of their churches, both Pius VII and Pius XI nevertheless achieved a reconciliation with their adversaries. Above all, they guaranteed that the Church's ministry could continue: Napoleon recognized the Catholic Church if not as the state religion then at least the religion of 'the majority of French citizens'; Mussolini recognized the Catholic Church as the established religion of Italy. The preservation of the Church was undoubtedly Sergii's principal motivation for his declaration of loyalty. To say that he failed is not necessarily to impute to him a lack of moral courage or of political judgement (though he has been accused of both). But fail he did. The Church was all but extinguished in the 1930s; it took the demands of the 'great patriotic' war against Nazi Germany to provoke Stalin to concede some small

---

12   The phrase 'oral concordat' is Sergei Hackels's: see his essay on the Orthodox Churches in J. McManners (ed.), *The Oxford Illustrated History of Christianity*, Oxford, 1990, pp. 519-49 (541). The following paragraph draws on Owen Chadwick, *The Popes and European Revolution*, Oxford, 1981, and D.A. Binchey, *Church and State in Fascist Italy*, Oxford, 1941.

13   I owe this point, and much else, to a course of lectures given by Professor Owen Chadwick in the Faculty of History, University of Cambridge, 1981-82.

measure of regularization to ecclesiastical life. Meanwhile, in Sergii's declaration, a world accustomed (wrongly) to thinking of the Russian church as the handmaiden of the tsarist state saw only further evidence of abject subservience to the secular power — a brush with which the episcopate of the offical Moscow Patriarchate has been indelibly tarred ever since. So far from enjoying establishment, the Russian Orthodox Church now faces a potential period of revival under the handicap of being led by a widely (if sometimes unjustly) discredited hierarchy.[14]

The second comparative point worth making concerns the scale of reconstruction facing the Russian Orthodox Church. To quote Olwen Hufton on Revolutionary France: 'Between 1790 and 1796 a church was dismantled: between 1790 and 1801 popular demand ... made its restoration a political necessity'. The French Concordat, in other words, was the 'recognition of a *fait accompli*'.[15] Popular demand for the restoration of the Russian church there may now be; but it cannot be said that restoration is guaranteed. There is, in the first place, a sharp contrast between the relatively short period of destruction and recovery in France and the much longer period of repression in the Soviet Union. Whereas in France in 1800 a flourishing institutional church was in everyone's living memory, in the contemporary Soviet Union there can now be few who remember it (and their view may be distorted by the rose-coloured spectacles of hindsight). In the second place, the French church benefited from being part of a supranational Catholic Church with international influence and considerable material resources. By comparison, the regionalist ecumenical structure of the Orthodox Church has more often acted as a 'cover for separatism' by rival autocephalous national churches than as an institutional basis for communion.[16] Certainly, the ecumenical Orthodox Church has been unable to offer the Russian church security or protection. Significantly, it is to the Vatican that the Moscow Patriarchate has turned in recent months for a reliable supply of Bibles and for help in restoring its clerical schools. Third, and perhaps most important of all, the French Catholic Church was able to embark on the practical process of ecclesiastical

---

14 The standard account of episcopal subservience is now Jane Ellis, *The Russian Orthodox Church: A Contemporary History*, London, 1986, pp. 257-84. See 'Documents on the Election of a New Russian Partiarch', *Religion in Communist Lands*, 18, Autumn 1990, 3, pp. 266-74, for a venomous attack on Aleksi (Ridiger) made by Father Georgi Edelstein in *Russkaia mysl'* just before the election — in which Aleksi is condemned as a 'hardened stoolpigeon' who 'for decades ... co-operated with the godless authorities in persecuting the church and believers', ibid., pp. 268-69.
15 Olwen Hufton, 'The Reconstruction of a Church 1796-1807', in G. Lewis and C. Lucas (eds), *Beyond the Terror: Essays in French Regional and Social History 1794-1815*, Cambridge, 1983, pp. 21-51 (25), an essay which prompted the reflections in this paragraph.
16 See J. Meyendorff, 'Ecclesiastical Regionalism: Structures of Communion or Cover for Separatism', in *idem, The Byzantine Legacy in the Orthodox Church*, New York, 1982, pp. 217-33.

restoration — be it in the matter of 'externals' such as the restoration of parish life, the strengthening and expansion of the priesthood, or 'internal' questions of faith — in a Europe whose population remained overwhelmingly rural, and a Europe in which religion retained central cultural significance. The Soviet Union, on the other hand, is no longer self-evidently a peasant society: it has undergone since 1917 a process of rapid urbanization and militant secularization in a world in which the central place of religion has almost everywhere been lost.[17] The Russian Empire proved unable to maintain either serfdom or autocracy in a Europe in which others had abandoned them. Can the contemporary Russian church now alone restore religion in adverse circumstances? No church has found it easy to combat the combined forces of urbanization, industrialization and secularization. It is difficult to imagine that the Russian Orthodox Church will find it easy to succeed where others have failed.[18]

The grounds for pessimism increase when we turn to our third comparison, between the position of the Catholic Church before the French Revolution and *before* the Fascist takeover, and the position of the Russian church under the tsars. What is it that Orthodox believers are hoping to revive and restore? All three churches were weakened by significant internal divisions. The eighteenth-century French church was plagued by both Jansenist-Jesuit rivalry and grass-roots clerical Richerism; Modernism and the commitment to social and political action disturbed the Italian church at the turn of the nineteenth century. By 1917, the Russian church was split both intellectually and socially. The Old Believer *raskol* had separated since the mid-seventeenth century an unknown (but undoubtedly large) percentage of the population from the church. Within the ranks of its own priesthood, the 'white' parish clergy resented the influence and wealth of the 'black' monastic clergy from whom the episcopate was exclusively drawn. But the 'white' clergy was also riven by internal tensions: in particular, ill-educated rural men envied the more comfortable lifestyle of their more sophisticated urban contemporaries. Such social division found partial (though not complete) reflection in theological disputes (over the degree to which it was right to draw on Western theology) and disputes about the administration of the church. There was widespread support for a restoration of *sobornost´* in place of Synodal control. But while bishops supported conciliarism in the hope of emancipating episcopal authority from bureaucratic inertia, parish priests advocated it in the hope rather of giving their own voice (and that of the laity) greater prominence in ecclesiastical affairs and consequently of reducing

---

17   M. Lewin, indeed, places urbanization at the crux of *The Gorbachev Phenomenon*, London, 1988.
18   To extend these points we need a survey of Eastern Europe to complement the invaluable H. McLeod, *Religion and the People of Western Europe, 1789-1970*, Oxford, 1981 — a survey which would have to account for the exceptional case of Poland.

episcopal influence. Each claimed canonical authority for incompatible opinions.

Two things made the consequences of internal division more severe for the Russian Orthodox Church than for the Roman Catholic. First, in its structure of separate orders, the Catholic Church had an inbuilt institutional mechanism for coping with division. Indeed, this mechanism could be turned to positive effect (witness the productive rivalry between missionary, philanthropic and educational orders in the post-Tridentine Church). The Russian church, by contrast, has no such internal mechanism, and its combined stress on spiritual harmony and 'wholeness' and on organic, conciliar decision-making has in the past made it difficult (and shows every sign of continuing to make it difficult) for the Orthodox to absorb and exploit those fundamental differences of opinion and approach which are hard to avoid in matters of pastoral practice. The second reason for believing the Russian church to have been peculiarly damaged by division is in the testimony of the 1920s. Whereas the evidence of continuity between Jansenism and Richerism and loyalty to the revolutionary Civil Constitution of the Clergy is debatable,[19] there can be no doubt that divisions within the Russian church before the Revolution persisted beyond it, and were crucial in defining the schisms which did so much to undermine the Church's authority in the early years of Soviet power and left it open to the Bolshevik policy of divide and rule.[20] The controversies which divided the Living Church from the League for the Regeneration of the Church, and the whole 'left schism' from the official church hierarchy, had their roots in pre-revolutionary arguments about the means by which the church should re-Christianize society. Here, in other words, we come full circle: there is a direct link between these disputes over church government, theology and pastoral work and the 'oral concordat' between Sergii and Stalin, which did so much to discredit the church hierarchy.

It has been important to dwell on the origins of the 1920s' schisms precisely in order to demonstrate, as we turn now to the practical pastoral means by which the Orthodox Church proposes to minister to its flock in the 1990s, that it is the very issues at the root of those splits that are now said to offer the basis for revival. Churchmen now speak, just as they did in the late nineteenth century, of the need for evangelization and re-Christianization, of the need for widespread Christian social action at parochial level, and

---

19 T. Tackett, *Religion, Revolution, and Regional Culture in Eighteenth-Century France: The Ecclesiastical Oath of 1791*, Princeton, 1986, esp. ch. 6.

20 A full exploration of the continuities, both personal and ideological, would require a comprehensive history of the church between 1870 and 1930. The problems of access to sources have so far prevented an enterprise. But the early chapters of D. Pospielovsky, *The Russian Church under the Soviet Regime, 1917-1982*, 2 vols, New York, 1984, provide the best extant account.

especially of the need for religious education among the young.[21] Indeed Patriarch Aleksi stressed in an interview with the Italian press in November 1990 that one of the most important obligations facing the church is the provision of catechetical teaching.[22] The official Moscow Patriarchate is therefore now advocating the homiletic role which has long been urged on it by dissident priests dissatisfied with its apparently supine inactivity.[23] But there is little evidence to suppose that the potential for disruption created by those evangelist ideals is any smaller now than it was seventy years ago. Indeed, it may even have been increased: first by the hardening of what might perhaps best be termed sectional emphasis of Orthodox thought during the period when it has been deprived of the chance of pastoral activity. The need to return from contemplation to action seems likely to provoke the same awkwardness that has bedevilled the pastoral work of the Church in the past.

The crucial difficulty is that the strength of the Orthodox Church has never lain in intensive pastoral activity. Orthodoxy is not a naturally evangelist faith: its distinctive emphases are apophatic, contemplative and mystical. It has in the past (especially in the seventeenth and nineteenth centuries) turned to evangelism only when under pressure from godlessness and from religious rivals within the empire. In the nineteenth century, when forced to combat the challenge of Baltic Protestantism, Polish Catholicism, Tatar Islam and multifarious sectarianism, the Russian church (relying on a Romantic conception of the relationship between 'external' form and 'internal' essence) adopted a number of its rivals' most successful evangelist techniques — such as preaching, temperance societies and organized social charitable work — attempting simultaneously to infuse them with an authentically Orthodox content.[24] The moral imperative of this pastoral enterprise was profound. But the historical scholarship which underpinned it by endeavouring to establish an Orthodox 'tradition' in such matters gave rise to vituperative debate within the church. In canonical terms, the new pastoral initiative was still more controversial, especially in its implications for liturgical reform. (Renova-

---

21 Significantly, the newly-emancipated Romanian Orthodox Church has published a similar list of evangelist *pia desideria*, calling for increased homiletic activity from its clergy — 'sermons and catechisms are needed now more than ever before. There should be no Romanian Orthodox church without the priest delivering sermons' — and for missionary work from the laity, especially from women. See *Romanian Orthodox Church News*, 1990, 1, Jan-Feb., p. 6, editorial by Rev. Prof. M. Pacuriariu.
22 'I russia ritorniana in chiesa', *Corriere della Sera*, 19 November 1990. I owe this reference to Professor Derek Beales. (The published version of the interview seems to have been pruned.)
23 Compare Father Gleb Yakunin's 1979 report to the Christian Committee to Defend the Rights of Believers in the USSR, in S. Pushkarev, V. Rusak and G. Yakunin, *Christianity and Government in Russia and the Soviet Union*, Boulder, Colorado, 1989, esp. pp. 135-42.
24 I have outlined some of these experiments in my essay 'The Church's Social Role in St Petersburg, 1880-1914', in G. A. Hosking (ed.), *Church, Nation and State in Russia and Ukraine*, London, 1991.

tionists advocated a shortened liturgy, sung in Russian rather than Church Slavonic, in the cause of comprehension and accessibility — two crucial attractions of the rival evangelical protestant sects.) Had the Russian church been capable of taking a relaxed view of such matters, things might have been different. Yet, as John Meyendorff has remarked, this is scarcely the case: 'If there is a feature of "Russian" Orthodoxy which can be seen as a contrast to the Byzantine perception of Christianity, it is the nervous concern of the Russians in preserving the very letter of the tradition received from the Greeks.'[25] Paradoxically, therefore, a pastoral initiative on which the Russian church embarked in order to strengthen and defend itself in the face of interdenominational rivalry foundered on the rock of internal theological disputes.

Shock waves from these same disputes echo through current discussion. For one outspoken Moscow priest, Father Viacheslav Polosin, writing in the *émigré* journal *Grani* in 1990, the tensions within the contemporary Russian church threaten 'in the worst case' to erupt in a tripartite *raskol*.[26] Polosin sketches two currents of religious social thought. The first he calls Renovationist. Though he is anxious to distinguish this tendency from the divisive *obnovlentsy* of the 1920s, their emphasis on the use of the Russian language in the cause of comprehension and accessibility is familiar. By contrast, Polosin's second group advocates a 'traditional-canonical' approach said to have much in common with the Russian church abroad. Polosin places both the 'renovationist' and 'traditional-canonical' currents in opposition to the official Moscow patriarchate (which he summarily dismisses as uncanonical, apostate and Shamanist, and from which he believes the Church must be defended). Though the tone of his article is hardly conciliatory, Polosin suggests that schism might be avoided by a compromise. He acknowledges the need for the Church to communicate more effectively with its flock, and nods in the direction of renovationism by advocating that priests be more clearly audible and visible during the service (instead of emerging 'at rare moments through windows and doors like a cuckoo clock', as Evelyn Waugh put it after his first visit to the Russian Orthodox Church in London).[27] Yet he cannot accept the use of Russian, arguing instead for an adapted version of Church Slavonic and a canonical approach closest to the Russian Church Abroad, with whom his sympathies seem to lie. Such sympathies, however, seem unlikely to meet with instant approval from Patriarch Aleksi, who remarked with some bitterness in an interview with *Izvestiia* on 16 June 1990 that 'it is easy for the representatives of the Russian Church Abroad to criticise when they were

---

25 J. Meyendorff, *Byzantium and the Rise of Russia: A Study of Byzanto-Russian Relations in the Fourteenth Century*, Cambridge, 1981, p. 25.
26 Sviashch. V. Polosin, 'Razmyshleniia o teokratii v Rossii', *Grani*, 1990, 157, pp. 229-57. The first part of this article was published under the pseudonym Sergei Ventsel in ibid., 156, 1990, pp. 232-55.
27 M. Davie (ed.), *The Diaries of Evelyn Waugh*, London, 1976. Entry for 29 June 1924.

sitting pretty, having left Russia in the difficult days of the Revolution and having escaped Stalinism'.[28]

Orthodox face the problem not only of restoring a parish network, but even more fundamentally of creating for the first time since the eighteenth century a real sense of parochial community. In the turbulent years around 1900, Father Gapon, who later became notorious in another context, was only one among many students of the Russian ecclesiastical academies who, stimulated by Slavophilism, wrote a dissertation contrasting the 'living' independence of Bulgarian and Serbian parishes with their stultified post-Petrine Russian counterparts. And it was not only the other Slavonic churches who succeeded where Russians had failed. Still more ominous was the success on Russian soil of rival faiths, notably Baptists, Pashkovtsy and Old Believers. As the diocesan consistory of St Petersburg ruefully confessed in 1908:

> Every schismatic considers himself a master in his own society. His vote and his opinion count for something. Without his direct participation, not one ecclesiastical issue is decided. When he goes to his prayer-house, he feels at home: he reads, he sings, and if he does not like something, he expresses his displeasure straightaway. Not so an Orthodox. He is no more than a guest in church and takes practically no part in either the service or the business of the church. As a result, our parishioners become uninterested in the affairs of the parish, and as a consequence of their lack of interest, become cold in their relationship with their parish church in general and affairs of the faith in particular.[29]

Many of the same fears live on. Of course, it cannot be denied that some old hostilities have given way to a more self-consciously eirenical approach to interdenominational relationships. Orthodox have long been engaged in ecumenical discussions with representatives of the Western Christian churches. Under the new conditions of *perestroika*, moreover, there has been an unprecedented opportunity to extend collaboration from the theoretical to the practical level. Such co-operation has even extended to joint undertaking by Orthodox and Muslim clergy in Azerbaidzhan. In 1989 a new mosque was built in Baku with material support from the Russian church, and the two churches have also worked together on charitable relief in the stricken area of Nagornyi-Karabakh.[30] The new chairman of the Moscow Patriarchate's Department of External Affairs, the energetic Kirill, archbishop of Smolensk

---

28   'Documents on the election of a new Patriarch', p. 267 (see n. 14 above).
29   Annual report from the Diocesan Consistory of St Peterburg to the Holy Synod in 1908. Tsentral´nyi Gosudarstvennyi Istoricheskii Arkhiv, f. 796, op. 442, d. 2290, 1908g., pp. 207-08.
30   O. Antic, 'The Russian Orthodox Church and Islam', *Radio Liberty: Report on the USSR*, 2, 4 May 1990, 18, pp. 10-11.

and Kaliningrad, had already by the time of his appointment embarked on a joint programme with the German Protestant Churches to restore the former Königsberg Cathedral for use by different religious confessions.[31] At a more general level, Patriarch Aleksi was anxious to stress in his interview with the *Corriere della Sera* in November 1990 that ecumenical collaboration since the Second World War had done much to promote the evangelization of Europe, and to combat not only the vices of drugs and prostitution but also the danger of nuclear war.[32]

Yet rivalry cannot be extinguished, The problem was stated in particularly acute form by a clerical historian of the diocese of St Petersburg, referring in 1871 to a long heritage of religious conflict in the area:

> When two religions, or even two confessions within the same faith meet one another in the same place, then there will be a struggle between them, which, being reflected in the souls of their followers, in turn increases the number of believers on one side at the expense of the other.[33]

No amount of ecumenical reassurance could drown the echoes of this fundamental assumption in Kirill of Smolensk's frank summary of the problem posed for his church in the 1990s by the Ukrainian Catholics:

> These new Uniate parishes are not cropping up on empty spaces, in a new area. These are not parishes that are emerging in Siberia. And these are not parishes that need to be opened and restored. We are talking about the registration of Catholic parishes on the site of Orthodox parishes. This means that it is necessary to liquidate an Orthodox parish and establish a Catholic parish in its place.[34]

Kirill has made it clear that he sees the Ukrainian Uniate question as a matter to be resolved by bilateral agreement between the Russian Orthodox Church and the Vatican, without the need for state intervention. But Metropolitan Aleksi's view is more ambiguous. And there remains, in the heritage of the Byzantine and patristic tradition, a vast reservoir of

---

31 *Idem*, 'New "Foreign Minister" of the Russian Orthodox Church', ibid., 1, 5 January 1990.
32 *Corriere della Sera*, 19 November 1990, p. 5.
33 Sviashch. M. F. Arkhangel'skii, *Istoriia pravoslavnoi tserkvi v predelakh nyneshnei S-Peterburgskoi Eparkhii*, St Petersburg, 1871, p. 9.
34 Interview on Soviet Central Television, 14 December 1989. Quoted (and translated) by Roman Solchanyk, 'Church and State Split on Ukrainian Catholic Issue', *Radio Liberty: Report on the USSR*, 2, 5 January 1990, 1, pp. 10-12.

canonically respectable support for intervention by the secular power in support of the true church against the heretics.

In its quest for ecclesiastical restoration and religious revival, the Russian church is still faced with a dilemma which has caused much strife in the past. If, on the one hand, emancipation from state control of its internal affairs is eminently desirable, any general acceptance by the State of toleration or freedom of conscience has uncomfortable implications for Russian Orthodoxy since it will release the energies of rivals who have in the past demonstrated a more successful and more coherent commitment to pastoral influence. So long as the Soviet Union remains intact as a multinational state, it is difficult to see how this state of affairs can be changed. *Perestroika* can make little difference. Perhaps only the secession of the Russian republic could resolve the dilemma. But this, in turn, might encourage the Russian church, and Russian culture generally, to retreat into introspection. This, however, must remain a matter for speculation. Speculation is no business of the historian. But he may nevertheless have a role in setting out, as I have tried to do here, some of the historical influences which seem most likely to shape the Russian church's reaction to future developments, and which lead one to believe that an optimistic view of imminent revival is misleading. It is not only economic history which is best understood in the '*very* long term'.[35] It may be that ecclesiastical history is even more suited to such an approach, for only by seeing its history in the *very* long term can we demonstrate the truth of the maxim that the Russian Orthodox Church thinks in centuries.

---

35 The term was first used by R. M. Hartwell, 'Economic Growth in England before the Industrial Revolution: Some Methodological Issues', *Journal of Economic History*, 29, 1969, pp. 13-31.

CHAPTER TEN

The Post-Revolution Conflict Between the Orthodox and Eastern-Rite Catholics in Romania

Fiona Tupper-Carey

One of the effects of freedom in Romania has been the development of deep internal conflicts, which have sometimes become savage, between different sections of society. Groups of different ethnic origin, of different social class, or of different political affiliation are engaged in a war of words, which twice developed into street battles, in Tîrgu Mureş in March (1990), and in Bucharest in June (1990). In each case the bitterest conflict is between a majority and a minority group. Thus Romanians, as the majority ethnic group are in conflict with both the Hungarian and Gypsy minorities. The majority political party, the National Salvation Front, which won a crushing victory both in the parliamentary and presidential elections in May 1990, has been doing fierce political battle with the tiny opposition parties. Likewise the majority of Romania's workers have come to regard students and intellectuals as enemies of their own country.

Such a pattern has developed among Romania's religious denominations as well. The majority of the population, about seventy-five per cent, belong to the Romanian Orthodox Church. Inter-denominational conflict has arisen between the majority church and the minority denominations, in particular the Evangelical, that is Baptist, Pentecostal and Seventh Day Adventist denominations, and the Eastern-rite Catholic Church. As with the ethnic and political minority groups, these smaller denominations are perceived as a threat by the majority church, and portrayed in the Orthodox and secular press as a dangerous foreign influence, threatening the national identity of the Romanian people. It is the conflict between the Eastern-rite Catholic and Orthodox Churches which has the deepest historical roots and has proved to be the most politically divisive.

The Romanian Eastern-rite Catholic Church was founded in Transylvania in 1700. Transylvania, today a part of Romania, then belonged to the Austro-Hungarian Empire. Within this relatively independent province of the Empire, the Romanians were totally unrepresented in the local government, although they were the largest ethnic group. They were entirely dominated by the Magyars and Saxons, which made up the nobility in the province. This ruling nobility also tried to dominate the Romanians in matters of religion. The Romanians of Transylvania belonged to the Orthodox Church, like their ethnic brothers in Wallachia and Moldavia. Numerous attempts were made to convert the Romanians either to Protestantism or to Roman Catholicism, but they failed. However, during the seventeenth century, efforts by the Magyars to convert the Romanians to Calvinism increased. So, rather than face the loss of their national identity, which would have followed from conversion to Calvinism, the Romanians succumbed to an offer which was being made to them by Jesuit missionaries at the end of the seventeenth century.

The Jesuits proposed that the Romanian Orthodox accept the supremacy of the Pope, as well as three insignificant points of Catholic dogma, but retain all their Orthodox rites and customs, including a married clergy and the use of their own language, Romanian, rather than Latin, for services. The three points of dogma were: the Latin doctrine of the Trinity, that is the procession of the Holy Spirit from the Father and the Son — Orthodox doctrine is that the Holy Spirit proceeds from the Father; belief in Purgatory; and the acceptance of the use of unleavened bread at the liturgy. This new Catholic Church was called the Eastern-rite, or Byzantine-rite Catholic Church, or Greek Catholic Church, to distinguish it from the Roman Catholic Church. It was also called the Uniate or 'united' church, because it had united with Rome.

Prior to the formation of the Romanian Uniate Church were those of the Ruthenian and Ukrainian Uniate Churches earlier in the seventeenth century.

More importantly, conversion to the new church offered the prospect of material and political benefits to the Orthodox clergy. The Emperor, who endorsed the Jesuits' mission among the Romanians, guaranteed the Orthodox clergy equal rights with the Roman Catholic clergy in Transylvania, if they agreed to join the new church. To the Orthodox priests and high priest, who lived as the peasants did, tilling the land, paying tithes to a landlord, without the right to own property or collect money, or even build churches, this was truly a tempting offer. This was why the Bishop of Transylvania and the majority of the clergy accepted the Union with Rome — though the laity were very much opposed to it at the beginning.

In fact the creation of the new church did not bring the political advantages the Romanians had hoped for until the end of the nineteenth century. What the Eastern-rite Catholic Church did do was to allow the formation of an educated Romanian clergy, from which emerged several national leaders, whose ideas caused an awakening of Romanian national consciousness in the eighteenth and nineteenth centuries. The aspirations of this movement grew from cultural to political, and eventually it achieved the union of Transylvania with the other Romanian principalities in 1918.

Relations between the Orthodox and Eastern-rite Catholics were turbulent, particularly in the first century after the split. The Orthodox leaders in Wallachia and Moldavia published many articles condemning the Union with Rome. Two wandering Orthodox monks, Visarion and Sofronie, led a violent uprising against the Eastern-rite Catholic Church in 1744. In the nineteenth century, however, the Eastern-rite Catholics and Orthodox were forced to work together in their efforts to further national interests. Their common goals of education for their people and equal recognition with the other nations of Transylvania made the differences between them seem insignificant.

Despite their ability to work together harmoniously at certain critical moments of their history, some Orthodox always cherished the idea of the Eastern-rite Catholics' return to the Orthodox Church. Historical memories of the constant political pressure and persecution used to convert the Orthodox, plus the fundamental belief in a single true church, created a strong anti-Uniate element among Orthodox theologians and leaders.

It was this sentiment which the Romanian Communist government exploited in 1948 when it forced the reunion of the Eastern-rite Catholic Church with the Orthodox Church. This reunion in Romania was preceded by a union in similar circumstances of the Ukrainian Uniate Church with the Russian Orthodox Church, which was decreed by Stalin. In both cases, the objective of the Communists was to bring an influential, westward-looking church under the authority of the more easily controllable state church, the Orthodox Church. What was crucial to the Communists was to cut the Uniates' link with the Pope.

Another important motive of the Communist government was to win much-needed support from the Romanian Orthodox clergy and theologians, to counteract their opposition to many of the restrictions which they had begun to place on the Orthodox Church.

From accounts given by Uniate clergymen who experienced the persecution of their church in 1948, the Orthodox patriarch, Iustinian, played a willing part in the forced reunion. During the first years of Communist rule the hierarchy always maintained that the majority of the Eastern-rite Catholics had willingly united. The vast majority of the 2,000 Eastern-rite Catholic priests followed the advice of their bishops, which was to stay loyal to the head of their church, the Pope. For some, however, there was a conflict between this loyalty and loyalty to their parishioners. Some decided to sign at the request of their parishioners, who wished to keep their priest in the church, for those who refused to sign would be forced to give up the priesthood and let an Orthodox priest take over their church. The small number of Eastern-rite Catholic clergy who did sign were regarded as traitors by those who were sent to prison for their opposition to the reunion. Yet, for some, integration into the Orthodox Church was not difficult from a theological point of view.

Following the meeting of 1 October, which the Eastern-rite Catholics have always regarded as invalid, in December 1948 the Romanian government passed a decree which banned any form of Uniate worship. From this point the church was restricted to surviving only in the prison cells where its leaders were held, in towns and villages where priests dared to hold services in secret, and in people's memory, which grew more and more distant as the years passed. Secret services were held in priests' homes and attended by a few selected lay people, whom the priest knew he could trust. Most of the Eastern-rite Catholic laity either began attending mass in Hungarian in Roman Catholic churches or continued going to the same church building, where the liturgy was now taken by an Orthodox priest.

Throughout these years of underground activity the Eastern-rite Catholic church was defined by circumstances as a church of resistance. It was the only church in Romania which, as a body, rejected Communism and refused any compromise with Romania's new rulers. Its leaders came to regard the Orthodox Church as its joint persecutor, together with the Romanian Secret Police, because of the Orthodox hierarchy's complicity in carrying out the reunion. There is evidence that the Orthodox clergy was required by the hierarchy to inform on the activities of the clandestine Eastern-rite Catholic clergy under Ceauşescu. A copy of a questionnaire issued to the Orthodox clergy by the leadership in 1978 was smuggled out to the West by a group of Uniates. In the questionnaire, Orthodox priests were to answer specific questions about the Eastern-rite Catholic priests' attitude to the Orthodox Church. While the leadership of the Orthodox Church continued to maintain that the Eastern-rite Catholic Church had willingly united with the Orthodox Church and therefore no longer existed, theological works were published which justified the reunion of the two churches, and these anti-Uniate ideas filtered down the ranks and the generations of the Orthodox Church.

Since the revolution in December 1989 the attitude of the Orthodox Church has been the most serious obstacle to the re-emergence of the Eastern-rite Catholic Church. On 31 December, the new Vice-President of Romania, Dumitru Mazilu, passed a decree abolishing the decree of 1948, which had made the Eastern-rite Catholic Church illegal. Yet within weeks, an Eastern-rite Catholic priest who took a public service in Northern Transylvania was called into the local police station and asked by the Orthodox priest under what right he had held the service.

The Eastern-rite Catholics reacted swiftly to the fall of Nicolae Ceauşescu by coming straight to Bucharest to persuade the new government to re-legalize their church. Despite the revocation of the ban, however, the question of the Eastern-rite Catholics' property remained unresolved. When the revolution first happened, Romania's new political leaders were anxious to gain support from the whole country, including the Eastern-rite Catholics. They were particularly anxious to gain the support of the most important Romanian dissidents, one of whom was the Eastern-rite Catholic Professor from Cluj, Doina Cornea. It is rumoured that President Ion Iliescu, initially unwilling to re-legalize the Eastern-rite Catholic Church, agreed to do so only to win

Doina Cornea's public support for the National Salvation Front. Within the first month of the revolution there were significant changes in the new leadership, which then changed tactics to wooing the support of the majority groups. The new leadership was therefore more disposed to serving the interests of the seventeen-million-strong Orthodox Church than of the Uniate Church, whose membership a government minister estimated at 10,000. While some Orthodox supported the revocation of the ban, the main body of the Church did not want to see a resurgence of the Uniates. In January 1990 the Uniates had already begun to claim back all the property they had lost in 1949, which alarmed the Orthodox greatly.

At the end of January 1990 the government set up a Ministry for Religious Affairs. An historian with a dissident background and a practising member of the Orthodox Church, Nicolae Stoicescu, was appointed head of the Ministry. He then chaired a series of meetings between the leaders of the two churches at which the official Romanian press agency announced that an agreement had been reached that a referendum was to be held in individual parishes, to decide whether churches should be returned to the Eastern-rite Catholics or be retained by the Orthodox. Despite this public statement, Eastern-rite Catholic Metropolitan Alexandru Todea had not agreed to this at the meeting and subsequently issued a *communiqué* conveying the Eastern-rite Catholics' opposition to the idea.

The Eastern-rite Catholics opposed the idea of a referendum for the principal reason that they had no hope of regaining their churches in this way. They constitute a minority in many of the parishes and say they have little chance of attracting members when they have no church buildings for them to worship in. They thus feel they would be unfairly placed if it came to a contest between the two churches. They oppose the referendum also on the principle that the Orthodox's use of their property for the last forty years does not legally entitle them to ownership. After all, no referendum was held in 1948.

This disagreement has still not been resolved and the conflict has deepened as it has dragged on. The Eastern-rite Catholic leaders were affronted by the attitude of the Minister for Religious Affairs, who announced in January that the State did not recognize their church, and could not do so until it was satisfied with the ecclesiastical legitimacy of its leaders. The Vatican then came to the aid of the Eastern-rite Catholics by reaffirming in March the leaders who had been secretly consecrated and appointing bishops to all the posts which were unfilled.

Following this, President Iliescu then issued a decree in April 1990 which gave legal recognition to the Eastern-rite Catholic Church and pledged the State to return all the property still in its possession which it had confiscated from the Eastern-rite Catholic Church in 1948. The question of the property now owned by the Orthodox Church, however, was still not legally dealt with.

The leadership of the National Salvation Front, dominated by ex-Communists, began to understand fairly early on that it could not expect political support from the Eastern-rite Catholics, whether it forced the Orthodox to return its property or not. The anti-Communist feeling among the Uniate leaders, who had endured years of continual harassment, was too strong. As a church which had made a stand against the Communist leadership of Romania for the last forty years, they were the only church which had a clear political position prior to the elections of 20 May. It was virtually unanimously on the side of the opposition, rather than of the National Salvation Front.

At the outbreak of the conflict, the Eastern-rite Catholic Church began to fall victim to severe criticism in the Orthodox religious press. Orthodox hierarchs, priests and laity alike were deeply offended by public criticism of the Church's subservient role under Communism. Such criticism came from the West, but also from certain sections of Romanian society, particularly intellectuals and especially from the Eastern-rite Catholics and other religious denominations. In the *Romanian Orthodox Church News*, the highly influential theologian Dumitru Staniloaie, who was imprisoned from 1958 to 1964, wrote that other religious denominations, including the Eastern-rite Catholics, who had been publicly criticizing the role of the Orthodox Church under Ceauşescu, wanted to destroy the very existence of the Romanian people.

The Orthodox Church went through a crisis of its own immediately after the revolution, due to the compromised position of its real leader, Patriarch Teoctist, whom Ceauşescu regularly used for propaganda purposes. Teoctist retired at the end of January, only to return as Patriarch at the beginning of April to prevent a potentially divisive contest for the leadership. During the period in which the Church had no leader, a renewal group of formerly dissident clergy and laity tried to assert its influence and give a sense of direction to the Church. It favoured the renewal of the hierarchy, though without jeopardizing the stability of the Church. One of the new figures appointed to join the hierarchy in 1990 was a member of this group. He is Daniel Ciobotea, appointed a Bishop in February, then Metropolitan of Moldavia in May, a post which traditionally leads to that of Patriarch. At forty years old, he is seen as a new young hope for the Church and the people. He is untainted by associations with the past regime, and, having spent ten years at the Ecumenical Institute of Bossey in Switzerland, he is said to have a more Western outlook than some of the other elderly church hierarchs. Yet his position on the Uniate Church is deeply traditional.

In an article in the *Romanian Orthodox Church News* he does not recognize the validity of the Uniate Church at all. While recognizing that the reunion with the Orthodox Church was forced in 1948, he calls on the Vatican to reconsider the principle of Uniatism. He talks of the need for reconciliation, but only in the context of relations between the Vatican and the Orthodox Church. 'It must be made public, in all sincerity, that Uniatism was and continues to be an action of annexation and domination of Orthodoxy by

Rome, with no brotherly theological dialogue with the Orthodox.'

In the secular press, particularly that controlled by the National Salvation Front, the Eastern-rite Catholic Church is portrayed as a greedy, proselytizing church wanting to force Orthodox congregations out of their churches. Public opinion tends not to have much sympathy for this church of martyrs, which is seen as priding itself on its position of no-compromise throughout the Communist era. Many people find their demands of *restitutio in integrum* unrealistic and are unattracted by the Eastern-rite Catholic leaders' constant emphasis on the glorious past of their church and its saintly suffering.

Eastern-rite Catholic priests around the area of Cluj report that a small number of Orthodox priests have warned their congregations that anyone who goes over to the Eastern-rite Catholic church will receive eternal damnation and the graves of their families will be exhumed. Meanwhile, an incident occurred in a village near Baia Mare in July which is typical of the sort of head-on confrontation which is happening in the villages. In this particular village the Eastern-rite Catholics hold their Sunday services in the village cemetery, as their former church is now used by an Orthodox priest and his congregation. The incident happened when an Eastern-rite couple were due to be married. When the wedding party arrived at the cemetery it was decided that a cemetery was not the most appropriate of places to have a wedding service, and they decided to go to the house of the Orthodox priest to ask for his permission to use the church. The whole wedding party arrived at the priest's front door and asked to be given the keys of the church, on the condition that they would return them after the wedding was over. The priest refused to relinquish the keys, at which point the Eastern-rite Catholics decided to remain outside his door until he did so. Eventually they decided to perform the wedding on the steps of the church. As they were doing this a number of people arrived, apparently drunk, and began to disrupt the wedding by shouting and trying to overturn the table on the steps which were being used as an altar. As the procession moved away from the church, the last four members of it were attacked and seriously wounded with knives. The Eastern-rite Catholics believe that the Orthodox priest was responsible for calling in these drunken and violent people.

The future looks bleak for the Eastern-rite Catholic Church at the moment. Unpopular with the general population, distrusted by the Orthodox Church and only very reluctantly recognized by the State, Eastern-rite Catholic leaders are placing all their hope on Western support for their cause. Initial support from the Roman Catholic Church in Romania has dried up and they have no allies in Romania. They are calling on Western governments to make aid to Romania conditional on the legal resolution of the situation. The Vatican is reluctant to intervene, perhaps for fear of damaging its relations with the Romanian Orthodox Church.

Meanwhile, with the onset of the cold winter weather, as well as the anniversary of the Romanian revolution, the Eastern-rite Catholics' frustration is increasing. In November 1990 a group of Eastern-rite Catholics began a sit-in protest inside the town hall of Baia Mare for the return of their cathedrals and churches in that county. Scuffles occurred when Eastern-rite Catholics demonstrated outside their former cathedral in Baia Mare as a new Orthodox bishop was being enthroned inside. Only a large police presence and appeals for calm by leaders of both denominations prevented any worse violence. The majority of the Eastern-rite Catholics are in no mood to back down on their demands, though the Vatican may try to encourage them towards some sort of compromise. The only way of resolving the conflict is through an independent mediator who would not share the interests of either denomination. The only mediator they have had so far is the Romanian government, which has political interests at stake in the conflict. The longer the conflict drags on the more the Eastern-rite Catholics will suffer in terms of their public credibility and status, and the more it will contribute to the divisive and confrontational atmosphere so prevalent in Romanian society today.

CHAPTER ELEVEN

Convergence versus Divergence in Romania: the Role of the Vatra Românească Movement in Transylvania

Dennis Deletant

'A Fascist organization', so Imre Szokai, a Deputy Foreign Minister of Hungary, was quoted as describing Vatra Românească in an article published in *The Times* on 22 March 1990 following the ethnic clashes in the Transylvanian town of Tîrgu Mureş in March 1990. Polemical attributions are understandable when people are the casualties of ethnic hatred, even more so when hopes of inter-ethnic reconciliation are brutally dashed.[1] The victims of Tîrgu Mureş, eight dead and over three hundred injured, cast a shadow over the euphoria of the overthrow of Nicolae Ceauşescu, which was sparked off by a protest of ethnic solidarity by Hungarians and Romanians against the expulsion of a Hungarian pastor, László Tőkés, from Timişoara. Coupled with the invasion of Bucharest by vigilante miners in June and their terrorization of the opposition and the city's inhabitants, the violence in Tîrgu Mureş convinced many that the nationalist attitudes and instruments of repression, fostered by the Ceauşescu tyranny, had not been discarded. Ceauşescu had temporarily united Romanians and Hungarians in opposition, but the *coup d'état* of December divided them.

---

1 Some of my Hungarian acquaintances in Romania have suggested to me that the very name Vatra has Fascistic connotations. Their argument is based on the link between Vatra Românească, the administrative and cultural centre of American Orthodox Romanians in Grass Lake, Michigan, and Valerian Trifa, Archbishop of the Romanian Orthodox Episcopate of America, who had his United States citizenship revoked in 1980 in the wake of a public outcry following his own admission that he was a member of the Iron Guard. Just how fanciful this claim is can be demonstrated by the fact that the centre was christened before Trifa entered the US in 1950. Furthermore, Vatra with its meaning of 'hearth' is not an unusual name for Romanian cultural foundations. In 1939, for example, the Romanian sociologist Dimitrie Gusti created the Social Service, an organization which brought together all existing cultural, economic and social bodies engaged in work for the peasants. Its aim was to build in every village a centre known as a Vatra Românească to serve as a focus of social life.

The emergence of Vatra Românească is symptomatic of this changed relationship and is emblematic of the force of Romanian nationalism. This force is emotional, being based on fear, but at the same time it is an ideology with a powerful mobilizatory capacity since it provides definition of group identity. As such it offers a ready-made vehicle to populist politicians who are willing to exploit its ability not only to include people within its definition, but also to exclude them. It was primarily fear which prompted the creation of Vatra, as indeed its President Radu Ceontea has pointed out.[2] Mistrust of Hungarian motives, fear of Hungarian revanchism, concern about an erosion of Romanian dominance in Transylvania and general unease about the economic future, have all contributed to create a climate of inter-ethnic tension which is by no means unique to Romania; we have only to look at neighbouring Serbia and Croatia, or even to Bulgaria, to find similar festering inter-ethnic rivalries and politicians only too willing to canalize resentment.

Buttressing these immediate problems lies the legacy of the different historical experience of Romanians and Hungarians. The lack of what we might call 'synchronization' between the essentially Western cultural experience of Hungarians and essentially Eastern Orthodox experience of the Romanians, and the resulting divergences in behavioural values, have fostered divergence rather than convergence between the two peoples. If we add to these considerations a belief, shared by most Hungarians, that after an era of the most abject totalitarianism, there should be more liberalism, and contrast this belief with a fear, held by many Romanians, that liberalism, unless checked, will bring anarchy, and bear in mind that since the Hungarians at present constitute the largest opposition party in Romania, opposition itself assumes an ethnic dimension, then we can see that the grounds for mutual respect and trust are slim indeed.

Against this background it is not difficult to comprehend why Romanian suspicion of Hungarian intentions was aroused by the rapidity and efficiency with which the Hungarian community in Transylvania organized and asserted itself after the overthrow of Ceaușescu. An association called the Hungarian Democratic Union of Romania (HDUR) was established in Cluj on 21 December 1989 and issued an appeal to 'our dear Romanian friends to unite in putting in end to evil':

> You should know that we, the Hungarians of Romania, are not driven by revenge. The suffering and humiliation to which we were subjected by the Ceaușescu clan's dictatorship has not blinded us. You will understand, we hope, our boundless pain at being called, particularly in the Ceaușescu era, 'fascists', 'Horthyists', 'revisionists', 'traitors', and at being cursed in every conceivable manner. In the dictator's speeches, and in the writings

---

2 *Cuvintal liber*, Tîrgu Mureș, 17 July 1990.

of his ideologues, we were declared extinct as a separate
nationality; we were denied the right to remain ourselves. Our
children were denied even the natural right of learning in their
own language. We Hungarians, together with the other national
minorities in Romania, were condemned to the fate of being a
herd of people destined to be forcibly assimilated.[3]

Two days later the HDUR issued a statement of its aims which included the
following demands:

The immediate development of an educational system which
guarantees the opportunity for minority language instruction at
every level ...

The re-establishment of the independent Hungarian University in
Kolozsvár [Cluj], the establishment of independent Hungarian
Schools of engineering, agriculture, medicine and pharmacology,
teaching and fine arts, and the re-opening of the centuries-old
Hungarian high schools ...

The introduction of mandatory bilingualism in Transylvania, with
administrative and judicial proceedings conducted in the
Romanian and Hungarian languages ...

The right of local government by democratically elected officials,
and the restoration of the Hungarian autonomous towns, regions
and counties where the majority of the population is Hungarian ...

The establishment of a Ministry of Nationalities and the
convening of a Hungarian Nationality Congress.[4]

To regain the ground lost by the Hungarian minority under the Ceauşescu
regime the HDUR's tactics were clearly to strike while the iron was hot, but
the haste with which they pressed their demands was regarded by many
Romanians in Transylvania as both indecent and sinister. Romanians' concern
at what they interpreted as a growing militancy on the part of the Hungarians
seemed to be confirmed by reports of revenge killings of six policemen in the
Hungarian-dominated county of Harghita at the turn of the year,[5] although the
HDUR swiftly criticized the murders. In the spirit of its initial appeal of 21

---

3 *Scînteia Poporului*, Bucharest, 24 December 1989.
4 G. Schöpflin and H. Poulton (eds), *Romania's Ethnic Hungarians*, London, 1990, p. 20.
5 *East European Newsletter*, Vol. 4, January 1990, No. 2.

December the leadership of the HDUR subordinated itself to the provisional government of the National Salvation Front (NSF), which included sixteen prominent Hungarians, among them László Tőkés, the pastor from Timişoara whose attempted arrest sparked off the revolution, Károly Király, a leading critic of Ceauşescu's policies, and Géza Domokos, the president of the HDUR.

The NSF soon took steps to restore Hungarian-language radio broadcasts, and four hours of national TV time were allocated programmes in Hungarian. A Transylvanian Hungarian, Attila Pálfalvi, was appointed Deputy Minister of Education in charge of minority schools and on 15 January 1990 he announced that the Hungarian Bolyai University in Cluj, mandatorily merged with the Romanian Babes University at a meeting presided over by the then Central Committee Secretary Nicolae Ceauşescu, would reopen in the autumn of 1990 and would take under its aegis the Hungarian Medical Institute in Tîrgu Mureş.[6] Five days later the Ministry of Education announced that it had begun to reorganize primary and secondary schools with a view to assuring education in their native tongue for the minorities.[7] The Ministry was indeed correct, but the speed and manner of this reorganization antagonized Romanians in Transylvania. In Cluj, for example, Romanian pupils of Lyceum no. 3, which had been a monolingual Hungarian secondary school until the 1960s when Romanian classes were introduced, were barred without notice from entering the school at the beginning of January and told to transfer to the former Party school in a different part of the town. Protesting Romanian parents complained to the Minister of Education Mihail Şora that they had not been consulted about these decisions and that the action taken by the local authorities was insensitive, coming as it did in the middle of the school year. Similar events were repeated in mixed language schools in Tîrgu Mureş and amidst the chorus of criticism from Romanians Pálfalvi was dismissed on 27 January for 'taking decisions on his own in such a manner that contributed to creating tension between the Magyar population and the Romanian population in some Transylvanian settlements',[8] and replaced by a Hungarian historian Lajos Demény. Education Minister Mihail Şora's statement, four days later, that agreements on the separation of exclusively Hungarian and Romanian schools which had been made 'in a spontaneous way in Transylvania' would be implemented, suggested that the provisional government had devolved the reorganization of schools to local authorities, but in what was clearly an attempt to forestall further agitation he announced that where local agreements had yet to be reached the question of separation would wait until the beginning of the academic year.

---

6   Budapest Home Service, 15 January 1990, in *Summary of World Broadcasts, Eastern Europe*, 0666 B/13, 19 January 1990.
7   *Rompres*, 20 January 1990, in *SWB*, EE/0673, B8, 27 January 1990.
8   *Rompres*, 27 January 1990, in *SWB*, EE/0676, B11, 31 January 1990.

Postponement of the process of reorganization merely angered the Hungarian population, who held demonstrations in the major towns of Transylvania calling for the separation of schools. Romanians opposed to these demands held counter protests and in Cluj several people were injured after clashes between rival groups on 8 February. Two days later an estimated 40,000 Hungarians marched peacefully through the centre of Tîrgu Mureş, a city of mixed Hungarian-Romanian population, in support of separate schools. It was against this background of demonstration and counter-demonstration that a group calling itself Uniunea Vatra Românească ('The Romanian Hearth' Union) emerged. The exact date of its constitution is not clear but one of its first, if not its first, public meetings was held on 1 February 1990 in the assembly hall of the Alexandru Papiu Ilarian secondary school in Tîrgu Mureş under the chairmanship of Radu Ceontea, a member of the editorial staff of the review *Vatra* (Hearth), in the presence of several hundred people.[9] A further meeting was held a week later in the larger premises of the Sala Sporturilor (Sports Hall) in Tîrgu Mureş and attracted an even larger audience.

It was clear from the speeches delivered on this second occasion that the question of separate Hungarian schools was regarded as the thin end of a wedge designed to truncate the Romanians' 'rights' in Transylvania and that the Hungarians' 'aggressiveness' in asserting their own 'rights', nowhere conceded by the Vatra speakers, had poisoned relations between the two communities in Tîrgu Mureş. Hungarian demands over schooling were seen as assuming the proportions of a general threat to the Romanians' own position in Transylvania. The problem, then, was not just one of language; behind it lay a mutual mistrust felt by the Hungarian and Romanian communities in Transylvania, which is the legacy of the province's position as part of the ancestral homeland of both peoples and, more basically, a differing conception of respect for minority rights. The Romanians feared that granting separate education in Hungarian would encourage the two million Transylvanian Hungarians to then press for greater political autonomy and for a closer association with Hungary, while the Hungarians felt that they could only reverse the process of forced assimilation and integration carried out by Ceauşescu by first protecting, and then asserting, their identity.

Here we come to the question of whether that identity should be regarded as 'national' or 'ethnic'; this is not just a matter of pedantry. If ethnic consciousness is seen as a cultural phenomenon it can consequently be argued that the Hungarians in Transylvania share a common culture with their fellow Hungarians in Hungary and nothing more; this is the view of the Romanian government for whom the Hungarian population in Transylvania is an 'ethnic' minority. National consciousness, on the other hand, may be seen as a political phenomenon, one which implies identity within a common government, and

---

9   *Europa si Neamul Romanesc*, XIX, April 1990, No. 214, p. 12.

for the Hungarian government the Transylvanian Hungarians are a 'national' minority.

Dr Zeno Opriş's address says a great deal about the Romanian attitudes which buttress Vatra's position:

> After the immense joy and warmth which filled Romanians' souls in December 1989, respectable people, after they had mourned and buried their dead, set themselves to work in order to get things moving again following their temporary interruption for the good and happiness of everyone. In Tîrgu Mureş things did not work out that way. Considering that 'now is the moment', that they must seize the advantage before things settle down, the Hungarian majority shamefacedly rushed at the mechanism of power, but the Romanians, tolerant and astonished, to avoid being accused of chauvinism in these confused times, found themselves pushed to one side, incredulous that the Romanian nation could become a minority in its own country![10]

This anger was echoed by a journalist Mariana Florea who defiantly declared:

> We will not accept the expulsion from schools of children and teachers whose only fault is that of being Romanians ... It is intolerable that the Romanian people should be placed in the position of demanding its rights in its own country! For we are in Romania! We have been, we are, and we shall continue to be![11]

By expressing the fear that the Romanians could become a minority in their own country Opriş was reflecting the Romanian conception of absolute sovereignty in the nation-state, embodied in the slogan coined by Ceauşescu's propagandists that 'Romanians must be masters in their own home'. The success of this slogan relied upon the interpretation that since Romanians were in their own home, they must therefore be masters in it, and the implicit corollary that the Hungarian minority were aliens. Such views, of course, completely ignore the position of the Transylvanian Hungarians, who also regard the province as their homeland since the logic of such an admission by the Romanians would lead to the conclusion that the Hungarian minority too should be 'masters in their own home'; and indeed they were before 1918, even though they were a minority. For the Romanians the idea of 'mastership' or supremacy was confirmed under Ceauşescu by the measures taken to place minority institutions, such as schools and institutes of higher education, under

---

10 Ibid., p. 7.
11 Ibid., p. 11.

the aegis of Romanian ones whose governing bodies were almost exclusively made up of Romanians.

The potency of the past was revealed in Ceontea's rhetoric: the formulation of Hungarian demands following the Revolution threatened yet again to expose Romanians in Transylvania to the 'injustice of history':

> Only five weeks after a bloody Christmas, here we are asking ourselves: will history, which has been so unjust to us Transylvanian Romanians down the centuries, also be consistent after the revolution of 22 December 1989?[12]

This brought Ceontea to the wider issue of the position of the Hungarian minority in Romania:

> but we ask only that these rights conform to the structure of the national unitary Romanian state, since Romania is not a multinational country. Let these rights be the same as those of the minorities in other civilized countries, not one of them greater...[13]

Ceontea's affirmation that Romania is not a multinational country should not be taken as a denial of the existence of minorities; he was merely echoing the official Romanian position that the country is not a 'multi-ethnic' state and that by definition its 'ethnic' minorities can owe no allegiance to a second 'national' state. For the Hungarians of Transylvania to whom I have spoken loyalty to the Romanian state, to have any meaning, must be one that is freely given and not coerced from them, and to give their loyalty they must not be placed in the position of 'second-class' citizens in the ancestral homeland which they share with the Romanians. Ceontea's begrudging concession of minority rights, 'not one of them greater' than 'in other civilized countries' typifies the mentality of those who see the relationship between Hungarians and Romanians in terms of subordination of the minority to the majority rather than co-ordination, or of tolerance rather than intolerance. In essence, Ceontea (and Vatra) seeks to maintain the Romanian position of supremacy in Transylvania and appeals to all those who still share Ceauşescu's aim of creating a uniform, homogenous state. When Ceontea advocates equal rights for everyone he is really saying that there should be no privileges for minorities.

Vatra's identification with Transylvania, the hearth (*vatra*) or ancestral homeland of the Romanian people, was underlined by one of its spokesmen, the judge Ioan Sabau:

---

12   Ibid.
13   Ibid.

> Vatra Românească, our ancestral hearth, thanks all of you, Romanians from these ancient regions of dream and legend, for coming to this meeting. We Romanians ... come from distant times of history, cogniscent of our purpose. That purpose we wish to carry further, here and nowhere else, in our ancestral maternal cradle of Transylvania, which has been so often covered in blood.[14]

The emphasis placed by Sabau on Transylvania's status as the birthplace of the Romanian people might be seen as a reflection of the role which the Romanian national historiography was called upon to play under Ceaușescu, that of justifying the nation's claim to its homeland, since the fate of the nation was perceived as being inextricably bound up with the promotion of this thesis. But it is the idea of mission and bloody sacrifice, taken in conjunction with Ceontea's appeal:

> We should all unite, let there not be a Transylvanian Romanian who is not a member of *Vatra Românească*, so that when we have more than six million members and more there will be no need to declare ourselves a party, because then we shall be the Romanian nation itself, dignified and free, upright and tolerant[15]

that recall the elements of an earlier nationalist ideology which has been labelled Fascism.

Vatra's attempt at identification with Romanian society as a whole received a helping hand from Orthodox priests, anxious no doubt to restore their moral authority amongst the Romanians following their church's collusion with the Ceaușescu regime. One of their number, Father Stefan Urda, the diocesan inspector from Alba Iulia, underlined at the 8 February meeting the unifying role the Church had played in preserving the identity of Transylvanian Romanians.[16] But Vatra's appeal is not solely as a defender of Romanian cultural interests. While this would explain the support it received from the urban intelligentsia, professional people such as teachers, doctors, writers and the clergy, it cannot account for the large numbers of industrial workers who attended Vatra meetings. Many of them were resettled from other parts of Romania during the last two decades as industry expanded in Transylvania and now fear the loss of their jobs if economic reform is implemented. Restoration of Hungarian cultural autonomy represents for them a step towards greater Hungarian control of the local economy, which will in turn lead to positive discrimination in a diminishing job market in favour of the Hungarians.

---

14 Ibid., p. 10.
15 Ibid., p. 12.
16 Ibid.

Vatra's manipulation of these fears has contributed in a major way to the ethnic unrest in Transylvania.

Alongside this one must consider the traditional political attitude in Romania, one inherited and exploited by the Communist regime. Distrust of authority, unfamiliarity with the idea of civic responsibility and acceptance of corruption in political life have created a political void which a nationalist ideology can fill. In these conditions an appeal to nationalism in the hands of demagogues can lift the audience beyond unimportant internal political struggles which were deemed injurious to the nation; at the same time a movement which can purport to show that government is insensitive to a 'national' problem, has every chance of attracting support.

For supporters of Vatra the Bucharest government's failing was its weakness in having made concessions in January over the Hungarian demands for separate schools; for the HDUR the government had gone back on its initial promise to introduce Hungarian schools by postponing implementation until September 1990. Education Minister Șora's announcement to this effect prompted a series of peaceful demonstrations by Hungarians in Tîrgu Mureș, but tension increased after celebrations on 15 March of Hungary's national holiday, which marks the day in 1848 when serfdom and privileges were abolished and the Union of Transylvania with Hungary was proclaimed. Several thousand Hungarians from Hungary joined relatives in Transylvania to celebrate this event, draping buildings with both Hungarian and Romanian flags as a sign of communal solidarity. In Tîrgu Mureș, however, where anti-Hungarian sentiment had been allegedly whipped up by Vatra speakers addressing meetings at factories and in surrounding villages earlier in March, the celebrations of the 1848 proclamation of Union with Hungary were deemed by many Romanians to be overtly provocative.[17] On the following day there were fist fights in the city when Vatra supporters, riled by two bilingual banners that read 'Schools in Hungarian' and 'Justice for Minorities', jostled Hungarians in the streets. On 17 March tension rose as a Hungarian shopkeeper displayed a notice allegedly saying that she would only serve customers who spoke Hungarian and a drunken Hungarian driver ran his car into a group of Romanians. Student rallies were held outside Transylvania in Bucharest, Iași, Craiova and Contanța where Romanian students rejected the

---

17 An example of the primitive atavistic character of the pronouncements by certain leading figures in the movement was that of Justinian, Orthodox bishop of the diocese of Vad, Cluj and Feleac who declares his devotion to Transylvania in a section devoted to Vatra in the Cluj newspaper *Adevarul in libertate* (1 March 1990) in these terms: 'The earth and sky here is at one with us, the forests and mountains have proudly defended us, toppling, at our behest on to hungry, haughty hordes who, if they had the sense would have shown shame at the crimes which they committed against this [Romanian] people, one of the oldest in Europe.'

call of Hungarian students at the medical institute in Tîrgu Mureş for separate Hungarian schools, considering it inimical to inter-ethnic harmony.[18]

On the morning of 19 March several hundred Romanians marched into the Square of Roses in Tîrgu Mureş in peaceful protest at what they regarded as the connivance of local Hungarian officials in staging the 15 March celebrations, which they considered provocative. The protest was swelled by large numbers of Vatra supporters who began chanting defiantly that they would not cede Transylvania and demanded the resignation of prominent Hungarian officials in the country of Mureş. As they laid siege to the building of the city council and the local headquarters of the HDUR a mass of about 1,000 peasants, mostly from the two neighbouring villages of Hodac and Ibăneşti situated some 50km to the north-east of Tîrgu Mureş, were brought to the city centre in the late afternoon in buses and lorries commandeered by the local mayors and officials and began attacking Hungarians in the street with clubs and axes which they had been given *en route*. Several bus drivers reported that mobs of workers and peasants had hijacked their buses *en route* to the city and had then stopped at prearranged sites to collect staves and axes. These attackers stormed the HDUR headquarters and after sacking the building they beat party officials as they tried to leave, including the prominent Hungarian Transylvania writer András Sütö, who was blinded in one eye. At the same time the local headquarters of the predominantly Romanian National Liberal Party were attacked by the mob.

On the following day, as an estimated crowd of some 20,000 Hungarians and Romanians staged a peaceful rally in the same Square of Roses to protest against the violence of the previous evening and to demand an official enquiry, Vatra supporters again assembled and were joined by villagers who had been bussed back into the city. When the rally broke up the Romanian demonstrators attacked the departing Hungarians, but this time the latter retaliated by assembling in large groups and counter-attacking with the help of the local Hungarian-speaking Gypsy community. Army and police units finally appeared on the scene at midnight and broke up the clashes. In the two days of violence eight people were left dead and more than three hundred injured. It was only after the bloodshed that the Army intervened with tanks to separate the rival groups.

Given the clear evidence that the violence was stage-managed, the question inevitably arose 'by whom?'. A number of young simple Romanians who were apprehended on the evening of 20 March after attacks on Hungarians revealed under questioning that they were from Hodac and Ibăneşti and that they had been promised sums of up to 3,000 lei (the average manual monthly wage) by the mayor to defend Romanians in Tîrgu Mureş where, they were told, they

---

18 V. Socor, 'Forces of Old Resurface in Romania: the Ethnic Clashes in Tirgu Mures' (hereafter Socor, 'Forces of old resurface in Romania'), *Radio Free Europe Report on Eastern Europe*, 1, 13 April 1990, 15, p. 38.

were being attacked by Hungarians. On closer questioning it emerged that the 'payment' consisted of exemption from a local 'tax' which the mayor had allegedly introduced. The young men's allegations highlight the power which unscrupulous Romanian officials can exert over a society in which only lip service has been paid to the rule of law during the last half-century and where the voice of authority still commands unquestioning obedience from the compliant. Vatra leaflets were found on many Romanians telling the Hungarians in abusive language to 'return' to Hungary if they did not like conditions in Transylvania. There is little doubt that supporters of Vatra organized the transport of villagers and provided them with their primitive weapons, and it is obvious that these supporters occupied positions of authority; this inevitably brings us to a further question as to their identity.

For an answer we need to consider the evolution of the regional structures of power which emerged after the overthrow of Ceaușescu. The local councils of the provisional government, the National Salvation Front (NSF), were largely constituted from the *nomenklatura* of the Communist Party who were naturally reluctant to lose a position of influence and patronage in the post-Ceaușescu period. In those Transylvanian counties with a predominantly Hungarian population, such as Covasna and Harghita, many of the Romanian *nomenklatura* have been replaced by figures less compromised in the eyes of the Hungarians, but in the county of Mureș, which has a more balanced mix of population, the Romanian *nomenklatura* have continued to exert influence by joining the Vatra bandwagon and thus presenting themselves as defenders of Romanian interests. Amongst this *nomenklatura* are large numbers of the *securitate* who played a vital role in overseeing the application of Ceaușescu's draconian repressive measures of the police state which had, and have yet, to be dismantled. The attributes of the *securitate* included supervision of the crude weapons used in Ceaușescu's civilian defense units to arm the patriotic guards. Stores in factories, these weapons included axes and scythes and it is likely that such primitive arsenals were supplied to the villagers of Hodac and Ibănești on the orders of *securitate* members sympathetic to Vatra. Suspicions that the *securitate*'s hand was involved in the Tîrgu Mureș violence were fuelled by the failure of the authorities, both at local and national level, to take any action before and during the clashes. The catalogue of inaction suggests either crass government incompetence and complacency, or collusion. No precautionary measures were adopted to prevent disturbances, despite warnings from the HDUR and the Romanian opposition parties about the increase in tension on 16 March, and there was no intervention by the police or army until the evening of 20 March, that is until after two days of bloody street fighting. In statements characteristic of the NSF's indecisiveness and lack of authority interim President Ion Iliescu and Prime Minister Petre Roman blandly referred to the clashes as 'regrettable events' and avoided mention of the dead and injured. A government statement, while charging that the violence had been 'provoked' by Hungarian citizens who had crossed the border on 15 March to celebrate the anniversary of the 1848 revolution,[19] made no mention of the attacks by Vatra supporters on Hungarians on 16 March, nor of the bussing of villagers from Hodac and Ibăneşti, nor of the sacking on 20 March by a mob carrying Vatra placards of the Tîrgu Mureş headquarters of the National Liberal and of the Social Democratic parties, both of which had adopted a more conciliatory approach to the question of separate Hungarian schools.

Also overlooked were intemperate statements made by Vatra president Radu Ceontea in an interview published in *România Liberă* on 17 March. When asked to describe the characteristic features of the Hungarian minority's demands he gave this answer:

> After almost a thousand years of foreign domination of Transylvania it is fairly difficult for them [the Hungarians] to forget their behaviour as rulers. These absurd claims, in support of which they blithely wander around Bucharest, knocking at the doors of power, are designed to give them rapidly not only rights which they had, which they have and which they will have — extended in line with the new democratic statute of Romania — but also 'special' rights which are not specific to minorities. They demand rights specific to communities with a federative status, like those in the Swiss Federation to which they often refer. All the comparisons are misplaced since we are talking about different historical situations. Perhaps if we too had the neighbours which Switzerland has we could discuss matters in another way ... Romania is not a multinational state, but a national unitary state in which different percentages of minorities live. And no minority is permitted to have favours just because their ancestors were oppressors for centuries!

The language of the last sentence recalled the tired old slogans of Ceauşescu and added further force to the arguments of those who saw Vatra as the haven of those anxious to retain a grip on power. In the approach to national elections the provisional NSF government seemed anxious, judging from its first statement on the Tîrgu Mureş violence on 20 March mentioned above, not to alienate Vatra supporters nor to be outflanked by its leaders, especially as the organization had spawned its own political party in mid-March under the name of the Alliance for National Unity of Romanians in Transylvania. The statement wrongly accused Hungarian President Mátyás Szürös of calling upon 'Hungarians in Transylvania to intensify their activity and to organize themselves in accordance with the idea that Transylvania is an ancient Hungarian land' when in fact Szürös had said in a speech on 18 March that, if

---

19 *Rompres*, 21 March 1990.

Ilie Ceaușescu, the former President's brother, could claim that Transylvania was 'an ancient Romanian land', then Hungarians were also entitled to say that it was 'an ancient Magyar land'. This did not mean that Hungary had designs on Transylvania, merely that 'we have a right to demand the assurance of individual and collective rights for the Hungarians as a nationality'.[20]

Yet Roman, whilst playing to the Vatra gallery,[21] appeared anxious not to antagonize the Hungarians in Transylvania and a two-sided policy began to crystallize; one of reconciliation towards the Hungarians in Transylvania, and one of hostility towards the Hungarian government. On 23 March, Prime Minister Roman spoke to representatives from the Hungarian-dominated counties of Harghita and Covasna and then issued a statement saying that accusations in pro-NSF newspapers that the two counties intended 'to maim Romania's territorial integrity' were 'groundless' and that measures would be taken against those who published material capable of 'inciting ... hatred and violence between ... ethnic communities'.[22] Signs that reconciliation was in the air appeared to be reinforced by a meeting between interim President Ion Iliescu and the President of the HDUR Géza Domokos.

In relations with Hungary the opposite was true. In a message sent out by Roman on that very same day, 23 March, to international leaders, including the UN Secretary-General, he alleged that 10,000 Hungarian citizens, i.e. from Hungary, had participated in the incidents in Tîrgu Mureș and, in the language of Ceaușescu, he warned of the 'gravity of nationalist-chauvinist and revisionist instigations carried out by certain circles from Hungary against Romania'. Asserting Romania's claim to absolute sovereignty he appealed to international leaders to use their influence with Hungary to 'put an end to all outside interference in Romania's internal affairs'.[23]

There is no doubt that Vatra made significant political progress as a result of the Tîrgu Mureș clashes. It attracted national and international attention, its nominees were appointed for the first time to the reconstituted urban and regional councils of Tîrgu Mureș and the county of Mureș, and its representatives were received by Iliescu and Roman. A measure of its influence can be detected in the vigorous rejoinders issued by the government to Hungary over her alleged interference in Romania's affairs. But at the same time the violence brought more liberal parliamentary and extra-parliamentary forces together in opposition to Vatra's posturings. On 22 March the National Liberal Party and the HDUR issued a joint statement, signed by their respective leaders Radu Campeanu and Géza Domokos, repudiating all internal and external 'Hungarian irredentist and Romanian extremist-nationalist' forces

---

20 M. Shafir, 'The Romanian Authorities' Reactions to the Violence in Tirgu Mures', *Radio Free Europe Report on Eastern Europe*, 1, 13 April 1990, 15, p. 45.
21 He continued to do so after the elections, see his declaration that 'Vatra was the wall which stopped the wave' (quoted in *Cuvintul liber*, Tirgu Mureș, 17 July 1990, p. 1.
22 Ibid.
23 *Rompres*, 24 March 1990.

and pledging respect for existing borders and for the cultural individuality of ethnic minorities. On the language question both leaders recognized Romanian as the language of the State but argued that 'the parallel use of native languages constitutes an important factor for Romania's liberal transformation'. On the same day eight youth groups in Tîrgu Mureş of mixed ethnic composition called upon the provisional parliament to bring the rights of Romania's ethnic minorities in line with the Helsinki Final Act, to monitor the application of such legislation and to bring to justice those responsible for the violence in the city.[24]

Sadly, the reintroduction of free elections and the adoption of a system of proportional representation, designed to ensure a fair reflection of views shared by smaller parties or interest groups, only polarized ethnic differences. A feature of the results of the May 1990 parliamentary elections in Romania was the emergence of the Hungarian Democratic Union as the joint second largest party in the lower house with 7.2% of the national vote and twenty-nine seats, and outright second largest party in the Senate with twelve senators. The almost one million votes which the HDUR received for the lower house, and their heavy concentration in the Hungarian-dominated counties of Covasna and Harghita, where they won 77% and 85% of votes, suggests that the Hungarian minority voted as an ethnic group, thus indicating that they regarded ethnic issues as more important than economic, social and political policies. Indeed, the HDUR's performance can be attributed to its umbrella character, representing a wide spectrum of political views, which enabled it to attract virtually the entire Hungarian vote. Its success demonstrates that the election for the Hungarian minority represented a declaration of ethnic loyalty rather than an expression of political choice.

By contrast, the Partidul pentru Unitatea Nationala a Romanilor din Transilvania (The Party for the National Unity of the Romanians in Transilvania), which was created shortly before the elections on what it called 'the socio-cultural principles of Vatra', received only 2.1% of the popular vote for the lower and upper houses of parliament, returning only nine members to the Chamber of Deputies and two to the Senate. The poor perfomance of the PUNRT, which campaigned nationally with the Partidul Romanilor (The Romanians' Party) under the umbrella of the Alianţa pentru Unitatea Românilor (AUR), should not be allowed to obscure the lesson of its victories in the counties of Cluj (three deputies and one senator) and Mureş (four deputies and one senator), for these were precisely the areas in which the transfer of Romanian pupils from reinstated Hungarian schools had been handled so insensitively. Signs that Romanian resentment over this issue, and therefore Vatra's ability to exploit it, was beginning to be soothed by government action emerged from the relatively poor attendance at Vatra meetings held in Satu Mare, Oradea, Arad, Cluj and Bucharest on 9 July to

---

24 Socor, 'Forces of Old Resurface in Romania', p. 41.

protest at what it claimed to be 'the frustration felt by Romanian pupils' at the number of places allocated to them in secondary schools in Transylvania. How misplaced this 'frustration' appears to have been can be judged from a perusal of the provision of school places made by the Ministry of Education for the year 1990-91 in the three counties with a significant Hungarian population. The statistics, published in a declaration of the Hungarian Democratic Union, show that Romanian pupils have a far better chance of continuing their education beyond the age of fourteen than their Hungarian colleagues (see annex). Vatra contested the accuracy of these figures, accusing the HDUR of falsifying them in respect of the Mureş county, although it failed to address the implication that the Romanian Ministry of Education, the source of the HDUR figures, was guilty of fabrication.

Resentment and fear are the two sentiments upon which Vatra feeds and therefore persistent criticism of the Romanian government's performance on minority issues runs the risk of playing into the hands of the ultra-nationalist lobby as well as of weakening the position of those Romanians who are prepared to take a conciliatory line. When I say to Vatra supporters that in my view Hungary has no territorial designs upon Transylvania they point to the display and sale of maps in Budapest of Greater Hungary with the incorporation of Transylvania. When I opine that the Hungarian government has distanced itself from the statements of ultra-nationalists in Hungary they will retort by quoting from the speech given by Hungarian Prime Minister Jószef Antall on 2 June, the seventieth anniversary of the Treaty of Trianon, to the Hungarian Democratic Forum's Third National Conference. Antall recalled that as a result of the treaty Hungary lost two-thirds of its historical territory and stated that 'while historically speaking we condemn the Peace Treaty, as a country which signed the Helsinki Basic Document, we nevertheless have foregone the violent changing of borders. At the same time we insist on what was also part of the Peace Treaty, namely guaranteeing the rights of national minorities.' There was nothing new in these words of the Prime Minister but then he went on to say that he wanted 'to be Prime Minister of fifteen million Hungarians'.[25] The implication here was that Antall saw himself as the representative of those Hungarians living beyond the frontiers of Hungary and in this sense he could be accused of challenging the sovereignty of neighbouring Czechoslovakia and Romania over their Hungarian minorities. It was precisely on this part of his speech that he was tackled in an interview on Hungarian radio. In answer to a question as to whether his words could be interpreted negatively, especially in the context of the anniversary of Trianon when Hungary was truncated within its present frontiers, Antall replied:

---

25 *SWB*, EE/0782, 5 June 1990, B/8.

A Hungarian government has a moral and spiritual duty to be responsible for every member of the 15 million Hungarian community, this means that we have to stand up for their human and minority rights, we must find a way to support their cultural aims, education and all other things connected with it.[26]

In both Czechoslovakia and Romania Antall's words were indeed interpreted negatively. Romanian Foregin Minister Adrian Nastase reminded his readers of them in an article in the Romanian weekly *Lumea* in which he was highly critical of recent official Hungarian pronouncements on the treatment of the Hungarian minority in Transylvania. Nastase pointed out that in the Declaration in the Helsinki Final Act regarding the principles which must govern relations between signatory states, the first principle records sovereign equality and respect for the rights inherent in sovereignty. In context this explicitly means, amongst other things, the right of each state to establish alone its laws and regulations. Prime Minister Antall, Nastase wrote, had received a mandate only from the citizens of Hungary, not from any other country in which 'citizens of Hungarian ethnicity lived'. 'On the territory of Romania', he went on, 'there exists no nation other than the Romanian one, only national minorities scattered over the whole area of the country.'[26] Here we have the reaffirmation of the principle of absolute sovereignty embodied in that creation of the Paris Peace Settlement of 1919-20, the nation-state.

Attacking 'Hungarian chauvinism', a favourite pastime of Ceaușescu, has become the main preoccupation of the weekly paper *Romania Mare* (Greater Romania), which, unlike the regional eponymous monthly of Vatra, is distributed nationally and has a print-run of 500,000 copies. Under the direction of Eugen Barbu and Corneliu Vadim Tudor, both notorious apologists of Ceaușescu, *Romania Mare* has become the mouthpiece of those same shadowy forces which have exploited Vatra's popularity. The very re-emergence of Barbu and Vadim Tudor is a clear signal that the ideas and faces dear to Ceaușescu have resurfaced after their temporary eclipse. Some idea of the sinister forces at work in Romanian society can be gleaned from a letter sent by Barbu at the end of April to the Prime Minister Petre Roman requesting permission to publish *Romania Mare*. Barbu is alleged to have written in the letter 'we have watched, we have waited and we now consider the time right to act. Within two weeks of our paper's appearance a huge silence will descend upon the country.'[27] If we bear in mind that 8 June saw the launch of *Romania Mare*, that 14 June saw the invasion of Bucharest by so-called 'miners' in an attempt to physically destroy the opposition, then it is tempting to see Barbu's alleged words as not so much a prophecy of, but

---

26   Ibid.
26   30 August 1990, p. 4.
27   Private information.

rather a conviction that, silence would be imposed by violent means. Indeed, it is very likely that the same people in Bucharest who applauded the miners' violence are the same people for whom *Romania Mare* is compulsory and compulsive reading. Opposition bludgeoned into silence, orchestrated terror, stridently trumpeted nationalism: these hallmarks of Ceauşescu's rule lead us to believe that the old forces of tyranny, drawn from the Communist Party *nomenklatura* and the *securitate*, still remain intact and use *Romania Mare* as their mouthpiece. The paper's use of information that can only come from state security files in an attempt to vilify opponents, and its reproduction of documents from the Central Committee archives, merely add strength to the conviction that it is the organ of the most conservative and chauvinist wing of the *securitate*. The calumnies printed by Barbu, Vadim Tudor and their associates are the expression of a despair born from a realization that they have lost the upper hand to the younger generation of reformers and their more outward-looking *securitate* supporters, and it is with columnists of Vatra Românească that they share an inability to accept opposition as adversarial rather than inimical, and an unwillingness to show that understanding from which tolerance is born. The accusation that the international press has been hoodwinked into believing that a minority problem exists in Romania, that certain Romanian intellectuals are guilty of contesting authority, in other words of failing to conform, are refrains shared by both papers.[28] But most explosive are the calculated attacks, occasionally with anti-Semitic undertones, delivered by *Romania Mare* on those who seek consensus, on those who advise moderation, and their attempts to create divisions between different social groups, such as Romanians and Hungarians, Romanians and Gypsies, and between the Romanian and Hungarian governments. Reading *Romania Mare* one would believe that both countries are on a war footing, that Transylvania is ready to explode and that Hungary is preparing to invade. By pouring petrol over the smouldering fire of ethnic resentment, *Romania Mare* threatens to stir the embers of discontent into a violent inferno.

How far the Romanian government is prepared to go to satisfy minority demands will depend on how willing it is to defy the organization Vatra. There is no doubt that ethnic harmony cannot be restored without muffling the wilful provocation and agitation of *Romania Mare*. An encouraging sign was the Statement of Intent made in February 1990 by Adrian Nastase, the Romanian representative on the UN Commission for Human Rights, now Romanian Foreign Minister. Mr Nastase announced plans to incorporate provisions for the protection of minority rights in the new Romanian Constitution and invited the Commission to assist the Romanian government in observing these provisions. Since acceptance of the European Convention on Human Rights is a condition of entry into the European Community,

---

28 See for example Elena Neagoe's article in *Vatra Romaneasca*, July-August 1990, no. 2, p. 1.

satisfaction of this condition will exert a powerful lever upon the Romanian government to comply not only in word, but also in deed, with the Convention. This means that the Romanian government will be obliged to allow legal cases to be brought against itself in the European Court of Human Rights and to accept that its treatment of national minorities is something that other states or citizens are entitled to comment on. All of this is anathema to Vatra and the ultra-nationalists of *Romania Mare* and represents a potential source of conflict with the NSF government. Upon its resolution hangs Romania's claim to be readmitted to the comity of European states.

As suggested earlier in this paper, the old fears and prejudices will not disappear as long as Romania's economic situation remains critical. It is of little use exhorting the Romanian government to ensure that there is no discrimination in employment, for example, if there are no new jobs available. A large amount of economic aid, allocated judiciously so that the minorities are not disadvantaged, will help to reduce inter-ethnic tension in Transylvania. Through economic progress and the introduction of a market economy the interests of citizens as producers and consumers are likely to transcend the claim of national identity. That appeal would be weakened if the Romanian fear of Hungarian revanchism were removed and this might be achieved if the Hungarian government's self-appointed right, embodied in Article VI of the Hungarian Constitution but contested by Romania, to monitor the treatment of the Hungarian minority in neighbouring states, were transferred from Hungary to other member states of the Conference on Security and Cooperation in Europe. Only the creation of mutual trust will diminish Vatra's appeal and enable the Hungarian minority and the Romanian majority in Transylvania to make their own distinct contribution to the development of a liberal democratic society in Romania.

ANNEX

Harghita County

	Completed class 8 (14 years)	*Places in class 9 (15 Years)*
Romanian stream	1123	1281 (+14%)
Hungarian stream	4734	2527 (- 47%)
	Completed class 10 (16 years)	*Places in class 11*
Romanian stream	1140	828 (- 38%)
Hungarian stream	4308	1714 (- 60%)

Covasna County

	Completed class 8	*Places in class 9*
Romanian stream	1052	1003 (-5%)
Hungarian stream	2594	1485 (- 43%)
	Completed class 10	*Places in class 11*
Romanian stream	1673	715 (- 57%)
Hungarian stream	1519	775 (- 49%)

Mureş County

	Completed class 8	Places in class 9
Romanian stream	3607 (5919)	3800 (+ 5%)
Hungarian stream	2030 (3432)	1827 (- 10%)
	Completed class 10	*Places in class 11*
Romanian stream	2653 (6600)	2940 (3053) (+ 10%)
Hungarian stream	1516 (2756)	1110 (1129) (- 27%)

Class 10 marks the end of compulsory secondary education.
Source: *România Liberă*, 14 July 1990. The figures in brackets under Mureş county are those supplied by the local school inspectorate, according to Vatra (*Vatra Romaneasca*, September 1990, no.3, p. 5).

CHAPTER TWELVE

Reconstruction as Deconstruction: the Case of Yugoslavia

Mark Wheeler

At the end of *We the People,* his eyewitness account of the 1989 revolutions in Warsaw, Budapest, Berlin and Prague, Timothy Garton Ash suggests an epitaph for East European Communism:

> *Nothing in his life*
> *Became him like the leaving it.*

Yugoslavia, as usual, was to be different. Not only was the collapse of Communism there postponed by a year, but nothing has so besmirched its life as the civil war unleashed by its death. Why the difference? Why did the demise of a regime lead inexorably to the break-up of a state? Did Yugoslavia fail because of Communism? Or conversely and unfashionably, did Communism fail because of Yugoslavia? And why, above all, has its dissolution had to be accomplished through a war which shows no sign of abating, which by the summer of 1991 had claimed at least 20,000 lives, and which has been waged by means of wanton cultural despoilation, unspeakable atrocities and the uprooting and flight of upwards of two and a half million people?

A cursory look at similar or potentially similar cases elsewhere in Central and Eastern Europe may help to refine the problems posed by such questions, although it is unlikely to answer them.

The Soviet Union was, of course, the potential and analogous nightmare which Western statesmen had in mind when they sought in recent years to support the Yugoslav federation and, then, in June 1991, to forestall secession by Slovenia and Croatia. And, indeed, the break-up of the USSR following the August 1991 *coup d'état* against Mikhail Gorbachev offers interesting parallels with the disintegration of Yugoslavia. I will mention a few of these later.

The German Democratic Republic also failed to survive its Communists, despite their ardent and long-standing pretensions to a separate and better German identity, and notwithstanding the growth of a substantial body of Western scholarship which tended to accept and amplify their claims. But everyone now agrees that the GDR was a special case. Unlike Austria, it turned out to have no *raison d'état* beyond the Soviet imperium.

Czechoslovakia (or the Czech and Slovak Federal Republic) is also expiring. Here, too, we encounter the national question (or the multinational question) in its centrifugal rather than its centripetal aspect. It is this tension, of course, which has been at the heart of Yugoslavia's turbulent life and death.

Both states were born in 1918, and will always and erroneously be widely viewed as the illegitimate issue of the Treaty of Versailles, despite coming into existence before the peacemakers of Paris set about their work. Both attempted to implant, nourish and reap the harvest of common Czechoslovak or Yugoslav national identities, ideologies and strategies of statecraft. As posited by what turned out to be only minorities, even among their respective intellectual and political élites, both state ideas were subsequently undermined by their largest nations' appropriations of the prerogatives and prerequisites of leadership. Both states were forsaken by their putative allies and by large sections of their populations before, during and after their destruction by Hitler. Both were reborn in Allied victory and either Communist-led resistance or pro-Soviet enthusiasm. Thereafter, both sought solutions to their national questions through frontier changes, expulsions of German minorities and, above all, Soviet-style Communism.

The Yugoslavs also embraced a Stalinist federalism which was destined to remain 'national in form, but socialist in content' even after the split with Stalin in 1948. In Czechoslovakia, on the other hand, the coup of 1948 was not followed by the introduction of a federal constitution — testimony both to Stalinist and Czech self-confidence.

By the 1960s, however, the re-emergence of their respective national questions helped engender liberal reform movements. Crushed by Soviet tanks, the Prague Spring proved in retrospect to be East Central European Communism's last chance to save itself. A formal federalism was only now — in 1969 — offered as a sop to the Slovaks.

In Yugoslavia, a Belgrade Summer (in 1968) and a Zagreb Spring (in 1971) appeared in their turn to threaten Communism and/or the state with Serbian and Slovenian liberalism, Croatian separatism and even new-left Maoism. But the supposed re-imposition of democratic centralism by Tito in 1971-72 led not to neo-Stalinist 'normalization' on the Czechoslovak model, but to the confederalization of party and state in the 1974 constitution. It was to be the challenge mounted by Slobodan Milošević and the Serbs to this last incarnation of Titoism that would destroy both Yugoslav Communism and the Yugoslav state, and to ignite civil war.

Yet if Czechoslovakia is also now dying it is not because of inflamed Czech nationalism, fear for the fate of Czech minorities in Slovakia or a rearguard

Czech effort to re-impose Communism and centralism. Nor is a Czech-Slovak war conceivable. Therefore the differences between Yugoslavia and Czechoslovakia may be as salient as the similarities.

Czechoslovakia's national composition was and is not only far less complex, but its Slav nations are fewer in number, are rarely inter-mixed and thus have scarcely any potential territorial claims on each other. From its inception Czechoslovakia also benefited from a more developed economy, a more modern society and — at least arguably — a more mature political culture than those inherited by Yugoslavia. (Like Garton Ash, I am dubious about the notion of a special and superior Central European culture.) There can be no arguing, however, that Czechoslovakia's inter-war experience was as conspicious for its relative success as Yugoslavia's was for its absolute failure. It was also more 'seemly', in that it was the secularized, urbanized and middle-class Czechs who lorded it over a priest-ridden Slovak peasantry. In Yugoslavia, on the other hand, it was the ostensibly 'oriental' and backward Serbs, with their swineherd dynasty, *putsch*-prone army, venal bureaucrats and domineering politicians, who rode roughshod over their supposedly more sophisticated but soft ex-Habsburg brethren.

In 1918 the Serbs had known what they wanted of the new state and found themselves in the happy position of being able to get it. But their satisfaction was short-lived. Parliamentary democracy and Serb centralism proved incompatible, and their king decided that the latter was more important than the former. King Alexander's ostensibly 'Yugoslav' dictatorship after 1929 administered a near-lethal blow to Yugoslavism. Under his effective successor, Prince Regent Paul, the regime managed to alienate even its Serb pillars. By destroying this Yugoslavia, and replacing it with something far worse, Hitler gave the Communists, the one pro-Yugoslav party which had not been contaminated by responsibility in the inter-war period, their chance.

Neither during the war nor thereafter did Czechoslovakia offer such unequivocal evidence of superiority. Beneš may well have been justified in boasting after the liberation that Prague's unblemished beauty was positive proof of his wisdom in accepting the Munich *diktat*, but 1948 was to throw a different light both on the Czechs' and Slovaks' undistinguished war record and on Beneš's own much-vaunted statesmanship.

For the Yugoslavs — like the Poles — the bloodbath of the Second World War was, simultaneously, a test heroically passed and a failure so horrific as to be unassimilable. The resistance to the Axis offered by the Communist-led Partisans, and their even more hard-fought victories over their pro-Axis and anti-Axis rivals, meant that Yugoslavia would be re-created, extended and revolutionized. It also meant that Tito and his comrades would enjoy a degree of legitimacy unparalleled elsewhere in Eastern Europe.

This was not just because they had won the war by mobilizing their compatriots' age-old hatred of alien oppression and resurrecting an all-Yugoslav patriotism, but also because they had appealed to them separately and innovatively as Croats, Slovenes, Muslims, Macedonians and Montenegrins. (The commitment of the Serbs to Yugoslavia — if not to them — the Communists could still take for granted.) They had also managed to enlist the rage and radicalism of such previously disregarded, abused or marginalized segments of the population as women, young people and the peasants of the food-deficit regions in which their crucial battles were largely fought.

Yet the Communists' triumph, complete as it seemed in 1945, and reinforced as it was by a second liberation and rebirth in 1948, was purchased at enormous cost and depended for its perpetuation on a set of circumstances and power relationships which could not and did not endure. The Communists had eviscerated their enemies, discredited the murderous chauvinism that had animated most of them and put an end to the wartime slaughter (albeit only after indulging in a final paroxysm of vengeance of their own), but they never represented more than the most formidable of Yugoslavia's many minorities.

The graveyard quietude over which the Communists presided in 1945 was thus both deceptive and dangerous. National hatreds, myths, stereotypes and grievances were suppressed rather than eradicated. In fact, they were put into a sort of historical deep-freeze, from which they would re-emerge with fresh virulence and insane cogency for a generation that could not remember the 1940s, once Communist power began to atrophy and the Cold War started to abate. For the Communists had won a war, not an argument; and their failures, ultimately, either to live up to their own propaganda of 'brotherhood and unity' or to redeem the promises of their ideology allowed both the argument and the war to recommence.

The Communists' situation in 1945, in 1948, in the 1950s and, indeed, throughout Tito's lifetime was far stronger than that of the pre-war state-makers. Their power was as unchallengeable as their certainty that they alone possessed, in Marxism-Leninism and, latterly, in its self-management recension, the key to all the mysteries. But they also had a unique asset in Tito: the architect of victory, the twice-over liberator of his peoples, the patriarch, taskmaster and judge, the high-living role model, the international statesman, the flywheel of stability and the cult of personality. Even in death his example and his myth had potency, and his otherwise shop-soiled party appeared to retain the political initiative well into the 1980s.

Indeed, it was the presence of Tito and the absence of any perceived or acceptable alternative to themselves that enabled the Communists to experiment so freely with their country. They were to make at least five attempts to get the Yugoslav and socialist formulas right. These might be identified as follows: (1) Stalinism, 1945-49; (2) anti-Stalinism, 1949-53; (3) Titoism, 1954-63; (4) Market Socialism, 1964-73; and (5) Confederalism, 1974-89.

In their headlong rush after 1945 to implement the Soviet model at home and to export their revolution to their neighbours the Communists not only incurred the wrath of their mentor in Moscow, they also sacrificed a large part of the domestic support they had won during the war. Paradoxically, however, only a thoroughly Stalinized party and state could have dared to defy Stalin, let alone have lived to start again.

Expulsion from the Cominform offered and required a new beginning. In the 1950s they tried a measure of devolution to the workplace and the commune, but without enhancing the purely formal authority of the republics or loosening the bonds of democratic centralism. The equally unacceptable extremes of Cominformism (i.e., surrender to the USSR) and Djilasism (i.e., surrender of their monopoly of power to the 'class enemy') were quashed. This, too, was the period when their confident claims to have solved the national question carried most weight. Socialism bid fair to create Yugoslav man. And the Cold War afforded their country an importance in the international system commensurate with the ambitions which Stalin had thwarted.

By the 1960s economic difficulties attendant upon the completion of the first phase of industrialization ushered in a second bout of reform. But what began as a debate inside the élite over investment strategies and the introduction of market mechanisms soon revealed that the national question remained undead. Disinterred both by the evangelists of the market (who hailed largely from the more developed northwest) and by the old believers in socialist orthodoxy (who represented the disadvantaged southeast), nationalism in a specifically republican guise was invoked to rally support and disarm opposition.

The party reformers and their technocratic allies won the argument (a victory marked by Tito's purge in 1966 of his Serbian heir-apparent and ex-secret police chief, Aleksandar Ranković), but lost the struggle to implement their policies. Having identified the party and federal bureaucracies and, increasingly, the banks and trading companies based in Belgrade as bastions of resistance to market socialism and the liberation of the economic potential of their republics, the reformers set about creating alternative and rival power bases in the republican capitals. Function was now following form; and constitutional amendments formalized the republics' (and Serbia's two autonomous provinces') new functions.

Republican and provincial nationalism proved a double-edged sword. It spurred a liberalization that made Yugoslavs the envy of other East Europeans; but it also bred chauvinism and party disarray, leading Tito to warn of civil war and to threaten use of the army. Prophetically, it was Albanian-inhabited Kosovo which erupted first in rioting in 1968.

By mid-1971 the Croatian *maspok* (mass movement) seemed to have swamped and supplanted that republic's party hierarchy. The newly empowered managers, bankers and technocrats, meanwhile, looked likely to marginalize the workers and their party without even having to pay heed to the supposed disciplines of the marketplace. Finally, 'rotten liberalism' appeared to have taken hold of the Serbian and Slovenian parties. Tito purged them all.

What happened next confounded expectations. Despite Tito's apocalyptic sermons and Stalinist vocabulary, there was no return to a neo-Stalinist ice age. Instead of a re-centralization of state and economic power equivalent to that which had supposedly taken place in the party, the search for viable, institutionalized and decentralized instruments of decision-making and resource-allocation continued. Tito's twilight years led not to the grooming of a new Tito, but to the total confederalization of the party as power bases continued to shift along with control over investment to the republican and provincial capitals. Not coincidentally, the rest of the 1970s were also years of giddy prosperity, consumer indulgence and profligate foreign borrowing.

With both euphoric nationalism and dissentient party factions laid low, the 1974 constitution (the world's longest, socialist Yugoslavia's fourth and the sixth since 1921) and the 1976 Law on Associated Labour sought to complete the creation of a self-managing society and economy. The aim was to strike a balance between competing national, regional, social and economic interests by establishing mechanisms for issue aggregation, conflict resolution, consensus-building and policy implementation that would neither require nor permit the emergence of another Tito. Rather, the integrity, unity and permanence of the socialist order would be guaranteed by the party (operating in and through every level of an atomized yet interlocking system), as well as by the army (charged with defending socialism as well as the state).

It did not work out that way. Not only did the system demand too much of those who were meant to operate it, but it introduced a mind-deadening political discourse which encouraged political infantilism in everyone else. Not only did it prove to require in Tito's continuing presence as arbiter just what it was meant to supplant, but it also presupposed continuing plenty (and plenty of foreign loans) in order to function at all. Not only did it confirm the apotheosis of nationalism as the primary and largely non-negotiable definer of identities and values in social, economic and political life, but it ensured that the republican and provincial Communist parties increasingly regarded each other almost as enemies. Lastly, not only did it appear to make Yugoslavia far less than the sum of its parts, but it came to be seen by Serbs as a dastardly plot against their interests, history, territory and nation.

Yugoslavia's crisis accelerated through the early and mid-1980s. Riots by and repression of the burgeoning Albanian majority in Serbia's semi-detached province of Kosovo testified to the mutual reinforcement of national and economic discontents. Bad debts, bad luck and paralysis at the federal level of party and state spawned a blizzard of inflation, impoverishment and beggar-thy-neighbour policies on the part of the republics. But Albanian rioters demanding republican status for Kosovo — or, for that matter, secession and unification with Albania — could not destroy Yugoslavia. Nor could Slovene peace movements, punk groups or economic nationalists. That right was reserved to the Serbs. Croats, meanwhile, maintained their post-1971 silence. By 1987 the Serbs' backlash against the ineluctable alienation of Kosovo, and the ever-widening perception that Tito's Yugoslavia had been an insidious plot to do them down was used by Milošević to topple the old guard in the Serbian party and to initiate what he was pleased to call an 'anti-bureaucratic revolution'. What this entailed was more thoroughgoing repression of the Albanians, a campaign of mass meetings demanding Serbia's 're-unification' (both with its provinces of Vojvodina and Kosovo and, in effect, with Montenegro), the incitement and mobilization of diaspora Serbs, and the perpetuation of Communist power in Serbia on the basis of anti-Titoism (i.e., historical anti-Communism!) and populist chauvinism. Milošević all the while proclaimed his devotion to Yugoslavia, if only the dysfunctional 1974 constitution could be replaced. It was a remarkable feat.

Trying to appease Milošević, and the unprecedented surge of mass hysteria he had whipped up, in 1988-89 the federal and republican leaderships acquiesced in his abolition of Kosovo's and Vojvodina's autonomy and in the overthrow of the Montenegrin government. This was a big mistake. For one thing, it handed Milošević potential dominion of the collective federal and party presidencies (where he would now have half the votes). For another, it underscored and justified historically-conditioned fears of Serbian hegemonism on the part of non-Serbs. Finally, it discredited their still-Communist leaderships among peoples now inclined to see the fate of Kosovo's Albanians as the shape of things to come for them too. Realizing their error and hoping to escape the whirlwind sweeping the rest of Eastern Europe, the Slovenian and Croatian Communists walked out of the last federal party congress in January 1990, changed their names and sought new legitimacy in free elections of spring 1990.

They fared better in Slovenia than in Croatia, but lost in both republics to more convincingly uncompromised nationalists. At the end of 1990 in Slovenia, and in spring 1991 in Croatia, the new governments secured impressive popular endorsements in referenda of their plans to secede if agreement to transform Yugoslavia into a loose alliance of sovereign republics were not reached by June 1991. This turned out to be no bluff, notwithstanding ample warnings by Croatia's 600,000-strong Serb minority that they must be counted out.

Milošević, meanwhile, aided by an Albanian boycott, had secured an equally impressive democratic mandate for his re-named Communists in late 1990 elections. (His Montenegrin minions managed to triumph even without abandoning the Communist label.) In Bosnia and Hercegovina the Communists lost to Muslim, Serb and Croat nationalist parties which formed a fragile coalition government proportionate to their numbers; while in Macedonia the result was a hung parliament and a coalition under ex-Communist leadership.

All this meant that Yugoslavia's break-up was more than likely by 1991. But it did not mean that civil war had to follow, even though the spread of violent revolts by Croatia's Serbs against an intransigent government in Zagreb — and the federal army's connivance in them — were ominous. Yugoslavs had lived with crisis for years. Crying wolf was an all-national pastime; and last-minute fixes a speciality. The experience both immediately after Tito's death in 1980 and, again, during Ante Marković's premiership in 1989-90 had seemed to demonstrate either that a confederal system could, at a pinch, be made to work or that the confederation might survive its Communists by relying on a competent, technocratic and internationally esteemed government at the centre. In fact, it was not until the army moved to vitiate Slovenia's 25 June declaration of independence by seizing its frontier posts that the game was finally up.

States, like individuals, can have good or bad deaths. Yugoslavia's, obviously, has been just about the worst imaginable. The equanimity with which Slovenes, Croats and their foreign friends anticipated a blessed release in spring 1991 proved misplaced. The short burst of pain which accompanied the Slovenes' parting ensured that there would be little mourning there, and that Slovenia's ceremonial international baptism would quickly follow. But the week-long Slovene war of independence also contributed to making the death throes of the residual Yugoslavia more agonizing and prolonged. Croatia, Macedonia and, above all, Bosnia and Hercegovina were never going to be permitted such a clean break.

Czechoslovakia's death, if it comes, will be marked by tedium rather than pain. The obituarists will note that it expired for lack of interest, and the experiment in Czech-Slovak cohabitation — to mix the metaphor — will be seen as a temporarily convenient if ill-matched liaison that was ended by mutual consent.

The Soviet Union's dissolution has and will be messier. As was the case in Yugoslavia, the Communists commanded a revolutionary legitimacy which was not revealed as bankrupt until it was abandoned. But the CPSU — and the Russians — also disposed of an imperial legacy, deriving both from the tsars and from Stalin, which was not available to the Yugoslav Communists — nor to the Serbs, however much they might have acted as if it were.

The Baltic republics escaped with Slovene-like ease. The Confederation of Independent States may well provide a useful mechanism for managing the departures of others, but especially of Ukraine. As a Russian officer serving with the UN peace-keeping forces in Croatia (and whose family lives in Ukraine) remarked to *The Times*, 'the differences between the Russians and Ukrainians will never come to this'. He added, however, that he and his wife were getting a divorce.

In the south of the ex-USSR, and occupying an arc of discord stretching from Moldavia, through the Crimea and Caucasus to Central Asia, the bust-up has been assuming Yugoslav ferocity. It was symptomatic that the Russian foreign minister should have abandoned a peace mission to the Yugoslav republics in May 1992 because his presence was required to deal with a worsening crisis in the Crimea. As has been the case with the Serbs, the widespread Russian diaspora, its members' support for neo- or still-Communist leaderships, ex-Red Army support for them and the real or imagined threat of Islamic fundamentalism envenom the state-making process. There is thus much scope for the emergence of a Russian Milošević.

There are, naturally enough, very few unashamed unreconstructed defenders of the Yugoslav idea and state to be found these days. The kindest thing it seems possible to say about Yugoslavia is that it offered a necessary if uncomfortable bolt hole to the South Slavs as they made their tortuous passage to modernity, the nation-state and, perhaps, to 'Europe' through the ruins of the Habsburg and Ottoman empires, the barbarism of Fascism and National Socialism and the worst excesses of Marxism-Leninism.

About Tito's Yugoslavia, the best that can nowadays be said is that it was in many ways an improvement on the first Yugoslavia, and certainly better than anything else on offer during the Second World War. Federalism, however notional at the outset, was a step forward. Confederalism might have worked had it been accompanied by democracy. But Tito and his party clung to power and outlived their usefulness, surviving to become themselves the principal regenerators and manipulators of national-chauvinist exclusivity, intolerance and hate. Alas, they were not also the principal victims.

The more common line — whether propagated by leader writers, Oxbridge dons or the South Slavs themselves — is that Yugoslavia was from the beginning a mistake (if not actually a crime against nature) which was decreed by for their own selfish purposes by arrogant and ill-informed great powers. The Communists, in their turn, are viewed as an unmitigated disaster, but one for which foreigners (and Winston Churchill in particular) were again primarily responsible. Similarly, Yugoslavia's 1991 dissolution, the outbreak of war, the mutilation of Croatia's territorial integrity in the Vance peace plan and the strangulation of an independent Bosnia and Hercegovina virtually at birth are — in ascending order of plausibility — also laid at the foot of a malevolent and/or purblind international community. (The conflagrations to come in Kosovo and Macedonia will be more justifiably blamed on outside powers.)

The fact that Serbs, Croats, Slovenes and Bosnian Muslims each subscribe to this self-exculpatory thesis ought, however, to give us pause. South Slavs — and East Europeans generally — should not be allowed to blame all their misfortunes on others. Nor should we forget that the ideologically homogenizing, ethnically-cleansing and state-worshipping nationalisms of the South Slavs are different only in degree — and in the degree to which history and geography has placed them cheek by jowl — from those of other Central and East Europeans.

Although I have yet to see much sign of it in print, we can expect eventually a good deal of lamentation over Yugoslavia's collapse. Tito, whose centenary has come too early for the rehabilitation process, will once more be

regarded as a statesman of genius and his party hailed (as during the Cold War
— and as King Alexander was in his time) as the one thing that kept Yugoslavs
from each other's throats. Such condescension will be as otiose as that which
would blame 'Versailles' for Yugoslavia, Churchill for Tito's Communism
and the European Community for 'ethnic cleansing'.

As the agony of Bosnia and Hercegovina unfolds, and as the spread of war
into Kosovo, Macedonia and beyond become more likely, we will have ample
opportunity to reflect that there was much to be said in favour of Yugoslavia.
It may have been unlucky in its human, physical and economic geography. It
was certainly ill-served by its rulers and their ruling doctrines. But, most of
all, its timing was wrong: it came too late to create Yugoslavs and too early to
make Europeans.

LANGUAGE: DEATH AND RESURRECTION

CHAPTER FOURTEEN

Language and Politics in Bulgaria

Blaga Dimitrova

Language is something like a scanner for discovering cancerous diseases in society. Pressures applied on society by totalitarian authorities create malignant tumours. Rather like metastasis, empty words and phrases creep into speech and deaden our thinking. An inflation of pompous epithets, heroification, militarization, bombastic expressions, pomposity, falseness, blatant lies, ritual phrases and clichés comes about. This phenomenon was associated with the Third Reich; it was brilliantly analysed by Viktor Klemperer in his book *LTI* (1946). The Nazis, after only twelve years' rule, inflicted profound traumas on the language. It is difficult to describe the result of a period four times longer than that, namely forty-six years of vacuity, in a brief essay like this. I shall nevertheless try to demonstrate some aspects of the Bulgarian language during the last years of totalitarianism.

Linguistic prognosis
I have noticed a hidden regularity in our language during the last decade, which was a sign of the critical state of health of the regime. This regularity had as a characteristic the hypocritical persecution of foreign words (naturally, mainly Turkisms which have become an integral part of our speech). This persecution was not coincidental. Nationalist passions are inflamed artificially when the ruling political authorities feel threatened and seek to consolidate their ranks. Imperceptibly, semantic contradictions emerge, produced by nausea induced by an official language which has atrophied semantically.

Cynical ambiguity develops: one thing is said but something else is understood implicitly. For instance, the ever-increasing use of the term нормализиране (normalization) immediately evokes alarm as there must be some dysfunction in the body politic; the same applies to единство (unity), сплотеност (cohesion), единомислие (unanimity), спонтанно (spontaneous -ly) or откровено (sincerely). Възродителен процес (process of rebirth) was the official definition of the forced renaming and naturalization of the Bulgarian Turks (1986-89).

The language of the press, as disseminated by the Bulgarian News Agency, revealed diseased equivocation, and this in turn led to equivocal emotions and desires and, finally, to apathy. Absurd, mutually antagonistic weeds of speech erupt, like the divided self of a schizophrenic:

Корекция на цените (price adjustments) instead of поскъпване (price rises)
самооблагане (self-taxation) instead of наложен данък (imposed tax)
осведомител (informant) instead of доносник по служба (professional informer)
по целесъобразност (due to expedience) instead of по некадърност (due to inability)
духовни ценности (spiritual values) as opposed to the total devaluation of spiritual values.

The superlative form НАЙ-

To what extent the totalitarian regime was alien to the Bulgarian character can be convincingly seen in the flooding of the Bulgarian language by epithets in the superlative, which are intrinsically alien to the ordinary Bulgarian who can pronounce them only with a wry wink, which means: 'That good, is it?' And the speeches of Party officials abounded with the prefix най-:

най-големи успехи (greatest success)
най-светлият празник (the brightest feast)
най-щастливото детство (the happiest childhood)
най-ведрото небе (the most serene sky)

and so forth.

In the spirit of 'leaping progress' we climb upstairs, jumping every other step, by jumping over the positive and comparative levels, and get straight to the superlative. A rapacious regime does not acknowledge gradualness. The 'most humane' society is super-aggressive.

We can judge by the following hilarious phenomenon the kind of breach of linguistic logic which follows: epithets are introduced in their superlative form, which are in essence superlatives already:

най-грандиозни строежи (most sublime constructions)
най-величави проекти (most majestic projects)
най-прекрасни образи (most 'most beautiful' figures)
най-висш комунистически морал (the supernal Communist morale)
най-мъдрото учение (the wisest teaching)
най-вярната дружба (the truest friendship)
най-прогресивният строи (the most progressive regime)
най-бляскава перспектива (most brilliant prospects)
най-неотменна грижа за човека (most ineluctable care of people)
най-кристалиа чистота (most crystalline purity)
най-безпримерният: подвиг (the most unparalleled exploit)
най-истинският живот (the realest life)

единственият най-правилен път (the only truest way) ...

The 'most supreme' peak was never reached!

The verb as a key to time
Similar deformities of speech occurred in all countries which were subjected to totalitarianism. Bulgarian, however, has its own peculiarity. This is the verb with all its tenses, moods and aspects, the verb which could provide us with the secret key to the era which used to be praised as great, unheard-of, a 'golden age', uninterruptedly in the ascendant, victorious, heroic, optimistic and coursing towards a brilliant future.

Changes in linguistic expression take place somewhere in the back of our minds. We are not aware of them in everyday usage. So, for example, whilst I was gathering material for my *Sofia under the Ruins* describing the World War II bombings, I once found in the press of that period a verb form which otherwise has disappeared from contemporary Bulgarian: 'We understand from a reliable source that the new German weapon "щяло да доведе" [is said to lead] to a blitz'.

This reported future mood is hardly to be found in today's language. But how and where did it disappear? Without noticing it, we have accepted that, for example, the great weapon of Marxist teaching would not щяло да доведе (would reportedly lead) to complete victory but ще доведе (will lead). All promises of success, all magnificent plans, audacious foresights, impressive aspirations are rendered by the tough and doubtless ще, ще, ще (will, will, will).

A similar categorical standpoint is imposed by another form of the verb which has otherwise disappeared: the reported past mood. For example, I found in old newspapers: 'Some witness claims that he бил видял [has seen]'. Even more indisputably: 'Someone claims that something is a fact'.

The conditional mood disappears
One has to consider the origins of the psychosis which swept away the richness of the Bulgarian verb. There are grounds for thinking about the impact of the semi-official Russian language of the press on this phenomenon. One might discover certain tendencies in the *Gleichschaltung* of life, which led to the impoverishment of the language. But the reasons go deeper than that: they lie in the very procedure of manipulating people's minds. Everything which 'comes from above' as the result of a certain decision cannot be disputed. There is not and cannot be any doubt that the message from above is true. In this way the conditional mood, which the Polish poet Wysława Szymborska calls the 'record of the human speech' in her poem 'Sto pociech' (One hundred amusements), disappears. But why does it disappear?

Simply because Communist language has been deprived of a former doubt: 'with hard labour we бихме постигнали [would achieve] great success'. No!

'With hard labour ще постигнем [we will achieve] great, unseen and unheard-of success!' This absoluteness coarsens not only one's language but also one's spirit. It turns one into a creature without tonality, without nuances, without inner plasticity. One's speech acquires the uncompromising character of a military command. This is assisted particularly by a commonplace verb that was turned into a key word of dictatorship: Трябва! (one has to! or I/you/he/) etc. must!).

If we undertake a statistical analysis of only one issue of the official Party newspaper *Rabotnichesko delo*, we will discover a large number of трябва in state decrees, accounts of measures taken by the Central Committee, speeches, programmes, plans, and even in the regular reports from factories or cooperative farms. Трябва in the imperative has been hammered into our heads during these decades to an extent that we have stopped hearing it altogether. The verb has been so drummed into our heads that we have stopped hearing it altogether. This achieved the opposite effect of what was intended. Instead of inciting us to act, it lulled us into inaction.

Mutually exclusive trends

A phenomenon exists that becomes conspicuous to the eyes or rather to the ears, and which wholly seems to contradict the generally accepted patriotic procedure of purifying the language of its alien elements. Xenophobia is typical of closed and hypocritically pure societies.

Besides linguistic purges in Bulgarian, one had the aggressive use of foreign terms and verbs to demonstrate innovation and 'scientific' reconstruction. Ordinary people were driven to the verge of dementia by the new корелации (correlations), структури (structures) and инфраструктури (infrastructures). Foreign verbs act as a shock-wave to produce affected activity and modernity:

мултиплицирам (replicate)
интензифицирам (intensify)
модифицирам (rationalize)

and also the hilarious:

дефектирам (become defective)
самоперфорирам ('self-clip', when a passenger in a tram clips his own ticket)
отсервирам (clear the table)
деструктурирам (destructure)
дифузирам (diffuse)
ерозирам (erode)
инфилтрирам (infiltrate)
ескалирам (escalate).

The alien verb invokes associations of hostile agencies and contagion.

Some monstrous verbal nouns also occurred which bore witness to bureaucratic autocracy:

договорености (agreementation)
успеваемост (success-rate).

Such verbs were used to characterize in particular 'dangerous' anti-State activities.

Verbal tenses during the period of timeless totalitarianism
The attitude to time, as expressed in language, to a large extent, defines the manner of a given nation's thinking. The tenses in Bulgarian express time as the fourth dimension. And the numerous aspects, moods, voices and nuances of the Bulgarian verb display specific complicated relations between space and time, which are unknown in many other languages. Why are non-Bulgarians, however long they have lived in our country, however perfectly they master Bulgarian, always confused by the subtleties of the verb? Probably because their way of thinking contains no such matrix of concepts and interrelations. This is one of the 'mysteries' of Bulgarian: there are nine tenses, ten different moods, and a number of varieties achieved through affixes, suffixes, supplements, root alterations and syncope.

I have a naive, amateurish hypothesis, for which I hope linguists will forgive me. Perhaps the tenses in Bulgarian do not stem from the Slavonic midstream, nor from the neighbouring Balkan tributary, but from Proto-Bulgarian, Finno-Ugric and Turkic roots in the remote Asian steppes near Mongolia. The nomadic life spent on horseback probably created a particular psychological predisposition to dynamic speech, to constant change and activity. Academic linguistics tends to neglect the direct relation between language and habit. But that the fighting, wild stream of life has found its expression not in the descriptive characteristics of speech but, instead, in the multifaceted and multifluvial miracle-monger which is the verb. The verb contains the key to the secret of time.

The concord of tenses is one of the subterranean passages of consciousness. Case endings disappeared; other forms were shortened or simplified, but tenses and aspects lie in the spine of the language and at the essence of thinking. If they are dissipated, inner life also becomes diluted. The habit has been forgotten; the Bulgarian has long since stopped sleeping in the saddle; the verb, however, is still racing through time and space. The Bulgarian tenses have preserved an active feeling of time in their genetic memory. Every moment has a value of its own which changes according to the viewpoint of the individual; it is denoted in subtle verbal nuances.

An abundance of affixes makes the Bulgarian verb the bearer of various prolongations of time and relations between people: ЗАПРИказвам (to address someone by talking), РАЗПРИказвам се (talking too much, suddenly burst into eloquence), изпонаприказвам се (talk out something). The nuances are in the process of being slowly wiped out: more and more one hears изказвам се (to make a statement), which evokes time in stagnation. Nevertheless, the following distinctive forms have not yet disappeared: 'Someone каза' (said, i.e. I was there and I heard it with my own ears) against 'Someone казал' ('is reported to have said' or 'apparently said', i.e. I did not hear him and am referring to secondary information). Yet there is another case which I mentioned at the beginning: the denotation of a stated and real fact: 'Someone said that the plan е изпълнен' (has been fulfilled) instead of бил изпълнен (is reported to have been fulfilled). I was not present at the fulfilment of the plan). Or 'an accident е избегната' (is averted) instead of 'е била избегната' (has been averted). These are statements beyond question: a truth arisen from the last instance of the spirit of dictatorship.

In this way the totalitarian regime cuts through the thousand-year-old trunk of the language. We have grown poorer without noticing what we are deprived of. The loss is irretrievable. But let us hope, in spite of all this, that that untiring inventor and creator, which is language, will engineer a system of compensation to fill the gaps left by the missing elements and forms. For example, certain jocular expressions now replace the aspects which have been lost:

> Би следвало да е било станало вчера (It ought to be concluded that it might have happened yesterday)

for which the young linguistic joker now says:

> Ще стане вчера (It will happen yesterday).

Or, instead of:

> Да би мирно седяло, не би чудо видяло (a proverb, literally: If you had been sitting quietly, you would not have seen the miracle)

now you hear:

> Мирно стой и се не бой! (Stand quietly and you will have nothing to be afraid of!).

This is short and clear.

Aggressive verbiage
In language, one side diminishes while another increases.

Whilst the polite verb forms моля (please), извинявайте (I'm sorry), съжалявам (I regret) are almost forgotten nowadays, a mass of aggressive verbs have arisen, such as изявявам се (to distinguish oneself), налагам се (to set oneself up), завоювам (to win), напредвам (to make an advance). Generally speaking, military concepts are forcing their way more and more directly into normal speech: превъоръжавам се (to re-arm oneself, e.g. with new thinking), атакувам (launch an onslaught on, e.g. the fortress of scholarship), сплотявам (to unify, to close ranks), рапортувам (to report, e.g. in a young pioneer camp). Even more impudent is the bursting of greed into speech: да придобиеш (to assume, e.g., a worldview, a title, a name, recognition); everything becomes acquisition, instead of the normal 'to gain experience', 'to build up a worldview', 'to achieve recognition', 'to deserve a title', 'to create oneself a name'. In one's schooldays one is constantly пришпорвам (spurred on) to catch up, to be ahead, and everything turns into competition. And there is the particularly important да води (to be a leader). Consequently there is a whole pile of derivatives, such as:

водещ жанр (leading genre — in literature!)
ръководна роля (leading role)
завеждащ отдел (leading person [head] of a department)
ръководни принципи (leading principles)
водещ отрасъл (leading branch) instead of главенн, основен (main, principal).

The aggressive imagery of totalitarianism is far-removed from 'market-led' aggression. One could take the verb пробивам (to penetrate) as the emblem of socialist conformism:

пробивам си път (to force one's way) and not проправям си път (make one's way)
пробивам с лакти напред (to elbow one's way forward)
пробивам в печата (to get into the press)

and, as the crown of break-throughs, the newly-concocted epithet пробивен (forceful). As opposed to the conflict person, the through-breaking one is the hero of our time. It is not the capable, not the educated, the experienced, the honest, the courageous, the hard-working, but ПРОБИВНИЯТ (the through-breaking) person.

Preoccupied as we were with our everyday breakthroughs, we did not notice how the verb успявам (to be successful) had been slightly marginalized by its present-day variant преуспявам (to be most successful). Like the English prefix 're-', the use of the prefix 'пре-' has increased *ad nauseam*:

преизпълнявам плана (to over-fulfil the plan)
презастраховам се (to re-reinsure oneself),
преквалифицирам се (to requalify)
преразпределям (to allocate)
пренасочвам (to reorientate)
преструктурирам (to restructure).

The escalation of pathos
Pathos is an infallible litmus test of totalitarianism.

Atanas Natev has analysed the 'fire-fighting' contemporary Bulgarian poetry which used to be pointed out by the official party critics as 'civic', 'optimistic' and 'inspiring the constant access of our development'.

On other linguistic levels, inflammatory verbs lead whole torch processions across reports, unctuous jubilee speeches, across newspaper columns and articles on the gathering of the уропжай (harvest — a Russicism), and even across the writings of candidate students:

> разгарям (to kindle, e.g. the spirit of competition)
> разискря се (becomes all sparks, e.g. the gaze of the leading tractor-driver)
> лумва (bursts into flames, e.g. a constructive argument)
> нажежава се (becomes red-hot, e.g. the enthusiasm of the young members of a brigade at work)
> разгорещява се (become hot, e.g. a creative discussion)
> разпалва се (flames up, e.g. the constructive energy of the masses)
> обжегват (burn, e.g. the words of the hero)
> изпепелява (burns to ashes, e.g. self-sacrificing commitment).

The stronger entropy becomes, the colder the sense of alienation, the more blazingly rages the fire of verbiage.

Magic spells
Magic spells are a fruitful object of sociolinguistic analysis. These spells aim at collective hypnosis, the stimulation of the masses, their adoption of marching by means of rhythmical slogans like the Leninist: 'Let us learn, let us learn, let us learn again!' This jingle provoked the opposite effect in the Bulgarian; it suggested a lullaby and made the Bulgarians lazy and indifferent, and discouraged the Bulgarians from reflection.

The *nomenklatura* particularly liked повишавам (to raise, increase). We constantly increase our mastery, increase quality (by now we ought to have reached perfection itself), increase crop production, and, especially, we wait to be 'raised' up the ladder of the hierarchy. The verbs of incitement have the effect of an anaesthesia: 'Let us increase discipline!' Similar stimulating appeals make our will drowsy. Our nervous system defends itself against any state intrusion: 'Let us increase vigilance!' 'Let us increase our qualifications!' 'Let us increase productivity!' Among analogous verbs one finds:

> завишавам (to raise), превишавам (to over-speed)
> надвишавам (to exceed, e.g. the norm)

and others.

Slogans often come in the form of stock pairs:

качество и ефективност, ефективност и качество
(quality and effectiveness, effectiveness and quality)
инициатива и взаимодеиствие, взаимодеиствие и инициатива
(initiative and interaction, interaction and initiative).

Why are they reversible? Their aim is to induce action not so much through their meaning as through their sound. However, the effect is the opposite: a dulling of receptiveness. Ordinary people react against the invasion of spell-like slogans with maxims like: 'Repetition is the mother of memory and the father of dulling.'

Flattery
In flattery of one's superiors one could display one's innovativeness, invention, spontaneity and irresistibility in a form which was accessible to the high-ranking to whom it was addressed. There are several sub-groups of this type of apostrophe: oral compliments whispered into the ear or in an intimate circle at meetings with the person in question; rhetorical flattery from a platform, long addresses at official receptions, or at meetings and jubilees, where the relevant name is repeated over and over again. The name is typically referred to in lectures and speeches with submissive gratitude for every breath of air and creative inspiration: 'I thank you for existing' — like the love poem of someone in a mid-life crisis.

The third most lasting kind of flattery consists of printed effusions, odes, memoirs, descriptions of travels or hunting experiences undertaken together, welcoming speeches, general glorifications. This was decisive for the ascent of any author. Eulogies addressed to the sovereign are a characteristic sign of an autocracy.

Perhaps one has to render due respect to historical truth: such respect has always been sought and has always been dearly paid for, according to court etiquette, but in Bulgaria flattery in unheard-of dimensions exists in literary life. In its linguistic tissue, quite apart from the use of the term 'genius', the epithet is the natural main ornament. The epithet, 'the prime', is used most of all: it contains the codified image of the state leader; he is first everywhere, at any time, and in any way. He is champion by birth until the end of eternity.

A number of verbs are offered:

твори (creates)
съзижда (builds up)
изваива (sculpts)
въздига (exalts)
възправя (raises)
претворява (recreates)
извисява (towers above)

which are all synonymous and, thus, interchangeable. There is nothing remarkable about them, apart from the ritual combination with the verbs:

кълнем се (we swear)
клетва сме дали (we have sworn an oath)
ние сме заклети (we are sworn).

My language, my enemy
The *nomenklatura* insisted on imposing its own system of signs.
Their newly-created verbs irritate the ear and provoke verbal allergy:

окрупнявам (to enlarge)
одържавявам (to nationalize)
омъдрнявам (to become wise).

A language within a language is created. This tendency to deform the meaning and sound of the word is typical of the totalitarian regime.

The energetic capacities се окрупняват (are increased) to unheard-of verbal dimensions, whereas in fact they melt. The leadership of the country омъдрява (becomes wise), whereas it turns out to be unable to cope with any of the problems. The regime се впечатлява (is impressed by itself) for existing in the glorifications of its functionaries and servants. They survive on miraculous formulae: вечна дружба (eternal friendship), от векове за векове (for ever and ever) — generally formulae expessing an eternal kingdom.

I would like to rephrase Acton's maxim: 'The word of the leadership corrupts but the word of totalitarianism corrupts totally.' Hyper-production. Hyper-crops. Hyper-gains. Hyper-plan. Hyper-words.

In the scanner of language fanfare phrases signal the malignant tumour in the last phase of the system's disease. Along with concepts like 'nationalizing', 'denationalizing', 'hyper-complicating' and 'superproduction', there is also a tendency to simplification and, thus, to colloquialism and playfulness. Language defends itself against the invasion of anti-language.

Robbed vocabulary
Totalitarianism seized the language and left it grey and coarse.
The appearance of such verbs as:

съгласувам (to co-ordinate)
контактувам (to make contact with)
договорирам (to conclude an agreement)
комуникирам (to communicate)
постановявам (to decree)
идеологизирам (to ideologize)
реабилитирам (to rehabilitate)

convert colloquial speech into hideous administrative newspeak:

Провеждам мероприятие (to carry out an activity)
заложили сме еталон (we have set up a model)
с оглед приложението (with a view to the application)
предвид указанията (bearing in mind the instructions).

Some words shift imperceptibly or narrow their semantic application. This is characteristic of the bureaucratization of the language. I was surprised to notice similar substitutions in Bulgarian. When I was preparing the second edition of my translation of Mickiewicz's *Pan Tadeusz* (the first appeared in 1959), I came across words which I would not use nowadays and which showed that I had myself been carried away by the inertia of the commonly accepted language. In my youth, странство used to mean 'other countries'. The root of this word produces the cognates странно (strange, foreign), странствуване (wandering), странник (stranger, foreigner): this sounds romantic. Today this alluring word has been forgotten entirely. Instead, the ideological centres imposed upon Bulgarians чужбина, contains a clear delimitation from foreign elements, which are prohibited and hostile. The magnetic странство was converted into the dangerous чужбина.

Until two or three decades ago, the word държава (country) was identical with родина (fatherland). We find in the newspapers of World War II, for example: 'The Bulgarian gardeners returned safely to our country.' This does not smack of institutionalism but sounds proud: we have a country, which is our refuge, however imperfect it is. The poet Georgi Bonev, who has for a long time been living in Vienna, said in one of his poems: 'I grieve, far away from my държава'. Today nobody would use this word which sounds solemnly comic and which has been turned into a fatherlandless and repugnantly institutionalized emblem; one would use the widespread, emotionally vacuous страна. Not only has the държава lost its connotations, but the very concept it expresses has become alien to Bulgarians and evokes repulsive associations.

A whole inventory of forgotten words was replaced by banal synonyms:

Младини (years of youth) by младост (youth),\
досежно (concerning) by относително (regarding),\
отрадно (encouragingly, pleasantly) by радостно (cheerfully).

And the avoidance of some commonplace foreign words is highly indicative of totalitarian dogmatism. For example, модерно (modern) is replaced by съвременно (contemporary) because модерно is associated with 'Western influence', 'sabotage', 'decadence'.

It is отрадно (encouraging, pleasant) that the young of today try to shake off 'state' language by using word-play. A whole dictionary could be produced of these words. They are supplemented also by the word-formations of satirists: другарго ('female comrade', contaminated with the word for 'crow', hence evoking 'silly socialist comrade'), думагогия ('logogogy', contaminated with 'word', hence evoking 'evil socialist demagogy'), всепобедно — все победно (throughout victoriously — getting poorer and poorer [word-play]), латернатива ('alternative', contaminated with 'street-organ', hence evoking 'evil socialist alternative'), доживотно — до животно (life-long — down to the state of an animal [word-play]), НРБ- на ръба (The People's Republic of Bulgaria — on the edge [word-play]), катастроика ('building', contaminated with 'catastrophe', hence suggesting the catastrophe behind *perestroika*), and finally: nowadays the verb стига (enough) has become a key word, the same as the previous трябва (one must or has to).

Language as a substitution for reality
The mechanism of the totalitarian system works in such a way that everything converts into its opposite. Proclaimed freedom is slavery; independence comes to mean total dependence; equality means the inequality of Party class structures; the 'classless society' becomes a feudal differentiation of classes and sub-classes. But the most amazing transformation is when honest people turn, unawares, into accomplices of totalitarian crimes through their industriousness, their discipline and loyalty; when personalities convert into nameless creatures and into faceless spectres. Language is one of the magic means of these metamorphoses.

I can still see a verbal euphoria: a 'new life', a 'new man', a 'new society', a 'new science', a 'new art', and even, despite it being inflationary, 'new money'. This mass hypnosis based on the 'new' has dragged us into the old trap of cruel obscurantism.

Boris Pasternak said: 'Reality is so horrifying that it has gone into hiding.' But where has it hidden? Behind words! Gradually, during the last four decades, words entirely replaced reality. Contemporaries, not without their own participation, were pushed into a verbal reality which had nothing in common with reality: 'the shining peaks of Communism', 'mature socialism', 'developed socialism', 'real socialism'. *Alice's Adventures in Wonderland* and *Through the Looking Glass* constitute works directed at the 'irrational' verbal world into which we fell. We were alive when we passed through the lemon-squeezer of Stalinism, whilst our foolish existence was realized in serial verbal campaigns. Our pseudo-existence was a projection of consecutive slogans and consecutive lies.

In Bulgaria this inertia of rhetorics lasted a long time, in spite of the efforts of a few intellectuals. One of the *last* magic spells of the Communist establishment was *glasnost´*. This word became a symbol. Even more schizophrenic was the Bulgarian attitude towards sweet home-made *glasnost´* which Bulgarians proclaimed on every possible occasion and was repeated mostly by those who used to drown the word in bureaucratic and editorial offices or at carefully controlled local meetings; a word which invaded the official press that was otherwise tightly safeguarded by the *cordon sanitaire* of censorship.

We knew very well that this *glasnost´* did not in reality exist. The amazing thing was that this haunting word veiled the space next to us. It was inside us as we were inside it. In this way we also became like spectres: voiceless, faceless, nameless and without legal defence. None the less this word engendered something that, for the time being, was much more important than anything else: the waking of the spirit — the self-revelation of the spirit which was shaking off chronic fear and authoritarian prejudice.

When people asked Confucius how he would adjust the world if he had the omnipotence of a god, he replied: 'First I would put the language in order.' I see the mission of the present-day writer precisely here: to return the primary meanings to words, to denounce the misuse of the word, to call spades spades, to liberate language from the monopoly of the solely right and irrevocable opinion which paralyses thought and action. By restoring the genuine functions of the language, a path to reality will be opened.

But we who are scalded by the crucible of language know that we will have to be wary of the danger of slipping into verbiage analogous to the socialist; that is, to do nothing else but launch loud declarations 'in the spirit of democracy'. Language is a tool for oppressing thought and action as well as a weapon to free the spirit.

CHAPTER FOURTEEN

Soviet Language Laws: 1989-1990

Michael Kirkwood

Soviet language policy under Lenin was in many ways enlightened. It is debatable whether Lenin was genuine in his apparent desire that all languages in the Soviet era should be equal (Soviet commentators think, on the whole, that he was; Western commentators have tended to think, unsurprisingly, that he was not), but the period from 1917 till the mid-1930s was a time of genuine commitment to such an ideal on the part of many educators and linguists. Lenin had insisted that people be taught in their native language. Since many languages in the Russian Empire had no written form, one of the first tasks of linguists was to produce alphabets and systems of rules of orthography for such languages and to simplify alphabets and spelling rules for those for which a written form was already available. For various reasons the Latin alphabet was chosen as the basis for new alphabets for many Turkic languages and during the 1920s and 1930s various Latin-based alphabets were devised and eventually unified under the rubric of the New Turkic Alphabet, then simply the New Alphabet. The alphabet consisted of a pool of some thirty-nine letters, the twenty-five standard ones plus several which had to be devised to represent particular sounds for which there was no equivalent symbol in the standard Latin alphabet. The writing systems of different languages drew on different groupings of letters from the standardized 'pool' and rules of spelling were codified, normally with reference to a particular dialect of a given language.

For reasons which have never satisfactorily been explained, the Latin-based alphabets were replaced by alphabets based on Cyrillic during the latter half of the 1930s. By the early 1940s the change-over was complete, except in the case of languages like Lithuanian and Estonian, which had traditionally used the Latin alphabet. In 1936 Russian became a compulsory school subject. This marked an obvious watershed in the fortunes of the other languages of the Soviet Union. If under the earlier Soviet period they had begun to thrive as a result of Leninist language policy, under Stalin they entered a period of decline, in the sense that they were no longer deemed to be 'equal' and it was clear that, for all practical purposes, the Soviet Union would require one language to operate as a *lingua franca* on its territory. Russian was the obvious choice.

The decline of Soviet languages other than Russian accelerated under Khrushchev and Brezhnev, both of whom promoted Russian at the expense of other languages. But it was not only the fact that Russian was promoted. The Russian people, first singled out by Stalin as being *primus inter pares*, or, indeed, just *primus*, became increasingly referred to as the 'velikii russkii narod' (the great Russian people) and as the elder brother in the fraternal family of Soviet peoples. The teaching of languages other than Russian declined, the use of Russian was extended ever further. Under Brezhnev the promotion of Russian at the expense of other languages was intensified and in addition there was the campaign to promote the concept of the 'Soviet People' as a 'new historic community', a policy which had as its aim the downgrading of individual nationalities. By the end of the 1970s Russian was being taught to children in kindergartens before they had properly mastered their own tongue.

When Gorbachev took power he was not aware that there was a particular 'nationalities' problem. Earlier speeches make practically no reference to the nationalities. Under *glasnost´*, however, the nationalities issue has become one of his most serious problems. What has been most interesting is the explosion of local initiative as regards language policy at Union Republican and occasionally Autonomous Republican level. It is not too much to suggest that local initiative, in fact, has outstripped the centre's ability to control it and this is nowhere better exemplified than in the language laws that every republic, bar the RSFSR, now has for the regulation of the languages spoken on its territory. The centre responded by passing a USSR law on languages during a meeting of the USSR Supreme Soviet in April of 1990.

Georgia, Armenia and Azerbaidzhan, up until recently, had been the only Republics to have included an article in their Constitution specifying that their national language was a state language on their territory. With the exception of the RSFSR, all the other republics have now followed suit, beginning with Estonia in January 1989. These laws have been the culmination of intense debate in the republics concerned and have been in every case the result of popular pressure, often in the teeth of strong resistance from the local Party chiefs and always with the disapproval of Moscow. It is quite clear that people everywhere have seized the opportunity offered by the conditions obtaining under *glasnost´* to push for a re-establishment of their own language and culture and to attempt to reduce the competitive power of Russian. In this respect some of the laws are particularly harsh as regards their treatment of Russian, others less so. What is less clear is whether in the long term new language policies enshrined in new laws will help rather than hinder the process of acquiring, or regaining, national independence.

The limitations of space preclude an examination of each new law, of which twelve have been passed since January 1989. We shall, instead, look at four: those of the republics of Estonia, Belorussia and Moldavia, and the USSR Law on Languages, passed in April 1990. On the basis of these examples we shall be able to draw some conclusions about developments in the future.

Estonia

It will be helpful to begin with some demographic and linguistic facts based on the Soviet censuses of 1979 and 1989. The following table gives data in percentage terms for Estonians and Russians living in Estonia, together with information about knowledge of Russian and Estonian respectively as second languages.

Table 1[1]

	Estonians as % of total population of Estonia	Russians as % of total population of Estonia	R as L2 (%)	E as L2 (%)
1979	64.7	23.0	23.0	3.9
1989	61.5	30.3	33.6	5.5

R as L2: Knowledge of Russian as a second language
E as L2: Knowledge of Estonian as a second language

The figures for R as L2 refer to Estonians who claim a knowledge of Russian as a second language whereas those for E as L2 refer to the non-Estonian population of Estonia as a whole. (The figures for non-Russians in Estonia claiming a knowledge of R as L2: 1979: 17.7%; 1989: 24.1%.)

We can see that the proportion of Estonians in the population of Estonia has declined over the decade between the censuses, whereas the proportion of Russians has increased, reflecting the policy of Russian in-migration fostered by central government during the earlier part of the period at least. We note also that, while still comparatively low in relation to other parts of the Soviet Union, the figure for those claiming a knowledge of Russian is quite

---

[1] All the percentages used in the tables in this paper are based on data contained in the following publications: (for 1989) *Vestnik statistiki*, 1990, 11, p. 73; 1991, 1, p. 72; 1991, 6, p. 76; (for 1979) *Chislennost' i sostav naseleniia SSSR*, 'Finansy i statistiki', Moscow, 1984, pp. 108, 128, 136.

significantly higher in 1989 than it was in 1979. However, in the context of the Estonian language law it is the figures in the final column which are of most interest. In 1979 just 3.9% of non-Estonians claimed a knowledge of Estonian, a figure which is still less than 6% in 1989. That 1989 figure gives some idea of the problems facing the Estonian government in its desire to promote Estonian as the state language. Nearly 40% of the population of Estonia are not native Estonians. If the 1989 population of Estonia is taken as 1,565,662, a rough calculation indicates that some half a million people do not know Estonian.

The picture is further complicated by the distribution of nationalities on the territory of Estonia. Industrial towns in the north-east of the territory have high percentages of non-Estonians: Narva — 95%, Kohtla-Jarve — 75%. In the capital Tallinn the percentage is fifty. Estonia was one of the earliest republics to raise the language issue openly. The Central Committee of the Estonian Communist Party (ECP) discussed language and nationality problems at a plenum in June 1987.[2] A long article criticizing official Soviet policy on Russian-national bilingualism by the Estonian linguist Mati Hint was published in two issues of *Raduga* in the same year and provoked an intense debate between 'radicals' and 'reactionaries' over the ensuing months.[3] An Estonian academician reported in February 1988 that new programmes were being drawn up for the study of Estonian at Russian language schools and that it had been decided to train bilingual personnel for work in the fields of services, medical institutions and law enforcement.[4] In September 1988 during a plenary session of the ECP it was stated that the Estonian language should have the status of state language for official business conducted on Estonian territory and that Estonian language, history and literature should be taught in all Estonian schools.[5] A Draft Language Law which was published in the summer reflected the determination to make the status of Estonian in Estonia paramount and provoked intense debate in the press, trade unions and intellectual circles and a hostile reaction on the part of non-Estonian speakers, particularly Russians. In December, the Estonian Supreme Soviet passed an amendment to the Estonian constitution making Estonian the state language on Estonian territory.[6] It did not however, pass a law on language but instead promised that a law would be passed on 18 January 1989. A second Draft Language Law was published on 10 December in which some of the more provocative pro-Estonian clauses were toned down, but by no means enough to prevent the continuation of the intense and acrimonious debate.[7] In an

---

2 *Summary of World Broadcasts (SWB)*, 1 June 1987.
3 M. Khint, 'Problema dvuiazychiia: vzgliad bez rozovykh ochkov', *Raduga*, 1987, nos 6-7.
4 TASS, 9 February 1988.
5 TASS, 10 September 1988.
6 TASS, 7 December 1988.
7 *SWB*, 14 January 1989.

article published in the morning edition of *Izvestiia* on 8 January 1989 two Soviet lawyers drew attention to the ways in which the Draft Law was at variance with USSR legislation, in particular with references to articles which appeared to discriminate against Russian in the spheres of education, business and the law.[8] This second draft however, was adopted at a session of the Estonian Supreme Soviet on 18 January and thus became law.

The law as a whole is to be enacted in full within four years. It goes a very long way towards establishing Estonian as the state language. It *ensures* throughout the territory of Estonia the provision of education in the Estonian language, whereas it merely acknowledges the 'right' of non-Estonians to the provision of state public education in the native language. Estonian becomes the language of internal office work in all institutions and enterprises and it will be the language of legal proceedings. There is no mention of Russian as the language of communication between nationalities and Russian is no longer a compulsory subject.[9]

Not surprisingly, the law has provoked reaction. Estonia's Interfront movement at its congress in March demanded a suspension of the language law, mindful that many of its provisions discriminated against non-Estonian speakers.[10] Baltic experts debating economic independence referred to the difficulties of translating all paperwork into Estonian as required by the new law. Some of the implications were rehearsed immediately after the law was passed by Estonian Deputy Premier Ain Doidla. Estonia would immediately need 100,000 typewriters with Latin fonts as all official documents would have to be in Estonian. By early 1990 it would be necessary for all offices, enterprises and organizations to have at least one employee who could serve an Estonian customer in his or her native tongue. All official forms and documents at present in Russian would have to be available in Estonian in two years' time, as would all operating instructions on equipment. All those in occupations serving the public would have to have a knowledge of Estonian in four years' time.[11] On the other hand, the resources which the republican government proposed to allocate came to no more that R300,000 to R500,000 per annum.[12]

According to the rough calculation above, Estonia will need to teach over half a million people to be proficient in Estonian within four years. A survey carried out in 1989 by the USSR Academy of Pedagogical Sciences Research Institute for the Teaching of Russian Language in the National School (NII PRIaNSh — the results of which have not yet been published as far as this author is aware, but a copy of which he has seen) shows that the infrastructure required for such a task is far from satisfactory. A centre for Estonian

---

8   Ibid.
9   *SWB*, 8 February 1989.
10   TASS, 6 March 1989
11   *SWB*, 20 January 1989, SU/0363 B/2.
12   Ibid., SU/0363 B/1.

language teaching has been created and there is a Republican commission for the teaching of Estonian in Russian language schools. According to information provided by the Estonian State Education Committee (GKNO ESSR) for 1988-89, 37.5% of schools in Estonia had Russian as the language of instruction. There were thirty-eight bilingual schools, of which twenty-five were in the towns. There was a serious shortage of teachers of Estonian in Russian language schools. In Narva, Estonian was taught in only 125 out of 281 classes. There was a general shortage of schools in Estonia. In Tallinn, in the last five years three of the four new schools had Russian as the language of instruction. Bilingual secondary school number thirty-nine had become a Russian language school. In Tartu, more than a thousand new places had opened in schools with Russian as the language of instruction, and over the last ten years the number of Russian pupils had grown several times over. The shortage of teachers of Estonian was aggravated by the fact that co-operatives could offer teachers higher salaries.

On the other hand GKNO ESSR has developed a plan for the teaching of Estonian in schools with special emphasis on those domains in which Estonian will be required by law. New textbooks are being written and there is already a programme for the production of phrase-books and books on the history of Estonian culture. In comprehensive schools Estonian language is taught for two hours per week and there are plans to increase the number of hours to equal the number of hours of Russian in Estonian schools (approximately four hours per week). Estonian is taught for one hour per week in specialized educational institutions and professional-technical colleges (PTU). Higher education institutions provide 150-200 hours of Estonian language instruction over the first two years of a student's course.

What are the chances of success for Estonia's new language policy? It is clear that there will be a substantial price to pay in economic terms. If 'success' means the restoration of pride in one's nationality, language and culture, the law may well achieve it. If 'success' also means 'success' in persuading non-Estonian speakers to learn Estonian (successfully!), the future is more doubtful. But the Estonian language law, by downgrading *de facto* as well as *de jure* the importance of Russian while enhancing the importance of Estonian, creates an environment in which people have an incentive (whether of the stick or carrot variety) to acquire a working knowledge of Estonian. What is doubtful, however, is whether incentive alone is enough. Estonian is not an easy language to learn. Russians are not used to having to learn someone else's language. In theory, with the passing of time, Russian influence should wane in favour of Estonian. It will be interesting to see whether that happens in practice.

Belorussia
The situation in Belorussia is quite different from that of Estonia as regards Russian and the indigenous language, as may be seen from the following table,

which shows percentages of Belorussians and Russians in the population of Belorussia in 1979 and 1989 together with percentages of those claiming respectively knowledge of Russian and Belorussian as a second language. The figures for R as L2 indicate Belorussians who claim a knowledge of Russian as a second language whereas the figures for Belorussian as a second language apply to the non-Belorussian population as a whole.

Table 2

	Belorussians as % of total population of Belorussia	Russians as % of total population of Belorussia	R as L2 (%)	B as L2 (%)
1979	79.3	11.8	53.4	4.7
1989	77.8	13.2	60.4	12.0

R as L2: Russian as a second language
B as L2: Belorussian as a second language

Belorussians make up a much larger percentage of the population of Belorussia than Estonians in Estonia, and Russians a much smaller, though not insignificant, percentage. The proportion of Belorussians claiming knowledge of Russian as a second language is also much higher than that of Estonians. It is also the case that in 1989 only 80% of Belorussians living in Belorussia claimed Belorussian as their mother-tongue, almost all of the remainder (19.7%) claiming as their mother-tongue Russian. In 1979 the corresponding figures were respectively 83.5 and 16.4. Russian in Belorussia, therefore, was a first or second language for about 80% of Belorussians in 1989. In 1979 Russian was a first or second language for 67.8% of Belorussians living in Belorussia, the difference between the two figures suggesting the rate of Russification of the republic during the ten-year period in question.

Belorussian has had a chequered career, the story of which has been well-told elsewhere.[13] Here we shall concentrate on the current situation to provide a context for an assessment of the Belorussian language law which was passed in January 1990.

---

13 Cf. A. Bembel', *Rodnae slova i maral'na-estetychny prahres*, London, 1985; P.N. Wexler, *Purism and Language: a Study in Modern Ukrainian and Belorussian Nationalism*, Bloomington, Indiana, 1974.

The NII PRIaNSh report alluded to above (which examined the Russian-national bilingualism in all of the Union Republics) makes for sombre reading. The current profile of Belorussian/Russian bilingualism in Belorussia is as follows. There is widespread use of Russian in all areas of activity. Russian is used among Belorussians themselves in practically all spheres. There has been a severe reduction in the domains in which Belorussian is used and a sharp decline in the use of Belorussian as a language of instruction in schools. There is a tendency for Belorussian pupils and parents to reject Belorussian. Furthermore, it appears that schools with Belorussian as the language of instruction are unpopular. Attempts to open schools with Belorussian encounter strong resistance, especially in the towns. Moreover, even in those which nominally teach in Belorussian, most of the subjects are in fact taught in Russian since there are not enough teachers with a sufficiently good command of Belorussian to teach in that language. Finally, there is the extent to which Russian colours Belorussian usage. Many people who claim to speak Belorussian in fact speak a kind of amalgam of Belorussian and Russian, known as 'triasanka'.[14]

The Belorussian law on languages was published in January 1990[15] after four months of intensive debate on a languages bill. Three points are important. First, Belorussian has become the state language (Article 2, para. 1). Secondly, Belorussia guarantees the status of Russian as the language of inter-ethnic contact (Article 2, para. 3). Thirdly, the law makes provision for the 'unconstrained' development and support of other languages of the USSR whose representatives live in the republic (Article 2, para. 4).

Given the profile of bilingualism in the Republic outlined above together with the 'condition' of Belorussian itself, it is a reasonable bet that the Belorussian language law is doomed to failure if the main aim behind it is to enhance the status of Belorussian. For Belorussian to gain a position of pre-eminence, it must gain it *de facto*, which means that ordinary people will want to use it, or perceive a need to use it, more than Russian. This is not likely to happen, given the provisions of the new law. The status of Russian as the language of inter-ethnic contact reinforces the *status quo* and undermines the claim of Belorussian to take over that role.

Moldavia

The linguistic debate has been nowhere more intense than in Moldavia. For most of 1989 the story is one of strong opinions vehemently expressed, public outcry, strikes, demonstrations, political infighting. It is all the more dramatic because hitherto the situation has been relatively stable. Moldavian was used

---

14 J. Dingley, 'Ukrainian and Belorussian: A Testing Ground', in M. Kirkwood (ed.), *Language Planning in the Soviet Union*, London, 1989, p. 186.
15 References to this law given in this paper are based on the text published in *Belarusskaia mova i literatura u shkole*, 4, 1990, pp. 3-6.

by Moldavians (95.4% of Moldavians in 1989 claimed Moldavian as their mother-tongue) and Russian was used as the language of inter-ethnic communication. Many Moldavians, of course, also knew Russian. The data for 1979 and 1989 expressed as percentages of the total population of Moldavia are as follows:

Table 3

	Moldavians as % of total population of Moldavia	Russians as % of total population of Moldavia	R as L2 (%)	M as L2 (%)
1979	63.9	12.8	40.6	4.0
1989	64.4	12.9	45.3	5.0

R as L2: Russian as a second language
M as L2: Moldavian as a second language

The stability of the linguistic situation in the intercensal period is reflected in the figures in Table 3. One notices that more than one third of the population is not Moldavian and that Moldavian is known by far fewer people in Moldavia than Russian. Any move to enhance the status of Moldavian was likely therefore to meet with substantial opposition.

On the other hand, what these figures do not show is the extent to which Russian had become entrenched. Moldavian had been increasingly replaced by Russian in the business and educational domains and even in the workplace the use of Moldavian was considered to be a manifestation of 'nationalism'. Moldavian was thus in danger of becoming merely a 'kitchen-table' language, i.e., of being restricted to the domestic sphere only.

In January 1989 an inter-departmental commission set up by the Moldavian Supreme Soviet proposed that Moldavian should be made the 'state language', but in a context of continuing Moldavian-Russian bilingualism.[16] This proposal, however, given that it left the *de facto* status of Russian unchanged, was met by a counter-proposal in the form of a 'draft law' by the Moldavian Writers' Union, published in the Moldavian newspaper *Literatura Shri Arta* on 16 March, which made provision for the extensive use of the Moldavian language in all fields, leaving Russian to be used only for business involving other republics or international relations.

---

16   TASS, 20 January 1989.

The official response from the authorities was to propose the drafts of two laws, one of which proposed that Moldavian be proclaimed the state language but that Russian should be the language of inter-ethnic communication within the republic, the other of which did not propose any particular status for Moldavian but which did propose that Russian should be an optional means of communication in practically every domain. A better recipe for the division of the population into warring camps could hardly have been invented. The result was mass rallies by Moldavians in support of Moldavian, and strikes and demonstrations by Russians, Ukrainians and others who favoured Russian. This split extended to the Party and the Supreme Soviet.

After intense lobbying from both sides (including an intervention from Gorbachev), the Supreme Soviet voted in August to make three amendments to the Constitution in relation to language. The first designated Moldavian as the state language of the Moldavian SSR, the second provided for the re-introduction of the Latin script and the third designated both Russian and Moldavian as languages of inter-ethnic communication.

It is difficult to imagine a less satisfactory outcome. Moldavian is the state language to be used in official business and education, but in a different script. On the other hand the use of Russian is still permitted. The economic cost of changing from Cyrillic to Latin will be very high (new typewriters, typographical arrangements, new street signs, new textbooks, new teaching materials, teacher-training, language learning courses, dictionaries, phrase-books, grammars, to name but the most obvious). Yet the change of script will hinder rather than facilitate the spread of Moldavian, given that it will give rise to problems in reading and writing for many who are used to Cyrillic. Despite the fact that Moldavian and Romanian are 'the same language', the Latin script is bound to be less familiar, although whether one could speak of 'instant illiteracy' is more doubtful. Above all, the fact that Russian may be used as a language of inter-ethnic communication will reinforce Russian in that role and at the same time undermine the chances of Moldavian as being able to compete (see the above figures for Moldavian as a second language compared with Russian). It is likely, therefore, that the new law will continue to act as a focus for inter-ethnic strife rather than as a blueprint for ethnic harmony.

The examples of Estonia, Belorussia and Moldavia give some idea of the range of different contexts, patterns of bilingualism and ethnic disharmony. The new language laws likewise differ in terms of their 'harshness' with respect to Russian and, more generally, the language rights of non-indigenous populations. At the 'hard' end stands Estonia, at the 'soft' end, Belorussia and Moldavia. Most of the other republican laws occupy a position within those two extremes. Broadly speaking one may say that the Baltic Republics as a whole are less compromising, those of Central Asia more accommodating.

In an effort to bring order into the growing chaos of Soviet language policy, the USSR Supreme Soviet on 24 April 1990 passed the Law on the

Languages of the USSR Peoples to take effect from 1 July 1990, with the exception of certain provisions which are to be phased in over the next four to ten years. Not surprisingly, it is at variance in important respects with many of the republican laws already adopted.

There had been a great deal of discussion of the language issue over the previous four years within central government and government institutions.[17] Throughout the debate the establishment line had not changed fundamentally, although increasingly lip service had been paid to the need to improve the teaching of indigenous languages and to the desirability of these languages being learned by non-native residents. Two pillars of long-standing Soviet policy remained firm: Russian must continue to be the language of inter-ethnic communication on the territory of the Soviet Union; the democratic right of parents to choose the language of instruction for their children must continue to be guaranteed.

These two pillars have been enshrined in the new law.[18] Article 4, which determines the legal status of languages, states: 'The union and autonomous republics have the right to determine the legal status of the languages of the republics, including their establishment as official languages', but then goes on to affirm that 'Russian is recognised on the territory of the USSR as the official language of the USSR and is used as the medium of inter-ethnic communication.' Finally, it states that 'infringement of the right of citizens of the USSR to use in various spheres of state and public life their native language and other languages of the peoples of the USSR is prohibited'. Article 6 guarantees the freedom of choice of language and education and tuition.

Various other articles are designed to reinforce the position of Russian (and Russians), either overtly or covertly. Article 7 stipulates that the teaching of Russian as the official language of the USSR is compulsory. Article 8 assures the right to work for citizens, regardless of knowledge of language. Article 13 relates to the use of languages of the peoples of the USSR in the service sphere and states that if 'knowledge of a language of address is not stipulated by the skills requirements for tenure of the corresponding positions, the official language of the USSR is employed. Refusal of service on the pretext of ignorance of the language is impermissible...'. Articles 16, 17 and 18 provide for the use of Russian as the official language of the USSR alongside official union and republican languages in such domains as legal documentation, elections, clerical work. Russian continues to be the language employed in the USSR armed forces.

---

17   For a review of this discussion, see M. Kirkwood, 'Glasnost´, the "National Question" and Soviet Language Policy', *Soviet Studies*, 43, 1991, 1, pp. 61-81.
18   An English translation of this law was published in *SWB*, 22 May 1990, SU/0770 C1/1-4. All quotations are from that source.

The USSR law applies throughout the territory of the USSR and takes precedence (Article 2) over union and autonomous republican laws. Many of the provisions of these laws are at variance with those of the USSR law and are consequently illegal.

The legal picture is thus one of total chaos. It is further complicated by an issue which has been beyond the scope of this discussion, yet is of great importance, namely the right granted by some of these laws, including the USSR law, to nationalities without their own territory but living in 'compact' groups to use their own language and to make provision for teaching it. *Glasnost´* has taken the lid off a subject that, as recently as 1985, was taboo — the question of the relationship between Russian and other Soviet languages. Since then, however, the periphery has sought to break away from central control and the centre has sought to retain it. Deep divisions have opened up in the domain of language policy which are irreconcilable. These have now been entrenched in conflicting laws. It may well be that the future cohesion of the Soviet Union is a matter of sufficient doubt for it to be premature to discuss the likely effects of these laws. They may well turn out to be irrelevant in the sense that they are unenforceable. The policies enshrined in the republican laws are very expensive and will require resources which could otherwise be allocated to other hard-pressed areas of the economy. It is likely that the training programmes and the infrastructural changes that will be required will not be adequately resourced. The pressure of Russian will continue — strengthened by a law which for the first time in Soviet history defines the legal status of that language. Language disputes are likely to increase. Estonians will insist that they have a legal right to use Estonian only. Russian residents in Estonia will insist that they have a legal right to use only Russian. That is only one of the many possible examples of conflict.

Will these laws make any difference to established patterns of national-Russian bilingualism? It is difficult to be sure. New trends will be slow to emerge, given the patterns which are already set in demographic concrete. Much will depend on the success of new language programmes but even more will depend on popular perception. People will learn a language if they need to and, with the exception of the linguistically-minded or gifted, not otherwise. Migration patterns favour the entrenchment of Russian in those areas where there are substantial Russian-speaking minorities. The invasion of Russian into the public domain will not be easily reversed. Policies which aim at the enhancement of the national language and which, at least on paper, have a chance, are those which seek to outlaw the use of Russian. Those which accommodate Russian, or tolerate it as a language of inter-ethnic contact, are much less likely to succeed, indeed are likely to fail dramatically. Thus one might, with fingers crossed, predict the possibility of success in the case of Estonia. Belorussia and Moldavia are highly unlikely to experience an early reverse in current trends. On the other hand, the fortunes of Russian in the republics of Central Asia, already not inspiring, are much less promising.

Russian has experienced more, largely passive, resistance in Central Asia than anywhere else. Laws which provide for the enhancement of indigenous languages and divert resources to that end undermine the position of Russian, and that will be most evident in republics like Uzbekistan, Turkmenistan and Kirghizia.

Postscriptum (August, 1992)
This paper was written in September 1990. Since then, the Baltic republics have gained their independence, the Soviet Union has collapsed and has been replaced by a smaller, much more loosely interconnected, fragmentary Commonwealth of Independent States (CIS). The Law on the Languages of the USSR Peoples discussed above has turned out to be a complete irrelevance. The linguistic problems, however, remain. In Estonia a new Language Department has been set up to watch over the implementation of Estonian language policy as enshrined in the Estonian language law.[19] Predictably, however, measures to facilitate the learning of Estonian have lagged behind what is required and the outcome to date is an unsatisfactory combination of pressure and capitulation on the part of government. Thus the Estonian State Language Department reminded the population in early January 1992 that from the first of that month all shop assistants are required by law to address clients in the state language and to continue in the language of the customer's choice (Estonian or Russian) on pain of dismissal.[20] On the other hand, the requirement to provide a certificate of proficiency in Estonian when applying for Estonian citizenship has been softened in the sense that such certificates can be supplied up to nine months after applying for citizenship.[21] The reasons given are practical, if reminiscent of the Soviet Union: lack of certificates; non-functioning of projected language training systems; the widespread non-functioning of state language examinations. Tensions connected with the language issue have been significantly exacerbated by the requirements of the Estonian citizenship law, an issue, however, which goes beyond the scope of this paper.

In Belorussia the linguistic situation continues to evolve in ways which are less dramatic, but which do not necessarily consolidate the status of Belorussian as the state language. The language law did not apply to the armed forces. However, in June 1992 the collegium of the Belorussian Ministry of Defence ratified a series of measures designed to effect the transition from Russian to Belorussian as the language of the armed forces, a process which, it is envisaged, will take at least six years. [22] On the other hand, Belorussia has also adopted a new education law, under the terms of which national

---

19   *SWB*, 11 October 1991.
20   *SWB*, 9 January 1992.
21   *SWB*, 11 April 1992.
22   *SWB*, 24 June 1992.

minorities living on the territory of Belorussia are guaranteed school education in their native language. [23] To the extent that such a law is practical, Belorussian will have to compete with other languages, notably Russian, but also perhaps Polish and Ukrainian as the language of education.

The political situation in Moldavia is currently much more serious. Moldavia is in a state of conflict with Russia over the 'Transdnestr Republic' issue. The linguistic situation, which appeared to be reasonably stable over the intercensal period reviewed in this paper, has radically changed, reflecting (but also significantly contributing to) the ethnic hatreds which are proving difficult to contain. Not only are the Russian and Moldavian communities split, the Gagauz minority has also mounted a separatist challenge.[24] In such situations linguistic issues provide ready badges of ethnic identity. The chances of linguistic harmony, already rendered difficult by the Moldavian language law (which has been incorporated into the draft constitution), have been virtually destroyed by political developments which have taken place since it was passed. In the circumstances in which Moldavia currently finds itself, linguistic differences emphasize ethnic differences and are likely to contribute to, rather than alleviate, ethnic tension.

23   *SWB*, 9 March 1992.
24   Associated Press, 29 June 1992.

CHAPTER FIFTEEN

Language and Nationalism in Georgia, and the West's Response[1]

B.G. Hewitt

Given the welter of pressing problems facing these countries of Eastern Europe, some may regard discussion of the fate of this or that language to be of trivial importance. One could, of course, examine the Causasus region, especially Georgia, from a number of standpoints — political, social, economic, etc. — but, as a linguist, I have chosen to take as my point of departure the issue of language. I will, I hope, be granted that a language is not merely a vehicle for certain academics to earn their livelihood, such that one or two fewer here or there does not really matter; there is unquestionably such an intimate bond between language and culture, that, if the language disappears, the distinctness of the associated culture must at the very least be threatened. With this in mind, I think that there is a cause for concern over the likely fate of a number of the thirty-eight (or so) indigenous languages of the Caucasus both generally and specifically in connection with extreme nationalist fever inside Georgia, as I hope to demonstrate.

Apart from various Indo-European and Turkic tongues that have come to be spoken in the Caucasus over the centuries, there are certainly three (possibly four) families that make up the indigenous languages of the region: N[orth] E[ast] C[aucasian] (*Avar*, Andi, Botlikh, Godoberi, Karata, Akhvakh,

---

[1] The original version of this paper, presented in summary at the 75th Anniversary Conference of London University's School of Slavonic and East European Studies in December 1990, was written at a time when Zviad Gamsakhurdia's star was in the ascendant and concentrated on two of Georgia's regions, Mingrelia and Abkhazia. The former section is here omitted, as interested readers now have available for consultation two separate articles dealing with language-aspects of Georgian nationalism *vis-à-vis* Mingrelia, namely Feuerstein and Enwall. As to Abkhazia, events are swiftly and tragically unfolding even as this final revision is taking place (end of August 1992). I have tried to update the paper as best I could, leaving essentially untouched (apart from appropriate changes of tense) whatever I judged to be still relevant.

Bagval, Tindi, Chamalal, Dido, Khvarsh, Hinukh, Bezhti, Hunzib, *Lak*, *Dargwa*, *Lezgian*, *Tabassaran*, Archi, Aghul, Rutul, Tsakhur, Budukh, Khinalugh, Udi, Kryts), N[orth] C[entral] C[aucasian] (*Chechen*, *Ingush*, Bats), N[orth] W[est] C[aucasian] (*West* and *East Circassian*, *Abkhaz*, *Abaza*, Ubykh), S[outh] C[aucasian] or Kartvelian (*Georgian*, Mingrelian, Laz, Svan) — the difficulty of differentiating between dialect and language accounts for why the total of thirty-eight is only approximate. Today Ubykh, spoken only in Turkey since tsarist Russia's conquest of the North Caucasus and the consequent expulsion of most of the North West Caucasians to the Ottoman Empire in 1864, is virtually extinct, whilst the others have speakers varying in number from 200[2] for Himukh up to four million for Georgian, the only one with (a) over even one million speakers, (b) its own unique script, and (c) a literary tradition (actually of fifteen centuries) pre-dating the nineteenth century. With a number of these languages being spoken by inhabitants of just a cluster of neighbouring villages, conditions were/are ripe for the development of bi-, tri- and quadri-lingualism — Adolf Dirr (1867-1930) described his informant for both Archi and Aghul as also competent in Lak, Avar, Kumykh, Russian and Arabic. The existence of naturally developed *linguae francae* will have played a part in the decisions as to which languages were to be accorded literary status in the early Soviet campaign towards eradicating illiteracy. The current literary languages are underlined in the above list — efforts to establish literatures for NEC Akhvakh, Tsakhur, Udi and SC Laz failed; for the fascinating question of Mingrelian, readers are referred to either Feuerstein[3] or Enwall.[4] Thus, many of the small peoples of Daghestan (NE Caucasus), like the Botlikh, in addition to their own language use Avar (or Russian, of course) for literary purposes; the Aghul have Lezgian, Dargwa or Tabassaran as inter-communal languages. However, a negative interpretation of Soviet treatment of the N. Caucasian languages is offered by Wixman.[5] His general thesis is summed up by one reviewer, Bernard Comrie,[6] thus: 'The establishment of new written languages for many of the peoples of the North Caucasus in the early post-Revolutionary years was an attempt to wean them away from other loyalties (e.g. to Arabic or a Turkic *lingua franca*); now that this aim has been at least in part achieved, these written languages are being phased out in favor of Russian.' Comrie himself, though, dismisses Wixman's theory partly on the grounds that the Soviets cannot win — 'if the Soviet

---

2 As reported by E.A. Bokarëv in 'Ginukhskii iazyk', *Iazyki narodov SSSR IV, Iberisko-kavkazskie iazyki*, Moscow, 1967, pp. 436-54.
3 W. Feuerstein, 'Mingrelisch, Lazisch, Swanisch: alte Sprachen und Kulturen der Kolchis vor dem baldingen Untergang', in B.G. Hewitt (ed.), *Caucasian Perspectives*, Unterschleissheim/Munich, 1992.
4 J. Enwall, 'Some Remarks on the Language Debate in the *q'azaxiši gazeti*' in ibid.
5 R. Wixman, *Language Aspects of Ethnic Patterns and Processes in the North Caucasus*, Chicago, 1980.
6 Writing for *American Anthropologist*.

authorities encourage a language, it is to divide and rule; if they discourage a language, it is to Russianize and unite' — and partly by adducing counter-evidence from regions of the USSR. N.W. Caucasian specialist Rieks Smeets could hardly differ more from Wixman: 'It is hardly feasible to find a more positive aspect of Soviet internal policy than the policy towards ethnic minorities. This policy is on the whole to be applauded.'[7] And on the whole, I rather incline towards this latter view. Quite simply, in modern conditions of a tendency to migrate from rural areas to urban centres and particularly of mass-communication (and entertainment) by means of broadcasting, which in the USSR is primarily in Russian with local alternatives in the shape of the respective union-republican languages, I believe that the long-term future for minority-languages can only stand even a chance of being safeguarded if they are awarded *some* level of literary status. Recent reports suggest that as a result of local initiatives some teaching of Rutul, Tsakhur and Aghul has already started.[8]

Wixman, of course, questions whether the title 'literary language' still has any real significance in the N. Caucasus. Literary status basically implies (a) publishing (of books, journals, newspapers), (b) schooling in the language up to a certain grade in local-language schools (though practices differ for each literary langue), and (c) some amount of radio- and TV-broadcasting (possibly for just a negligible amount of time per week). Regarding (a), Wixman dismissively states: 'One cannot call a language in which fewer than 100 different books are printed per year "literary".'[9] Regarding (b), he concludes: 'It is clear from current educational policies that there is now an attempt to completely replace native languages of the N. Caucasus, at least in terms of their use as literary languages, with the Russian tongue.'[10] He has in mind the School Reform of 1959, concerning which he quotes Conquest:[11] 'The language issue is essentially that of making the language of instruction voluntary from the parents' point of view ... In effect this means that ambitious parents try to get their children into Russian language schools, which are in any case of higher quality'. It may well be true that the effect here has been that in some areas there no longer exist local-language schools, i.e. schools where tuition for the first few grades is actually in the local language, and that where such teaching has survived, there is a switch to Russian after grade 2 — I believe literary languages are still taught as a discipline within regional Russian schools regardless — but I think Wixman's judgement on publishing is too severe. It would obviously be foolish to claim that all is well even for the literary languages of the N. Caucasus — evidence

7 R. Smeets, *Studies in West Circassian Phonology and Morphology*, Leiden, 1984, pp. 59-60.
8 Personal communication to the author by Rieks Smeets and Simon Crisp.
9 Wixman, p. 157.
10 Ibid., p. 155.
11 R. Conquest, *The Nation Killers*, London, 1970, p. 137.

is available that both NEC Avar[12] and NWC West Circassian[13] are being squeezed in terms of their functional viability — but I see the problem more as one of accidental neglect than deliberate open hostility on the part of the (Russian) authorities, though I could of course be wrong and remain open to persuasion; I am, for instance, told[14] that the Academy authorities have a central policy not to fund all publications relating to the non-literary languages, with the result that the Bezhti-Russian dictionary that exists in manuscript form is unlikely to appear in print. If true, this is indeed a matter for regret.

In the case of the already established literary languages, the basis is there for a revival. Assuming that the N. Caucasian territories will remain part of some continuing Russian Federation whether in the guise of today's mixture of autonomous regions and republics or conceivably as a reconstituted Mountain Caucasian Republic, it is likely that in the prevailing climate of self-awareness and self-determination the various peoples themselves will soon start to claim their ethnic/linguistic rights — such moves will be even more marked if the regions follow the example of Dudaev's Chechenia in not only pressing for but actually achieving their independence from Russia. And so, as post-Soviet society opens up to further contact with the West, academic bodies and cultural organizations here should encourage the relevant authorities to facilitate the re-invigoration of the minority languages and cultures. A campaign to remind people of the importance of re-introducing and/or strengthening the local languages in education would have to be accompanied by measures to improve the quality of teaching in the relevant schools to ensure at least the same standards as in Russian schools. This almost certainly would have to be accompanied by radical improvements to the primers already in existence both for the local languages themselves as well as for disciplines taught in them. Linguistics would have to be involved to ensure that the local languages were endowed with technical vocabularies appropriate to both the relevant subjects and adequate for the level to which these subjects were to be taught. New scripts might even have to be devised. All this would take effort, time and money. Since the economy across the whole former USSR is today in many ways as parlous as it was in the early days when many of the literary languages were first created and when, differently from today, there existed the pressing need to eradicate illiteracy, it would be understandable if these concerns were not exactly accorded top priority for funding. But if all interested parties (the local peoples, the relevant authorities, and Western institutions and funding-agencies) agreed that such a project

---

12 See Simon Crisp, 'Language Planning and the Development of Written Avar Syntax', unpublished DPhil thesis, University of Oxford, 1982.
13 Olag Lalor, 'Languages in Contact in North West Caucasian Communities', Unpublished PhD thesis, University of London, 1990.
14 Personal communication to the author by Rieks Smeets.

should be undertaken, could not funding be targetted by appropriate sources from the West?

As to the more numerous non-literary languages, I am convinced that, unless some sort of albeit elementary provision is made for underpinning them at nursery and primary schools, there is just no way they are going to survive in the long term, given the demands of modern life and the all-intrusive influence on television with its major language (Russian). I was delighted that in the paper he had hoped to read on behalf of himself and his collaborator R. Radzhabov at the Vth Caucasian Colloquium at London's School of Oriental and African Studies (SOAS) in June 1990 the distinguished Russian Caucasologist M. Alekseev himself argued the case for provision to be created for the NEC Dido language (population = 8,500). This generous attitude is to be contrasted with that obtaining in the Transcaucasian Republic of Georgia, to which we now turn our attention.

Georgia presents a complex picture. It incorporates (apart from Georgian itself) the NWC literary language Abkhaz, which was included in his book by Wixman even though it is not spoken in what is geographically the N. Caucasus, the non-literary NCC Bats and SC Mingrelian, Svan and Laz (spoken by only a negligible number within Georgia since the traditional Laz homeland falls today inside Turkey's borders), as well as a variety of other languages which are also spoken elsewhere within the former USSR (including Ossetic, Azeri, Armenian, Russian, Ukrainian, Avar, Udi and Greek). The position of Georgia's sister-languages is particularly intriguing, and, even though we shall not be looking at this problem in detail, some basic information is necessary to help with an understanding of some terminology in what follows.

In the 1926 Soviet census 242,990 declared Mingrelian nationality (with a further 40,000 stating Mingrelian to be their native language); 13,218 described themselves as Svans.[15] Today there are no precise figures for the numbers of Mingrelians and Svans or for those having first- or second-speaker knowledge of these languages. Some time around 1930 it seems to have been decided that these people were simply to be classified as 'Georgians', and the result is that, since all Svans and virtually all Mingrelians educated during the Soviet period have studied in Georgian-language schools, most have been apparently happy to call themselves 'Georgians' hitherto.[16] Within the Georgian language although there is the term *kartveluri* 'Kartvelian' to describe the family to which the four SC languages belong, the equivalent human adjective (*kartveleli) does not (yet!) exist, and so the term *kartveli* 'Georgian' is used instead. There is no excuse for continuing this

---

15 These figures are quoted from Wixman.
16 Following the virtual war that Georgian forces conducted in parts of Mingrelia against supporters of Zviad Gamsakhurdia in the first half of 1992 there are reports of growing Mingrelian self-awareness and a movement for some regional autonomy (personal communication to the author by Nugzar Dzhodzhua).

terminological inaccuracy in English, where 'Kartvelian' should be used to refer generically to any of the four peoples, whilst Georgian be properly reserved for the largest of the four. Introduction of the designation *kartveleli into the Georgian language would provide a rough equivalent to the term 'British', leaving the ethnonyms *kartveli, megreli, svani* and *lazi* free to play the same roles as the terms 'English', 'Scots', 'Welsh' and 'Irish' in the British Isles. Even to raise the question of differences beween Mingrelians and Georgians produces a hostile response from Georgians; indeed, those few Mingrelians who have proclaimed their ethnic distinctness since 1989 have been lambasted in the Georgian media. This extreme sensitivity can, to my mind, only be explained by pointing to the fact that, for all its vaunted antiquity and culture, Georgia, as a *modern* nation-state, is barely 100 years old, when the 'positive' nationalism of men like Prince (now Saint) Ilia Ch'avch'avadze struggled to give the regions a sense of national identity and self-respect at a time of oppressive tsarist domination. This state-immaturity results in a collective lack of self-confidence about what it means to be a 'Georgian' with accompanying fears of threats to national unity and territorial integrity[17] — of the 3,787,393 'Georgians' in Georgia in 1989, constituting 70.1% of the republic's population, maybe one million were really Mingrelians! Even if the above is the correct diagnosis of part of the Georgians' abrasive self-assertiveness today, it does not excuse their denial of legitimate rights (linguistic, cultural, political) to any of the country's ethnic minorities, be they fellow Kartvelians or North West Caucasian Abkhazians. And it is to Abkhazia that we now turn our attention in earnest.

One of the nastiest aspects of modern chauvinism (and there can be no doubt that that is what it is) in Georgia is revealed in the recent history of Abkhazia and should be viewed with alarm by all who regard the protection of minorities as a worthy cause — the situation in the (formerly Autonomous) Republic of Abkhazia has many sad parallels with that obtaining in Georgia's (formerly Autonomous) Region of South Ossetia, the autonomous status of which was abolished by Gamsakhurdia in December 1990. In a remarkably daring article by railwayman Sergo Panculaia (a Mingrelian, according to the

---

17   Some two years after coming to this conclusion I was bemused when I came across the following observation written in 1913: 'Take the Georgians, for instance. The Georgians before the Reform inhabited a common territory and spoke one language. Nevertheless, they did not, strictly speaking, constitute one nation, for, being split up into a number of disconnected principalities, they could not share a common economic life; for centuries they waged war against each other and pillaged each other by inciting the Persians and Turks against each other ... Georgia came on to the scene as a nation only in the latter half of the nineteenth century, when the fall of serfdom and the growth of the economic life of the country ... bound them together into a single whole.' The author was none other than Joseph Stalin! And it is clear from his constant references to chauvinism against the minorities in his home-republic throughout his collected articles and speeches (*Marxism and the National and Colonial Question*, London, n.d. [hereafter *Marxism...*]) that what is happening today in Georgia is regrettably no new phenomenon.

form of his surname),[18] he perceptively observed: 'By the way, it was only when the issue of the state-language came on the agenda that nationalism exploded in the republic [Georgia].' What is the significance of this observation? There is, unhappily, a long and sad history of tension between the Abkhazians and their Kartvelian neighbours, which goes back, in modern times at any rate, to the already mentioned migration of many N. Caucasians to the Ottoman Empire in 1864 — there are perhaps half a million or more Abkhazians today in Turkey. This partial evacuation of their territory led to competition for rights to the fertile land along this stretch of the Black Sea coast with its favourable climate, which lends it today such potential for rich pickings from the lucrative tourist-trade. There is no time here to detail the history of this conflict.[19] Suffice it to say that the repression suffered in Abkhazia under Beria and his successors in Tbilisi from 1937 to 1953 is especially significant to an appreciation of current difficulties since it not only included mass-importations of Kartvelians and others in order to reduce the Abkhazian percentage of the population but also saw the closure of Abkhaz-language schools as well as both the prohibition of teaching of Abkhaz and restrictions on publishing in it from 1945 to 1953 (*mutatis mutandis* the same restrictions were applied in S. Ossetia) with children being simply transferred to Georgian-language schools[20] — this rather crucial fact is strangely not mentioned by Wixman. Ever since then the Abkhazians have been particularly concerned about safeguarding their language and stress the struggle they have had to achieve other advances, such as access to broadcasting and the creation of the so-called Abkhazian State University in Sukhum in 1978 (the largest of the three sectors was always the Georgian one at about 40%, although Kartvelian propaganda always talks of this university in such a way as to lead the innocent reader into the erroneous belief that it was established solely to *cater* for the Abkhazians, who thus, the imputation goes, can have no justification for their claim of cultural repression) — these concessions followed the request to secede from Georgia and join the RSFSR. By June 1988 an eighty-seven-page document, the so-called *Abkhazian Letter*, signed by sixty leading Abkhazians and prepared in the early heady days of *perestroika*, was ready for submission to the Kremlin seeking restoration of

---

18 Published in *Veteran*, 1990, no. 27.
19 For convenient sources in English reference may be made to the relevant articles in *Index on Censorship* (January 1990, pp. 23-25; May 1990, pp. 29-31) and *The Central Asia and Caucasus Chronicle* (March 1990, pp. 16-18), as well as to a forthcoming issue of *The Nationalities' Journal* (New York), which will contain my own 'Abkhazia: a Problem of Identity and Possession'.
20 The conclusion of the relevant commission's report of 12 March 1945 reads: 'Knowledge of the Georgian language by a significant part of the Abkhazian populace, the lexical similarity of the Georgian and Abkhaz languages, and their shared alphabet [the Abkhaz alphabet was changed from Latin to Georgian only in 1938] dictate the necessity of switching and teaching in Abkhazian schools to the Georgian language' (*Istoriia Abkhazii*, Sukhum, 1991, p. 360).

the status enjoyed by Abkhazia from 1921 to 1931.[21] Then towards the end of 1988 the Georgians published the draft of the State Programme for the Georgian Language, which advocated the obligatory teaching of Georgian in all schools in the republic — the final version promulgated in 1989 adds that access to higher education in Georgia will be dependent on passing a test in Georgian language and literature. Thus, it was immediately abundantly clear to any informed observer that following this there would be even more trouble, for Georgian is poorly known among Abkhazians (that is, apart from those who had it forced on them in the years 1945-53). This may come as a surprise to many people, but it is entirely natural for the following reason: for a number of years Georgian, Russian, Armenian, Azeri, Ossetic, Abkhaz and Avar schools have been operating in relevant parts of Georgia. In non-Georgian schools Georgian has always been an optional subject, Russian obligatory, since knowledge of Russian was essential for inter-communal intercourse throughout the Union. Within Abkhazia Georgian is little heard for the simple reason that there are relatively few Georgians resident there — although Kartvelians make up 45.7% of the population, almost all of these are Mingrelians, who still tend to speak Mingrelian amongst themselves. Those Abkhazians who live in close contact with Mingrelians (i.e. the southern Abkhazians) have tended to speak this Kartvelian language, with Russian as their third tongue — today Russian occupies second position, Mingrelian a definite third — whereas in the north of the region Abkhaz and Russian generally suffice. If Georgian is not deemed necessary for purposes of day-to-day life, who is willingly going to study it? To make it obligatory in all republican schools, regardless of local circumstances and merely to satisfy the pride of the Georgians, is just to invite hostility, because under prevailing conditions, where Russian remains essential and will remain essential as long as Abkhazia (if not Georgia proper) remains closely associated with Russia/CIS, the casualty will in the long run be Abkhaz (or Ossetic, as the case may be). The State Programme for the Georgian Language was a blunder of the first magnitude — it makes no mention of provision for *any* other of the many languages spoken in Georgia, as would surely have been expected from a worthy leadership aware of its responsibilities to all of the republic's peoples. When the S. Ossetian organization *Adæmon Nexas* (Popular Shrine) complains of just this omission as a principal cause of alarm, it is no good people like Roman Miminoshvili reacting in November 1989 with such withering remarks as: 'In the Programme there is nothing said about co-operatives, and no single mention is made of the increase in the hole in the ozone over Antarctica; there is talk only of the Georgian language — so

---

21 Abkhazia's status at this time, albeit (from December 1921) with special treaty-ties to Georgia, along with its right to secede from both the Transcaucasian Federation and the USSR, was enshrined in articles 4 and 5 of its 1925 constitution, reprinted in 1992 from *S'ezdy Sovetovsoiuza SSR. soiuznykh i autonomnykh sovetskukh sotsualisticheskikh respublik*, Moscow, 1964, pp. 686-700.

what?'²² The problem lies precisely in this restriction and the shortsightedness which caused it! In two issues from 1989 *The Central Asia and Caucasus Chronicle* included translations of the parallel documents from the Central Asian republics of Uzbekistan and Tadzhikistan. As both the translations themselves and the discussion appended thereto make clear, the Uzbekistan law is much more liberal and generous in its attitude to the rights of local non-Uzbeks and their languages than the Tadzhikistan equivalent and for this reason apparently gave rise to much criticism within certain Uzbek circles. However, the drafters of even the Tadzhiki document saw fit to incorporate certain rights for the local non-Tadzhikis and their languages. In the Georgian programme, on the other hand, only the needs of Georgian are addressed.

This Programme cannot, of course, be viewed in isolation. The inexorable rise through 1987-88 of more and more unofficial groups, taking ever more extreme stands on the national question with slogans such as 'Georgia for the Georgians!' [i.e. Kartvelians] has continued to this day, so that, as my colleague Donald Rayfield has observed,²³ even the most respectable (i.e. least reactionary) party, Nodar Natadze's National/Popular Front, did not baulk at suggesting that Georgian citizenship should be available only to those with a command of Georgian, a policy adopted by nationalists in other republics (as noted by Mike Kirkwood in his contribution to SSEES's 1990 conference), where, to my mind, it is just as unacceptable. A notorious article by Revaz Mishveladze in *Axalgazrda K'omunist'i*²⁴ (Young Communist) proposed that Georgia should tolerate only 5% of 'guests' (i.e. non-Kartvelians) on its territory, and in the following year the poetess Medea K'akhidze wrote in *Lit'erat'uli Sakartvelo*²⁵ (Literary Georgia): 'I hate no-one, but I firmly believe that everyone should live in his own homeland', noting that one of the Avar villages in K'akheti (E. Georgia), Tkhilists'q'aro, had already been vacated — the residents clearly preferred the peace of Daghestan to continuing pressure from Georgian nationalists. Why should this last have been viewed with concern in Abkhazia? The response to the *Abkhazian Letter* and the subsequent Lykhny Declaration (March 1989) was explosive. There was no attempt to ask whether there might be some justification to the dissatisfaction with their treatment from Tbilisi over recent decades²⁶ — regardless of their

---

22 *Lit'erat'uli Sakartvelo*, 17 November 1989, p. 4.
23 In a seminar paper delivered at SOAS in Spring 1990.
24 29 July 1989.
25 7 September 1990, p. 4.
26 Instead of searching for the reason why the Abkhazians and South Ossetians did not spontaneously embrace the cause of Georgian independence, the propaganda-machine tried to argue for the benefit of foreign consumption that these peoples, especially the Abkhazians, are in fact pampered and privileged. If so, one has to conclude that the Abkhazians and South Ossetians must be the first people in history to seek separation from masters whose beneficence is so generous! The question is posed, for example, as to why, when South Ossetians have language schools with tuition in Ossetic to grade 5,

constant bickering over other questions, the whole plethora of Kartvelian parties, with the possible exception of Irak'li Shengelaia's Federalist Party, have been virtually united in viewing the Abkhazians (and S. Ossetians) as traitors or dupes of Moscow — even otherwise sane individuals, as visitors to Georgia since 1989 unanimously agree, find self-restraint difficult when the issue of Abkhazia is raised. The viciousness of the attacks on both Abkhazians and Ossetians across the whole Georgian-language media from at least early 1989 onwards has to be read/heard to be believed — indeed, one can hardly avoid the conclusion that this initially was nothing other than a cynical attempt to create internal enemies so as to rouse support for the nationalists' cause; in other words, this was precisely the same sort of perversion of patriotism practised for decades previously by the very Bolsheviks the nationalists claimed to despise. Especially pernicious has been the vigour with which the discredited ideas of P'avle Ingoroq'va (dating from the bleak late 1940s) have been re-disseminated not merely by politicians like Zviad Gamsakhurdia and writers (such as Rost'om Chkheidze and Revaz Mishveladze) but even by scholars in the disciplines of history (e.g. Davit Muskhelishvili) and philology (e.g. the Svan linguist Aleksandre Oniani and the Georgian Givi Nebieridze). The sorry argument is that even the 300 years of residence on Georgian [*sic*!] territory that such tendentious commentators allow the Abkhazians give them no entitlement to rights — for the Ossetians even the accepted minimum of 600 years is not enough! The paper I gave at the Vth Caucasian Colloquium[27] addressed this particular question, since no serious scholar in the West doubts that the Abkhazians have occupied their present territory for at the very least 2,000 years, though this in no way implies, nor have the Abkhazians ever

---

they seek union with North Ossetia, where reportedly there is only Russian schooling. The Abkhazians too have Abkhaz teaching to grade 5 in local-language schools, whereas since 1959 the situation has been more restricted in the North Caucasus. I strongly suspect that the avoidance of cut-backs in local-language tuition in Abkhazia and South Ossetia will have been conditioned by the fact that at the time these schools had only been open again for five to six years, whilst the North Caucasian local-language schools had suffered no parallel closure from 1945 to 1953. To restrict or shut them once more so soon would, then, have been too risky. If this is indeed the explanation, their survival to the present will have owed more to historical accident than the positive fostering of two minority languages by Tbilisi. Rejection of a proposal to introduce ten years of schooling in Abkhaz resulted, as I understand it, from suspicions that this suggestion could not be taken seriously when no appropriate course or textbooks had been designed, so that to transfer suddenly from five to ten years, with consequent reduction in both teaching and competence in Russian, would have had the understandable effect of holding the children back from a still essential knowledge of Russian without any compensatory advantages, since the children would still be unable to play any greater role in Georgian society. Increase in, and consolidation of, local-language teaching for all of the relevant languages in the multilingual Caucasus will thus have to achieve a careful balance between the needs of the local language and whatever major language (Russian, Georgian, Azeri) is important in the life of this relevant minority.

27 B.G. Hewitt, 'Languages in Contact in North West Georgia: Fact or Fiction', in *idem* (ed.), *Caucasian Perspectives*.

claimed that it does, that *only* the Abkhazians have rights in Abkhazia. However, the implication behind this imputation of late arrival, an insult in itself, is not lost on the Abkhazians when repatriation (to where?!) has become no longer a mere abstract concept as noted above for the Daghestanis of E. Georgia. All of this was accompanied by demands for the abolition of autonomous status for both Abkhazia and S. Ossetia (now achieved in the case of this latter), and meanwhile local Kartvelians have been encouraged to avoid associating with Abkhazians and Ossetians in any club, society or organization in which both communities previously participated (e.g. the Writers' Union or, most notoriously of all, since it led to the bloodshed in Abkhazia in July 1989, the splitting off of the Georgian sector from the Abkhazian University) in furtherance of what is a blatant policy of racial segregation on the part of Tbilisi.

Fearful that the process of Georgianization begun by the Mensheviks (1918-21) and compounded by Beria and others in the middle years of the century, a period which has been lauded by Gamsakhurdia for demonstrating the correct way to deal with the Abkhazians,[28] could be completed under resurgent chauvinism, S. Ossetia decided to seek union with N. Ossetia (part of Russia) and Abkhazia dared to declare itself independent from Georgia on 25 August 1990 — this declaration was immediately rescinded by the authorities in Tbilisi, though before the collapse of the USSR there were indications that the recognition of its republican status by the Kremlin was imminent. Indeed, the election to power on 28 October/11 November of the coalition known as the Round Table under the leadership of Zviad Gamsakhurdia and the subsequent election of Gamsakhurdia as state-president were from the very start in the view of many observers, including this one, certain to prove utterly disastrous to the well-being of Georgia. To those who only knew this person as the head of the Georgian Helsinki Group and were thus likely to think of him as manifestly a 'decent chap' it must surely have come as a nasty surprise to discover what he actually stood for *vis-à-vis* Georgia's ethnic minorities. In his interview with the Dutch journalist Laura Starink, published in *Zaterdags Bijvoegels* in January 1990 and subtitled with the quotation 'Our Way is the Way of Civil War', he baldly admitted that it was his intention to instil in the South Ossetians the same fear of the Kartvelians that had been instilled in the Abkhazians in 1989. The consequences for the 30% non-Kartvelian population were beyond doubt even for those with little or no knowledge of Georgian affairs in the West, and Georgia was (quite properly) not recognized by any significant Western country as long as Gamsakhurdia remained in power.

---

28 See 'An Open Letter to the Georgians of North West Georgia [*Abkhaz ASSR*]', in *Letopis'*, 1989, no. 4, for instructions to the Georgians on how to carry out anti-Abkhazian agitation.

If the message of this paper was depressing when it was first written, it remains so in late 1992. This is because I judge the developments in Georgia from around the middle of 1988, continuing to the present day and for the foreseeable future to be just that. There seemed originally to be a simplistic *credo* that, if only independence could be achieved, some form of heaven on earth would spring into being on Georgia's hallowed soil, wherein the various nationalities would live in harmonic bliss. This is surely belied by the hatred for, and suspicion of, the ethnic minorities that virtually all of the nationalist leaders, joined by a whole gamut of members of the Writers' Union and, I have to say, many academics, have been calculatedly stirring up throughout this period. Authors sense no internal contradictions when they write of 'the Georgian phenomenon', of 'humanitarianism residing in the blood' and even 'the genes' of the Georgian race, of 'the tolerance Georgians have always shown towards other peoples taking up refuge and residence on Georgian soil', whilst simultaneously attacking with glorious unrestraint be it Abkhazians, Ossetians, Avars (Leks, as they undiscriminatingly refer to the various tribes of Daghestan) or Azerbaijanis residing there — not to mention the Meskhians, whose desire to return home to S.W. Georgia after almost fifty years of Central Asian exile has been constantly thwarted not by Moscow but by Tbilisi; one feels it is just a matter of time before some conflict with Georgia's sizeable Armenian population bubbles up.[29] In their Open Letter addressed by the writer L. Khaindrava and film-director E. Shengelaia to Aleksandr Solzhenitsyn, occasioned by the latter's unflattering reference to Georgia in his advice on 'How to Organize Russia',[30] we were told the latest excuse for denying the Meskhians the right to return home. Since they are Turks [a matter that is surely in dispute], and the area in which they wish to reside is inhabited by Armenians, and since we know the history of Armeno-Turkish relations, the Kartvelians cannot allow their Armenian residents to face the danger that would result from the Meskhians' return! The suggestion that the authorities in Georgia have taken the stand they have out of altruism for the well-being of their Armenian community will bring a wry smile to the face of those who know only too well the usual attitude of the Kartvelians towards the Armenians!

I happen never to have held any truck with the view that blamed the whole series of the USSR's ethnic disputes on the conspiratorial role of Moscow and

---

29 It might be salutary to quote again from Stalin (*Marxism* ..., p. 160). Writing in 1923, twenty years before he himself became the large-scale practitioner of ethnic cleansing in the Caucasus during the war, he condemned this possibility with reference once more to his home-republic: 'Tbilisi is the capital of Georgia, but the Georgians there are not more than twenty-five per cent, the Armenians not less than thirty-five per cent, and the rest belong to other nationalities. There's a capital of Georgia for you! If Georgia were a separate republic, a certain transplantation of population might be effected — for instance, the Armenian population might be removed from Tbilisi.'

30 *Lit'erat'uli Sakartvelo*, 2 November 1990, p. 6.

regard with suspicion the view that, by allowing the Georgians (Kartvelians?) to play the roles of prosecutor, judge and jury in their own court, all the conflicts in this republic will achieve a fair resolution. There is virtual proof of this in the interview[31] with the Procurator of Georgia, Vakht'ang Razmadze,[32] if indeed further proof were needed after his statements on Georgian TV about a week after the killings in Sukhum in 1989 when he publicly pre-judged the guilt of the Abkhazians and threatened retribution. In general the article can best be interpreted as an attempt on the part of a functionary appointed under the old Communist regime to secure his post under former dissident Gamsakhurdia's presidency. In his introductory remarks the interviewer states: 'We know to what extent you personally fought agianst the Soviet Procurator removing from your jurisdiction the Abkhazian affair. We know too how the all-Union organs tried to make you indict the leaders of the national movement following the 9th April, to which your reply was that you would discuss such outstanding matters only after they first indicted Rodionov and the other guilty ones [i.e. for the deaths on 9 April 1989 in Tbilisi]. Not everyone knows this.' In fact, it was quite widely reported at the time. What does it show? It crucially shows that, although Razmadze evidently accepted there was a case for the nationalist leaders such as Gamsakhurdia, the late Merab K'ost'ava and others to answer, he would not act on this unless action was taken against the military commander in Tbilisi on the night of 9 April. In other words, justice for Razmadze, the Procurator of Georgia, was (and no doubt still is) nothing but a mere bargaining chip.

In 1990, when writing the original version of this paper, I dismissed the view of people like ITN's Moscow correspindent at the time, David Smith, that Georgia was equipped with the wherewithal to survive as a fully independent country. My concluding suggestion, in fact, was as follows: 'Thus, when the Georgian begging bowl is proferred, there is no reason why the West's response should not be simply to ignore it, making it plain that it will attract funds only when the hand holding the bowl behaves with dignity towards all the peoples on whose behalf it purports to be collecting. To those who argue that the surest way to defeat the evil of nationalistic repression of minorities is to help create that general prosperity in which tolerance of ethnic, linguistic, cultural and religious differences is more likely to exist, I would reply thus: while in general agreeing with the proposition, I feel that the situation has been brought to such a critical pitch by the words and actions of the Kartvelian nationalist leaders, backed by most of the so-called intelligentsia, that any unconditional injection of funds would be taken by them as a signal that the donors are in no way concerned with the internal ethnic

---

31 Ibid., pp. 3-4.
32 This official's term of office has stretched from the Communist era, through Gamsakhurdia's presidency, continuing into Shevardnadze's chairmanship of the State Council.

troubles of Georgia. Given, as they would see it, such a green light, they might well adopt such measures as would ensure that there were no ethnic minorities left to benefit from any long-term improvement in the economy, if indeed such improvement were ever to materialize in this notoriously corrupt society. There is no Western self-interest that I can see on the altar of which the rights of Georgia's minorities need to be sacrificed. If the Kartvelians themselves do not realize and rectify the error of their ways, they must be persuaded to by what may be the only leverage left open to us.'

It is interesting to compare the West's reaction to Georgia under (a) the legitimately elected President Zviad Gamsakhurdia and (b) the illegitimate State Council presided over since March 1992 by Eduard Shevardnadze that took power in a bloody coup in Tbilisi over the 1991-92 New Year. Gamsakhurdia's undisguised racism resulted in a world-response that essentially corresponded to my suggestion outlined above. However, once Gamsakhurdia was out of Georgia, the local propaganda-machine commenced laying the blame for Georgia's ethnic difficulties exclusively on him and his policies. This was a manifestly successful tactic (I saw no questioning of it in the British media), and within weeks of Shevardnadze's return home every major Western country was falling over itself in an unseemly, headlong rush both to recognize Georgia and to establish diplomatic relations with it. This was followed by Georgia's membership of such organizations as the International Monetary Fund, the Conference on Security and Co-operation in Europe and the United Nations. In the vanguard of those pressing for such positive steps were Prime Minister Major and Foreign Secretary Hurd. Was this wise? Anyone familiar with the Georgian scene since late 1988 would have pointed to the *universal* nature of racist intolerance towards the minorities, as highlighted earlier in this article. Such being the case, the only sensible course of action should have been to keep a watching-brief on events in Georgia, at least up to the time of the elections, announced for 11 October. The reward of recognition and the consequent flow of aid should have been held out as the carrot to the obstinate Georgian donkey on the specific condition that it mend its collective ways in respect of the minorities. This crucial chance to exercise a really positive influence was naïvely cast to the wind with the recognition that many observers strongly suspect was primarily an international 'thank-you' to Shevardnadze for five years of smiles as Gorbachev's international representative. The green light was assumed to have been given for the State Council, still without any popular mandate, to take what action it deemed necessary to deal with its own internationally recognized 'internal affairs'. After an intensification of the blitz in South Ossetia, the exhausted Ossetes agreed to a truce, which is still holding precariously. A virtual war was waged in parts of Mingrelia, on the grounds of rooting out support for Gamsakhurdia, especially by the Mkhedrioni of Shevardnadze's deputy, Dzhaba Ioseliani, who, to judge by the interview he gave to Georgian TV after the battle in Ts'alendzhikha, clearly relishes his war-games. Reportedly a plea was sent in mid-July to the United Nations by Mingrelian representatives seeking help against Georgian repression of the ancient peoples of Colchis (W. Georgia). And finally, the Abkhazian authorities declared on 23 July the re-instatement of their 1925 constitution, wherein their status of 1921-31 was legally laid down. Despite the fact that negotiations were in progress in Tbilisi on 13 August and due to resume in Sukhum the following day on the form of association between the independent states of Abkhazia and Georgia, the Georgian invasion-force went in with tanks and helicopters to crush the unilateral declaration of independence, as Defence Minister K'itovani himself admitted some days later. Two weeks after the event, as fierce fighting continues throughout the region, not a single Western political leader has spoken out against these actions of their friend Shevardnadze. The media, for the most part, are equally selective in the world's examples of racism that they choose to condemn, concentrating on Bosnia and Iraq. Tsarist Russia was responsible, as we have seen, for the decimation of the North West Caucasus in the last century, and the immediate response to this crisis by that empire's 'democratic' heir, Boris El'tsin, has been to try and close his border with Georgia to prevent Abkhazia's fellow-members of the North Caucasian Confederation helping to defend a region that has followed good democratic principles to achieve its goals against blatant agression from the present-day 'little empire' that is Georgia, this being the description applied to the country in a July 1989 issue of *Ogonek* by the late Andrei Sakharov.

This discussion was originally conceived in 1990 as a warning about the unfortunate fate that might await two of the peoples resident in (the then still marginally Soviet) Georgia (*viz*. the Mingrelians and the Abkhazians) in respect of the danger that I perceived to be threatening the continuing viability of their languages. As I complete the revision of this shorter version with its emphasis on the Abkhazians, it is not the viability of their language in its historical homeland that is at stake but the very existence of the Abkhazians themselves. Collapsing empires have always meant potential dangers for the peoples caught up in the shattering edifices. For decolonization to proceed smoothly a magnanimous attitude is surely essential on the part of the colonial power, preferably supported by informed perspicacity on the part of the world-community. The sixteen members of the Confederation of North Caucasian Peoples have claims for self-determination which at the very least merit investigation by experts in international law. Two of these peoples (the Abkhazians and the South Ossetians) are in conflict with Georgia, the rest with Russia. Both of these states have now been internationally recognized within their existing frontiers without any inquiry in appropriate world-fora as to the justness of the claims of these various minorities. This is a manifest recipe for future trouble. The specific lack of magnanimity on the part of the

Georgians/Kartvelians has been highlighted in the present account.[33] Had Western decisions concerning Georgia been taken unhurriedly and with foresight based on a careful consideration of known facts, the present tragedy in Abkhazia might have been avoided. As it is, the conflict could now well lead to a conflagration that will envelop the whole Caucasus. The proximate cause of this will have been the ordering in of the Georgian troops, but at least one of the ultimate causes must remain that communal act of hand-washing of any responsibility for securing minority rights in Georgia when the individual decisions to recognize this republic were predicated not on the noble principle of wise foresight based upon knowledge of all relevant facts, but rather on ignorance and a squalid readiness to allow the conduct of international relations between states to be determined by the personal relations obtaining between the ephemeral politicians of the day. The golden opportunity that the disappearance of Communism in Eastern Europe should have afforded has clearly been squandered in the Caucasus at large and in Georgia in particular principally by the collective failure of the world community to take appropriate prophylactic measures in response to the clearest danger-signals. This small-scale example does not bode well for the future conduct of international affairs in the East *or* West.

---

33 El´tsin's reponse to the Chechen leader Dudaev's declaration of independence was also to despatch troops, who, however, were promptly and unceremonioulsy sent packing by local forces!

CONCLUSION

A Europe of Nation-States: Interdependence, Nationalism and Security

Peter J. S. Duncan

Since the seventy-fifth anniversary conference of the School of Slavonic and East European Studies in December 1990, the region has continued to change at remarkable speed. This chapter will discuss the most recent developments in post-totalitarian Europe: the collapse of the USSR; the growth of nationalism and conflict in Central and Eastern Europe; and the impact of these events on Western Europe and its security concerns.

The countries of Western Europe and North America played an important role in the collapse of Communism in Eastern Europe and the Soviet Union. In the mid-1980s the contrast between the prosperity of Western Europe and the stagnation of the Communist economies became apparent to many representatives of the political élites in the East as well as to private citizens. Gorbachev's use of the slogan 'common European house' was in part a reflection of concern that the bloc in general and the Soviet Union in particular would lose out irretrievably if they were prevented from sharing in the fruits of economic integration, centred on the EC. The failure of the earlier policy of confrontation with the West and the inability of the Soviet Union to indulge in another twist to the arms race (threatened by President Reagan's Strategic Defense Initiative) forced the new Soviet leader to seek an accommodation with the West.

Gorbachev's desire for disarmament, co-operation, technology and credits from the West gave new life to the Conference on Security and Co-operation in Europe (CSCE), the series of meetings involving the European countries, the USA and Canada, which had become a forum for the revived Cold War in the latter Brezhnev years. Gorbachev and his Foreign Minister, Eduard Shevardnadze, discovered that this Helsinki process and in particular the human rights provisions, so obnoxious to previous Soviet leaders, could promote the democratization of the USSR (and Eastern Europe) which was central to *perestroika*.

Already in his address to the UN General Assembly in December 1988, Gorbachev emphasized the right of states to choose their own social systems. The refusal to use tanks to prevent the East Europeans from exercising that choice at the end of 1989 and the acquiescence in the unification of Germany in the summer of 1990 showed that the Soviet leaders gave more priority to improving relations with the West than to maintaining the buffer zone against it. Soviet support for the American-led war in the Gulf against Iraq in February 1991 seemed to confirm that the Kremlin had shifted to a general pro-Western position in hope of major aid grants from the leading capitalist countries.

The end of the Soviet Union
As far as Gorbachev was concerned, however, the new political thinking did not extend to the break-up of the Soviet Union. While recognizing the injustice of the Molotov-Ribbentrop Pact, Gorbachev resisted the demands of Estonia, Latvia and Lithuania for independence. When Lithuania declared independence in March 1990 the central authorities responded with a blockade. The position of the centre was severely weakened by the democrats' successes in the Russian elections and the victory of Boris El'tsin as Chairperson of the Russian Supreme Soviet, against Gorbachev's opposition. The Supreme Soviets of Russia and Ukraine echoed the Baltic desire for independence by passing declarations of sovereignty in the summer of 1990, for the first time claiming to place republican laws over Union laws. It was the fear of disintegration of the Soviet Union as much as concern over the social consequences of rapid privatization that led Gorbachev in October 1990 to reject the Shatalin Plan for a 500-day transition to a market economy, and side with conservatives in the leadership. With this Gorbachev became almost a prisoner of the Right in domestic affairs. By the time of the 75th Anniversary conference of the School of Slavonic and East European Studies in December 1990, the liberal Minister of Internal Affairs, Vadim Bakatin, had been sacked after conservative pressure. At the conference Galina Starovoitova, then an adviser to El'tsin, warned of the threats to the Foreign Minister; within a week Shevardnadze had resigned, predicting that the Soviet Union was heading for a dictatorship. In January 1991, in Vilnius and Riga, the Soviet security forces caused several deaths while repressing pro-independence activists, in what appeared in retrospect to be a rehearsal for the August coup.

Believing that the bulk of the Soviet population still wanted to maintain some form of Union, Gorbachev held a referendum on the future of the USSR on 17 March 1991. The Baltic States, Georgia, Armenia and Moldavia refused to participate. Support for the continuation of a reformed USSR was recorded in all the other republics, representing nine-tenths of the Soviet population, ranging from seventy per cent in Russia and Ukraine to over ninety per cent in Central Asia. On this basis, Gorbachev prepared a new Union Treaty. The

Russian and Ukrainian republican leaderships, however, each asked an additional question in the referendum: Russia proposed to establish a directly elected Presidency; and Ukraine asked for support for its declaration of state sovereignty. Both these propositions were carried, with the sovereignty declaration gaining even more support than Gorbachev's reformed Union in Ukraine. Overall, the referendum showed the strength of the democratic movement in Russia and the national movements in the European republics and Transcaucasia. This, together with the inability of the conservatives to halt the growing failure in production, led Gorbachev to begin to break with the conservatives and to form an alliance with El´tsin and the leaders of the republics. This was the basis of the '9 + 1' agreement, made at Novo-Ogarevo in April, when Gorbachev and the republics which had participated in the referendum agreed to replace the USSR with a looser confederation.

On 12 June Russia held its first-ever direct presidential election. El´tsin won easily with fifty-seven per cent of the vote. Striking at the basis of the continuing Communist domination of the Russian Federation, in July he banned Party cells in factories and state bodies under Russian jurisdiction. He even talked of banning cells in the Armed Forces and the KGB. The conservatives in the KGB, the Army, the Ministry of Internal Affairs, the CPSU Central Committee Secretariat and the defence industry could take no more. They had already watched Gorbachev give up Eastern Europe and allow Germany to be united within NATO and they considered the Union Treaty equivalent to the break-up of the USSR. They attempted their coup, arresting and deposing Gorbachev and declaring a state of emergency, on 19 August, the eve of the signing of the new Union Treaty which would have transferred power from the centre to the republics. The putschists were concerned not only with saving the Soviet Union, but with preserving their own privileges and the positions of their own institutions.

Even sixteen months after the coup, it is difficult to identify precisely why the attempt failed. It is tempting to see the coup as doomed in advance; Soviet society had changed too much in the years of *glasnost´* and democratization; people had lost their former fear of the authorities and would not tolerate the turning back of the clock. Hundreds of thousands followed El´tsin and demonstrated at the Russian parliament in Moscow and the Winter Palace in Leningrad. Most importantly, key sections of the security forces refused to turn their guns on Russians. On the other hand it must be admitted that by far the greater part of society responded to the coup with apathy. If the members of the Emergency Committee had been Stalinists they could have been ruthless by calling in more reliable forces and turning the parliament into a Tienanmen Square. Their failure to arrest El´tsin or indeed any leading democrats suggested a half-hearted approach. Some evidence from the interrogation of the plotters suggests that they expected Gorbachev to go along with them; his refusal left them in mid-air, forced to seek consolation in vodka.[1]

The coup made the failure of Gorbachev's project for a renewed Union probable but not inevitable. Gorbachev's initial unwillingness to abandon the Party eroded his support. El'tsin's decrees suspending and then banning the Communist Party in Russia destroyed the organization which had created and maintained the Soviet Union. The defeat of the coup unleashed a wave of support for El'tsin and for an independent Russia, while the apparent unwillingness of the Russian leaders to take over the central Union institutions alarmed the non-Russian republics and promoted their own desire for independence. Nationalist governments in the Baltic States and Georgia made their independence a reality, while in Ukraine, Azerbaijan and Central Asia the Communist leaders continued to seek to transform themselves into semi-nationalists to escape the waves of democratization and economic reform from Moscow and maintain their legitimacy in the post-Communist era.

The position of Ukraine was crucial. Leonid Kravchuk, Chairperson of the Ukrainian Supreme Soviet and the former ideology secretary of the Communist Party of Ukraine, used the traditional Communist means of control over the mass media to ensure a referendum vote of ninety per cent for Ukrainian independence and his own election as President of Ukraine on 1 December. Gorbachev had said that a Union without Ukraine would be unthinkable. On 8 December El'tsin and Kravchuk travelled to Minsk and together with the Chairperson of the Belorussian Supreme Soviet, Stanislau Shushkevich, declared the end of the USSR and the formation of the Commonwealth of Independent States (CIS). Gorbachev protested against the destruction of his plans, foreseeing not only the end of his presidential role but also the threat of ethnic strife between the new independent states as they acquired their own armed forces.[2] The leaders of all the other former Soviet republics, apart from the Baltic States and Georgia, acceded to the CIS under the Alma-Ata declaration of 21 December.

Crisis and conflict

The collapse of the Party machine and the dissolution of the USSR allowed the fifteen former Soviet republics to join the Central and East European states on the path of reform. All the post-Communist states of Europe shared similar problems. Much of the region was an ecological danger zone, poisoned by acid rain and contaminated by radioactive leaks. Communist industrialists, under pressure to fulfil the plan, did not so much neglect as violate the natural environment.

---

1 Similar points are made in William E. Odom, 'Alternative Perspectives on the August Coup', *Problems of Communism*, 40, November-December 1991, no. 6, pp. 13-19.
2 Mikhail Gorbachev, *Dekabr' - 91. Moia pozitisiia*, Moscow, 1992.

The economic stagnation of the last Communist years gave way to declining output as the established trading links of the CMEA and those between former Soviet republics were ruptured. The fall in the volume and value of Russia's energy exports meant the loss of the Soviet market for East European products. The low technological level of East European and Soviet industry made much of it uncompetitive in world markets, while the end of the Cold War removed the *raison d'être* of the massive arms industries. The already huge debts of these countries, especially in the USSR and Poland, and in some case their inability to service them made it much harder for them to borrow their way through the crisis. Leszek Balcerowicz in Poland and Václav Klaus in Czechoslovakia sought, with the approval of the IMF, to launch a programme of 'shock therapy' to stabilize the economy and then to privatize most of it. The risks were high; Lech Wałęsa and Václav Havel, as presidents of the two countries, sometimes expressed concern at the social costs involved in reduced real wages and high unemployment. The fear of the manipulation of social grievances by former Communists or by extreme nationalists was always present. In Russia El'tsin and his acting Prime Minister Egor Gaidar freed prices and sought to cut subsidies to state industry, as a prelude to large-scale privatization, but found themselves confronted with the opposition of the directors of state industry and the Supreme Soviet.

The creation of a post-Communist political leadership was a problem in some countries. In Russia, Ukraine, Belarus and the former Soviet Central Asia the Communist élites remained dominant, although they abandoned Marxism-Leninism. In Serbia, as in Ukraine and Central Asia, the Communist leader Slobodan Milošević re-legitimized his rule in nationalist terms. The National Salvation Front in Romania sought to ban the Communist Party, but former Communists continued to dominate the Front and the state, and Ion Iliescu, a former leading Communist, was comfortably re-elected President in 1992. Similarly, the banning of the Communist Party in Russia did not prevent many former Communist *apparatchiki* maintaining their positions in the republics and regions of the Russian Federation. From June 1992 El'tsin was effectively compelled to share power with them in the central government organs.

In Poland, Hungary, Czechoslovakia, Bulgaria, Slovenia, Croatia, Albania, the Baltic States, Transcaucasia and Moldavia opposition movements were able to come to power. Since the Communists had retained a monopoly for between forty and seventy years, most of these movements were led by politicians who had had no experience of any level of government. The Baltic States to some extent constituted exceptions, because of the fairly close relationships between the popular fronts and the republican Communist parties. Slovenia constituted a similar partial exception in that while the opposition DEMOS won the parliamentary elections of April 1990, the former Communist leader, Milan Kučan, was able to retain the post of President of the State Presidency. Wałęsa in Poland, as the head of Solidarity, had gained much experience in leadership and negotiation. Elsewhere, leaders of what had been small intellectual discussion groups were swept to office. Their lack of experience could have a price. Havel, the playwright in Czechoslovakia, and Zviad Gamsakhurdia, the specialist in American literature in Georgia, had both been imprisoned for their courageous defence of human rights. Yet Havel's inability to appreciate the strength of Slovak national feeling contributed to the dissolution of Czechoslovakia, and Gamsakhurdia's dictatorial tendencies provoked the Georgian opposition into civil war and his own downfall.

The factor common to most of Eastern Europe and the former Soviet Union after the fall of Communism was the upsurge in political nationalism. By the 1970s, there were few believing Communists left in any of the states in the region. The year 1989 brought new hopes in democracy: the competitive elections to the USSR Congress of People's Deputies and the fall of the East European regimes. Rejecting class politics, the new governments appealed to their electors in nationalist terms, highlighting the need to negotiate the withdrawal of foreign troops and regain control over the country's resources. While the democrats typically portrayed the Communist and renamed Communist parties as dupes of Moscow, the ex-Communists tried equally to present their opponents as agents of the West and the IMF, selling out resources cheaply to Western corporations. Anti-Semitic feelings in the population were also manipulated; in the Polish presidential campaign Tadeusz Mazowiecki was presented as being under Jewish influence, and elements in the Hungarian Democratic Forum were not always reticent about referring to the Jewish origins of some of the leaders of the Free Democrats.

The most obvious consequence of the growth of nationalism was, as Mark Wheeler notes in his chapter, the dissolution of all three federal or pseudo-federal Communist states, Yugoslavia, the Soviet Union and Czechoslovakia.[3] This seemed to be in marked contradiction to the progress towards federalism in the EC. Yugoslavia from the last years of Tito had been a collection of quarrelling republics and provinces. Tito left behind an arrangement to share power between the regions in the federal bodies, but the Yugoslav Army was dominated by Serbs and thus acted as a centralizing factor. The Soviet Union and Czechoslovakia were centralized states dominated by Moscow and Prague. There had been a transfer of resources from Russia to the poorer Soviet republics and from the Czech Republic to Slovakia (although the Communist military and state machine exploited everyone). In Yugoslavia, Slovenia and Croatia subsidized Serbia and the other poorer southern republics. The desire of the Slovenes and the Croats to reorient their economies away from the economically crisis-ridden Yugoslavia towards the expanding EC can be seen at the roots of their quest for independence. Similarly in the Soviet Union it was the most economically advanced republics, the Baltic States, which were

---

3 See also R. Lukic, 'Twilight of the Federations in East-Central Europe and the Soviet Union', *Journal of International Affairs*, 45, Winter 1992, no. 2, pp. 575-98.

most determined to achieve independence. Cultural factors were also highly important: the Slovenes, Croats, Estonians, Latvians and Lithuanians were all traditionally tied to Western Christianity (Catholic or Protestant) rather than Orthodoxy, and used the Latin alphabet rather than the Cyrillic. Slovenia and Croatia had belonged to the Habsburg Empire while most of the rest of Yugoslavia had been under Ottoman rule. In the Baltic, German influence had deep roots.

The dissolution of Czechoslovakia took place, according to opinion polls, against the wishes of a majority of the Czechs and of the Slovaks. The Slovak desire for more autonomy was enhanced by the desire to protect Slovakia where unemployment was already high from the consequences of Klaus's promised shock therapy. After the election of June 1992 Klaus's victorious Civic Democratic Party was unwilling to meet the demands of the parties winning majority support in Slovakia. The Czech liberals preferred a break with Slovakia rather than a brake on their economic reform programme by making concessions to the Slovaks. The consequences were the same in all three cases: the dissolution of the federations and the emergence of the constituent republics as nation-states. With the unification of Germany, the principle of 'one nation, one state' in the region was established to a greater degree than ever before.

Ethnic rivalry was not confined to the former federal states. For centuries millions of East Europeans have lived without or outside their own nation-states, creating chronic problems of minority rights and disputed borders. The ending of the Warsaw Pact and the Soviet policing role in Eastern Europe allowed old ethnic conflicts to be reopened. Large numbers of Hungarians, Serbs and Russians lived outside their nation-states, and the governments of the latter in different ways have taken an interest in the fate of their diasporas.

Hungary has established a 'Secretariat of Hungarians beyond the Borders' originally within the Prime Minister's Office. Significant numbers of Hungarians live in Romania (in Transylvania), in the Vojvodina province in Serbia, in Slovakia and in Ukraine, especially in Transcarpathia. The treatment of Hungarians in Romania had been an issue of concern while Ceauşescu ruled. His successors in the National Salvation Front, manipulating the Romanian nationalism analysed in Dennis Deletant's chapter, have backtracked on their promises of cultural rights to Hungarians. In Vojvodina Hungarians faced conscription into the Yugoslav Army to fight the Serb war against the Croats. The growth of Slovak nationalism led to tension in southern Slovakia between Hungarians and Slovaks. Tension there was increased by the Slovak decision to proceed with the construction of the Gobčitcovo Dam on the Danube, despite Hungarian objections on environmental and safety grounds.

The collapse of Yugoslavia and the USSR left nearly a million Serbs in Croatia and Bosnia-Hercegovina and twenty-five million Russians in the former Soviet republics outside the Russian Federation. The declarations of independence by Slovenia and Croatia and then Bosnia-Hercegovina allowed Milošević to extend his power into the post-Communist era by posing as the defender of the Serbs outside Serbia and waging war on the new states. As a Communist turned Serb nationalist, he received the backing of most of the officer corps of the Yugoslav Army. At first they attempted to crush Slovenia, but soon abandoned it to its independence; few Serbs lived there.

The real aim was to detach the predominantly Serb districts of southern and eastern Croatia from that republic. The Yugoslav Army, backed by local Serb militias, brought to Croatia the first protracted armed conflict on the European continent since the Greek Civil War. Names such as Vukovar and Osijek became known throughout Europe as synonymous with mass destruction and death. A ceasefire line, policed by the UN, represented Serbia's new *de facto* border. The Yugoslav Army was then free to support the activity of well-equipped, locally-based Serb forces in Bosnia-Hercegovina. The delicate power-sharing arrangements between the parties of the Muslims, Serbs and Croats were shattered. The Serbs seized control of territory where they could and laid siege to the capital, Sarajevo. In spite of the fact that Serbia was occupying parts of Croatia, the Croat and Serb forces strove to co-operate in the division of Bosnia-Hercegovina, leaving the Muslims in control only of small enclaves. The euphemism of 'ethnic cleansing' concealed the murder, rape, torture, expulsion or transfer to concentration camps of hundreds of thousands of Croats and Muslims in Serb-occupied areas. Half a million refugees escaped to Croatian-held territory.

At the time of writing it seemed likely that, unless decisive action was taken by outside powers, Milošević would move to consolidate the successes of Serb nationalism by imposing a crackdown in Kosovo. This might provoke the involvement of Albania in support of fellow Albanians and of Turkey in support of fellow Muslims. Any involvement of Turkey would alarm Greece, as a traditional enemy of Turkey and a friend of Serbia. Greece was already concerned at the emergence of an independent Macedonia, considering that it posed a threat to Greek Macedonia. Bulgaria was torn between fear of Serbia, the possibility of unrest among its own Turkish minority and its unwillingness to recognize the existence of a Macedonian nation on its borders. The possibility of the widening of the conflict could not fail to alarm the West, particularly if Iran or Saudi Arabia was to become involved on the side of the Muslims.[4]

El'tsin was not a Milošević. He had not tried to save his *nomenklatura* post by becoming a nationalist; rather, he had broken with the *nomenklatura* and fought his way back to power democratically. Far from trying to re-create an empire, he had done as much as any other Russian to destroy the USSR. In spite of the threat of his press secretary after the coup that any republic which

---

4 Franz-Lothar Altmann, 'Ex-Yugoslavia's Neighbours: Who Wants What?', *The World Today*, 48, August-September 1992, nos 8-9, pp. 163-65.

left the Union might have to renegotiate its frontiers with Russia (a threat which probably promoted separatism in Ukraine), El'tsin accepted the existing frontiers on the formation of the CIS.

Eleven million of the Russians outside the Russian Federation live in Ukraine. Since Kravchuk was prepared to recognize them as full citizens of Ukraine, and (at least in the first year of independence) to allow them the free use of the Russian language in the East and the South where they were concentrated, the Russians of Ukraine acquiesced in, and even welcomed, Ukrainian independence. Conservatives in the Russian parliament, seeking to embarrass El'tsin, demanded the return to Russia of the Crimea (which had been transferred to Ukraine in 1954). The majority of the local population and local *nomenklatura*, however, seemed to be satisfied with the degree of autonomy within Ukraine which Kiev was prepared to concede.

In Moldavia, on the other hand, it was not possible to avoid armed conflict. On the left bank of the Dniestr, where Russians and Ukrainians formed the majority of the population, the local *nomenklatura* had declared the formation of a Transdniestrian autonomous republic within Moldavia. This had happened in November 1990 in response to the language policies of the Moldavian government and to the fear that Moldavia would unite with Romania. In 1992 the Russian Fourteenth Army, stationed in Transdniestria, gave support to the local government in conflict with Moldavian forces, leading to perhaps 300 deaths in Bendery. The conflict highlighted both the uncertainty of central Russian government control over the armed forces, and the weakness of the CIS in solving disputes between member states. Moldavia requested CSCE intervention, but Russia opposed this. In July 1992 a joint Russian-Moldavian peacekeeping force was established; and it was agreed that, if Moldavia decided to unite with Romania, Transdniestria would have the right to opt out. The level of tension fell.

The Russian minorities in the Baltic States showed no sign in 1992 of turning to violence to defend their rights, but all shades of opinion in Russia showed increasing concern over the problem of citizenship rights in Estonia and Latvia. Estonia held a constitutional referendum and a general election in which only people who were citizens of Estonia in 1940 and their descendants were allowed to vote, thus excluding around one third of the population. Latvia was discussing a draft law establishing a sixteen-year residence requirement, a loyalty oath and the passing of a language test as preconditions for citizenship.[5] In response the Russian government was threatening to halt the withdrawal of Russian troops unless the rights of the Russian-speaking population were guaranteed.

The break-up of the USSR caused concern in the West over whether the Soviet-American strategic arms reduction treaty (START-I) would be

---

5   On citizenship laws in the Baltic States, see Henn-Juri Uibopuu, 'Dealing with the Minorities: a Baltic Perspective', *The World Today*, 48, June 1992, no. 6, pp. 108-12.

honoured, and over the security of Soviet nuclear weapons. It was agreed that the CIS would take control over all strategic weapons, and all nuclear weapons would be concentrated on Russian territory. Claiming to fear nuclear blackmail by Russia, some Ukrainian nationalist groups urged their country to maintain its own nuclear forces as part of the new Ukrainian Army being created. By the end of 1992 Ukraine had still not ratified the START-I agreement. There was still greater concern that the general chaos in the former Soviet Union might lead to the capture of nuclear weapons by groups fighting in the Caucasus or to the illegal sale of nuclear weapons to countries such as Iran, Iraq or Libya. The CIS had proved to be as powerless as its predecessor to stop the conflict between Armenia and Azerbaijan, which had begun over Nagornyi Karabakh but escalated to general border war. Efforts at mediation by Iran and Turkey proved equally fruitless. Meanwhile in Georgia Gamsakhurdia was violently overthrown and Shevardnadze returned to lead the republic in which he had earlier been Communist First Secretary. El´tsin and Shevardnadze succeeded in calming the conflict in the Georgian region of South Ossetia by instituting patrols by Russian, Georgian and South Ossetian forces. But in August 1992 Georgian forces entered Abkhazia and drove the government of the autonomous republic out of Sukhumi. In response, unofficial militias from the 'Confederation of Caucasian Mountain Peoples', based in the Russian Northern Caucasus, infiltrated into Georgia to help their fellow Caucasian Muslims, the Abkhaz. This in turn led to the direct involvement of the Russian Armed Forces in the conflict, in an attempt to contain it.

The danger facing the Russian authorities was that the multinational Russian Federation, with its twenty-one ethnically-based republics, might disintegrate as the USSR had done. Given that ethnic Russians formed eighty-three per cent of the population of the Russian Federation, the latter can be seen as an approximation to a Russian nation-state, albeit one with national sub-states occupying much of its territory. The coercive forces which had kept the Soviet Union together were in disarray after the coup. When a rebellion in Chechnia in the Northern Caucasus in October 1991 led to the overthrow of the republic's government and the proclamation of independence, El´tsin tried to use force but had to back down in the face of opposition from the Russian Supreme Soviet. The Federal Treaty of March 1992 was intended to meet the demands of the republics and provinces of Russia for greater self-government. Full independence for most of the republics was impractical; many were surrounded by Russia and in most the eponymous nationality was less than half the population. Tatarstan suffered from both these drawbacks. Tatarstan and Chechnia, however, refused to sign the Federal Treaty. By November 1992 the centre was showing more self-assurance, dispatching troops to the North Caucasus to help the North Ossetians against the Ingush.

However unjustified, there was a fear in Moscow that Islamic fundamentalism might unite the Muslim peoples of the Caucasus and the Volga

Tatars and Bashkirs against Russia. There was intense popular dislike of the Caucasian 'mafias' which many believed to control private trade in Moscow and St Petersburg, and a perceived danger of Chechen terrorism. At the military level, the Russian Army continued to seek to control the frontier between independent Tadzhikistan and Afghanistan to prevent the import of arms from the victorious Afghan *mujahidin*. At the political level, Russian diplomacy sometimes tried to appeal to the West by presenting Russia as a reliable ally against Islam. It was perhaps only in Russia that Serbian claims to be defending civilization against Islam in Bosnia were taken seriously.

The growth of nationalism and ethnic conflict created the refugee problem. Within the former Soviet Union, hundreds of thousands of Russians left Central Asia, Armenians fled from Azerbaijan and Azeris from Armenia. Many Germans and Jews used their privileged positions to emigrate to Germany and Israel respectively. German legislation allowed Germans from Poland, Romania and anywhere else to 'return' to a country which was already struggling to cope with the absorption of the former GDR. The war in former Yugoslavia qualitatively changed the dimensions of the migration problem. To the economic migrants seeking a better life in the West were added hundreds of thousands of Croat and Bosnian refugees, fleeing ethnic persecution and war. The liberal asylum law had already been leading two-thirds of all asylum-seekers entering the EC to head for Germany.[6] The entry of three million people into Germany over three years at a time of recession fuelled the racism of the neo-Nazis. Vicious attacks on Turkish migrant workers and refugee hostels and the desecration of Jewish cemeteries were accompanied by the growth of electoral support for the far right, especially but not only in Eastern Germany. The mainstream politicians promised to tighten up the asylum law, thus lending credence to the anti-foreigner propaganda of the neo-Nazis. The strength of the neo-Fascists of Jean-Marie Le Pen in France discouraged Paris from opening the doors to the refugees. The British government, although criticized at home and abroad for allowing only a small number of refugees in, preferred to maintain a cautious approach.

Towards a new security regime for Europe
The refugee crisis and the continuing threat of war in the Balkans showed that it was in the vital interests of Western Europe to maintain stability in the East. It was not obvious, however, what the best mechanism was to achieve this. This section will review the major structures involved.

The end of the Cold War had been marked by a CSCE summit held in Paris in November 1990. The meeting had adopted the 'Charter of Paris for a New Europe', which accepted German unification, promised the observance of human rights and the principles of a market economy, and made a statement of

---

6 Jochen Thies, 'Germany I: Into Turbulent Waters' (hereafter Thies), *The World Today*, 48, August-September 1992, nos 8-9, p. 149.

friendly relation between the participants. The institutionalization of the CSCE began. As well as inaugurating biennial summits and annual foreign ministers' meetings, the summit established a Committee of Senior Officials, a permanent secretariat in Prague, a Conflict Prevention Centre in Vienna and an Office of Free Elections in Warsaw.[7] In July 1991 the CSCE had an experts' meeting in Geneva on national minorities and the rights of members of national minorities, but neither this nor any other body was able to prevent the war in Yugoslavia.[8] Following the collapse of the Soviet Union, all the former Soviet republics were admitted as full members (including those in Central Asia). By joining the CSCE they formally accepted that frontiers between them could be changed only by agreement (a factor of some importance, given the existence of 160 border disputes between them). With the accession also of Albania, Slovenia, Croatia and Bosnia-Hercegovina the number of CSCE members rose to fifty-two. A drawback of the CSCE as a security mechanism is the requirement of unanimity. A single state violating human rights commitments would have the right to veto sanctions against it. To overcome this difficulty a 'consensus minus one' procedure has been proposed.[9] In practice the July 1992 CSCE summit in Helsinki (known as Helsinki-II) evaded the consensus rule by suspending the rump state of Yugoslavia (Serbia and Montenegro) before imposing sanctions on it. Helsinki-II made a step forward in establishing peace-keeping structures in Europe. Lacking forces of its own, it agreed that the CSCE would ask NATO or the Western European Union (WEU) to provide troops to deal with threats to European security where it considered this necessary. The CSCE became a 'regional organization' in the meaning of the UN Charter, facilitating the co-ordination of its work with the UN. Moreover, the meeting agreed to establish a high commissioner for minorities to investigate ethnic discrimination.

Similar work was already being done by an entirely separate body, the Council of Europe, which has been promoting the development of human rights in Central and Eastern Europe. Admission to the Council of Europe is conditional on an inspection into the human and civil rights of the inhabitants, including the rights of ethnic minorities. Bulgaria and Hungary have amended their constitutions and practices in order to join. Individuals living in member states can appeal to the European Court of Human Rights against decisions of their governments or courts.

---

7 US Commission on Security and Cooperation in Europe, *The Conference on Security and Cooperation in Europe: An Overview of the CSCE Process, Recent Meetings and Institutional Development*, Washington D.C., February 1992, p. 10.
8 US Commission on Security and Cooperation in Europe, *From Vienna to Helsinki: Reports on the Inter-Sessional Meetings of the CSCE Process*, Washington D.C., April 1992, pp. 133-49.
9 Christopher Anstis, 'CSCE Mark II: Back to Helsinki from Paris via Berlin and Prague', *NATO Review*, 40, April 1992, no. 2, p. 23.

The moves of the European Community towards political integration and its great economic weight and influence might appear to make it the most reliable vehicle for security in the East. Events up to now, however, suggest that it is as yet too divided to act coherently on the world stage. After the Iraqi invasion of Kuwait, France and Germany were slow to follow the US-British lead in enforcing the UN Security Council resolution for an Iraqi withdrawal. Above all the Community failed the test of Yugoslavia. To use the words of Jochen Thies, the EC's policy was a 'total fiasco'.[10] Against the advice of Britain and France, Germany recognized the independence of Slovenia and Croatia in December 1991, forcing the other EC states to follow suit.[11] The episode illustrated the strength of Germany within the Community, despite the problems of unification, and cast doubt on the usefulness of the EC as a means of controlling German ambitions in the post-Cold War era. Similar comments would apply to the WEU, to which France has been much more committed than Britain.

The end of the Cold War inevitably brought into question the future of NATO. Would the United States, with its own social problems, be willing indefinitely to continue to provide defence support for Western Europe? No less a figure than Admiral Sir James Eberle, a former NATO Commander-in-Chief, Eastern Atlantic, argued in early 1991 that 'NATO should remain in being only as long as is necessary to create the conditions that would allow it to be dissolved'. The WEU and EC should, he suggested, gradually take over NATO's defence planning.[12] Developments since then suggest that America is not in a mood to abandon its world responsibilities; in the Gulf, Somalia and the former Yugoslavia, Washington has continued to play an active role. The statement by President-elect Bill Clinton that US foreign policy will be guided by economic interests need not signify a major change; American economic interests are world-wide. The extension of Atlantic co-operation into Eastern Europe and the former Soviet Union with the establishment of the North Atlantic Co-operation Council gives further ground to suggest that NATO has long-term utility. On the European side (and not only on the Left) the desire for independent European defence is sometimes linked with a perception of the Americans as being trigger-happy and not wholly reliable. NATO and its associated structures, however, can provide a calming influence against American unilateralism. At the same time, as the conflict with Iraq showed, America can use the NATO structures to overcome divisions among the European allies and carry through policies about which some European members may be unenthusiastic.

---

10 Thies, p. 150.
11 Trevor C. Salmon, 'Testing Times for European Political Cooperation: The Gulf and Yugoslavia, 1990-1992', *International Affairs*, 68, April 1992, no. 2, pp. 252-53.
12 Sir James Eberle, 'The Security Interests of Western Europe', *The World Today*, 47, February 1991, no. 2, p. 35.

The role of the UN in settling conflicts in Africa, Asia and the Middle East has grown substantially since the impact of Gorbachev's new thinking. In Europe, as already pointed out, the CSCE has begun to play the role of a regional organization of the UN. The resources of the world body are fully stretched by existing peace-keeping operations, and there has been opposition in the Third World to the use of UN forces in wealthier Europe. The horrors of the Yugoslav war led the Security Council to impose economic sanctions on Serbia and to declare a 'no-fly zone' over Bosnia-Hercegovina, but without ensuring a mechanism of compliance. In December 1992 UN Forces were sent to Macedonia in an attempt to deter Serbia or Albania from action in Kosovo or Macedonia itself.

So long as Russia and America are willing to act together, the UN can probably be an effective agency of peace-making in Europe, if countries are prepared to carry out Security Council decisions. Russia still retains, however, a veto in the Security Council, and the UN could be paralysed in cases where Russia perceived its national interests to be threatened. This could arise in conflicts within the former Soviet Union or possibly in relation to Serbia and Bulgaria. It seems clear that neither the CSCE, EC, NATO nor the UN is capable on its own of preserving European security. Rather, as Adrian Hyde-Price has argued, a 'pluralist and multi-layered system' is needed in which the existing structures interact and develop as specific problems emerge.[13]

The end of the Cold War means that foreign policy will be determined much more than before by the pursuit of perceived national interests.[14] The growth of nationalism in Eastern Europe has promoted nationalism and regionalism at the sub-state level in Western Europe, for example in Scotland and Northern Italy. Equally pronounced has been the revival of attachment to the nation-state in Western Europe, in reaction to the moves towards federalism in the EC. The Maastricht Treaty looked forward to European Union, a common foreign and defence policy and a single European currency, held together by an untranslatable *acquis communautaire*.

The first Danish referendum rejecting Maastricht and the narrow margin of support for the treaty in the French referendum were indications of a shift in public opinion; the departure of the pound and the lira from the Exchange Rate Mechanism highlighted the difficulty of monetary union, and the growth of national feeling in Germany made it unlikely that any German government could abandon the Deutschmark. The EC majority have held it necessary to deepen integration before expanding geographically but this attempt seems to be breaking down now. When new members are admitted, Austria, Finland, Norway, Sweden and possibly Turkey will be the next in line. It is unlikely

---

[13] Adrian Hyde-Price, *European Security beyond the Cold War: Four Scenarios for the Year 2010*, London, 1991, p. 250.
[14] Peter M. E. Volten, 'Security Dimensions of Imperial Collapse', *Problems of Communism*, 41, January-April 1992, nos 1-2, p. 137.

that the countries of Central and Eastern Europe will be allowed in before the end of the century, unless the aims of Maastricht are postponed.

Denial of EC membership to Eastern Europe might not in itself be disastrous if there were alternative channels of support and if some access to the Community market was guaranteed. The good intentions and modest resources of the European Bank for the Reconstruction and Development of Eastern Europe are insufficient to underwrite the transition of command economies to the market, especially where the former Soviet Union is concerned. Adequate Western support for Gaidar's government in Russia never materialized, as the IMF insisted on prior conditions which it proved politically impossible to achieve. The defeat of Vytautas Landsbergis and the return of the former Communists under Algirdas Brazauskas in staunchly Catholic Lithuania, and the replacement of Gaidar by Viktor Chernomyrdin in December 1992, represented setbacks for Western policy. Without real and substantial help from the West to Moscow there is a clear danger of the resurgence of Russian imperialist nationalism.

At the same time much has already been achieved. In Eastern Europe and in most of the former Soviet Union progress towards pluralism and democratization has been more successful than seemed likely in 1989. Security co-operation between Russia and the NATO allies has continued to develop. The START-II treaty of January 1993 will bring a two-thirds reduction in long-range American and former Soviet nuclear weapons, if it is ratified and implemented. West Europeans are more aware of how their own security is linked with conflicts in the East. Nevertheless, the inadequate Western responses to challenges such as the war in Yugoslavia or the economic reform process in Russia show that there is a pressing need to develop the study of the nations of the East as they strive to create new communities.

NOTES ON CONTRIBUTORS

DENNIS DELETANT is Senior Lecturer in Romanian Studies at the School of Slavonic and East European Studies, University of London.

BLAGA DIMITROVA is a Bulgarian poet and novelist, and was vice-president of Bulgaria from 1992 to 1993.

SIMON DIXON is Lecturer in Modern History at the University of Glasgow.

PETER J.S. DUNCAN is Lecturer in Contemporary Russian Politics and Society at the School of Slavonic and East European Studies, University of London.

GEOFFREY HOSKING is Professor of Russian History at the School of Slavonic and East European Studies, University of London.

MICHAEL KIRKWOOD was Senior Lecturer in Russian at the School of Slavonic and East European Studies, University of London, and is now Professor of Slavonic Languages and Literatures at the University of Glasgow.

VÁCLAV KLAUS is Prime Minister of the Czech Republic and former Finance Minister of Czechoslovakia.

PAUL LEWIS is Senior Lecturer in Government at the Open University.

ELENA NEMIROVSKAIA is Director of the Moscow School of Political Studies.

GHIA NODIA is a Senior Fellow in the Institute of Philosophy at the Georgian Academy of Sciences, Tbilisi.

LÁSZLÓ PÉTER is Reader in Hungarian History at the School of Slavonic and East European Studies, University of London.

MARTYN RADY is Lecturer in Central European History at the School of Slavonic and East European Studies, University of London.

ANDREI SAKHAROV is Director of the Institute of Russian History at the Russian Academy of Sciences.

ANTHONY D. SMITH is Professor of Sociology at the London School of Economics and Political Science, University of London.

GALE STOKES is Professor of History at Rice University, Texas.

FIONA TUPPER-CAREY was a researcher at Keston College, Kent; she is now engaged in independent research in Italy.

MARK WHEELER is Lecturer in History at the School of Slavonic and East European Studies, University of London.